I JUST GET SO ... ANGRY!

*Dealing with anger and
other strong emotions
for teenagers*

By Timothy Bowden Postgrad Dip Psych
and Sandra Bowden M Ed (Couns Psych)

Illustrations by Sandra Bowden

EXISLE
PUBLISHING

First published 2013

Exisle Publishing Limited
'Moonrising', Narone Creek Road, Wollombi, NSW 2325, Australia
P.O. Box 60 490, Titirangi, Auckland 0642, New Zealand
www.exislepublishing.com

National Library of Australia Cataloguing-in-Publication Data:

Bowden, Tim.

I just get so ... angry! : dealing with anger and other strong emotions for teenagers / Timothy & Sandra Bowden

ISBN 9781921966217 (pbk.)

For secondary school age.

Anger in adolescence.
Anger.

Bowden, Sandra.

152.47

Designed by Alan Nixon
Typeset in DejaVu Sans 11/16
Printed in Shenzhen, China, by Ink Asia

This book uses paper sourced under ISO 14001 guidelines from well-managed forests and other controlled sources.

10 9 8 7 6 5 4 3 2 1

Once again, to our friends and family, our constant compass points — and Snuff, the Furious Rabbit, who has taught us much about rage and forgiveness ... and who may get to feature in our next book!

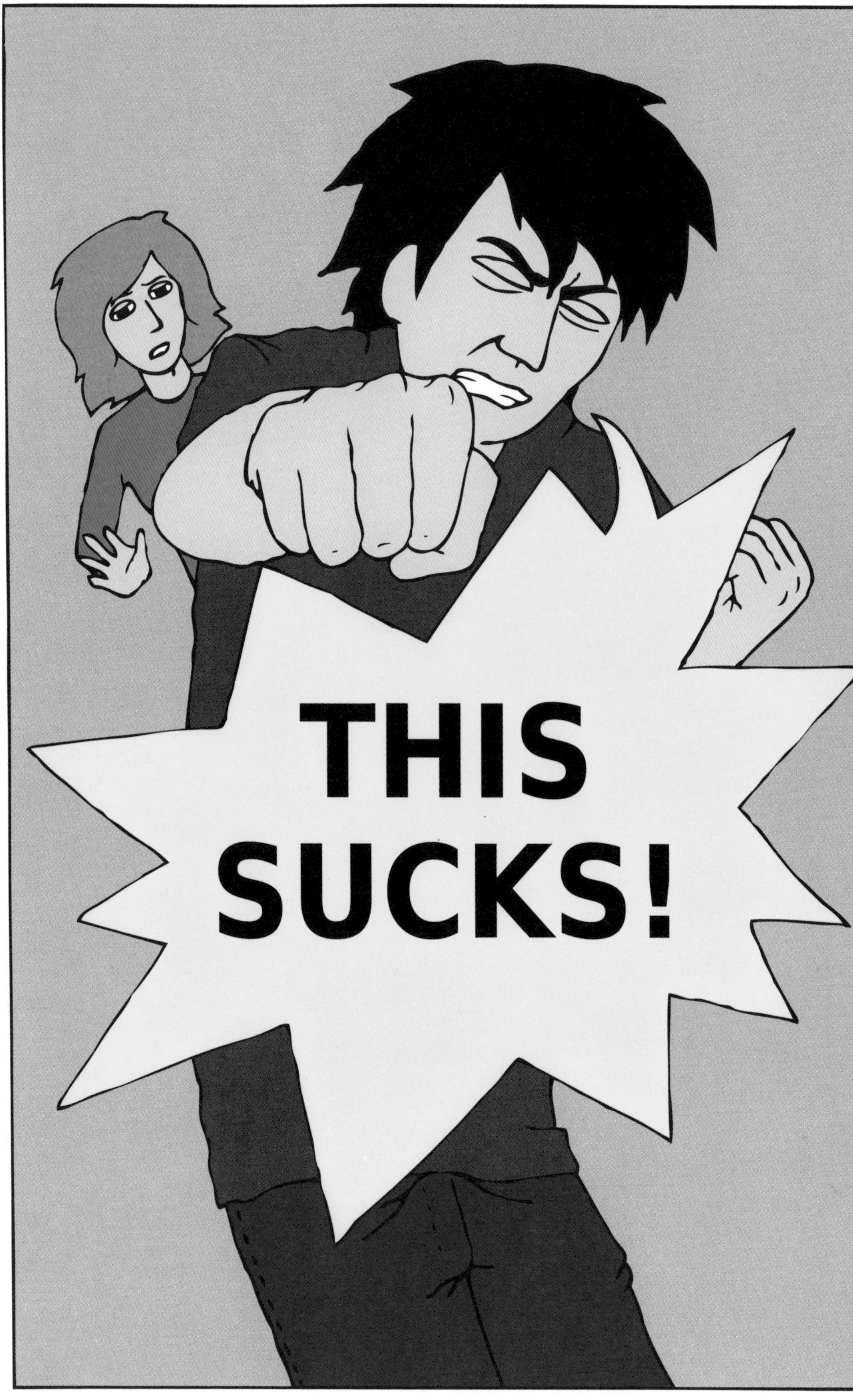
THIS SUCKS!

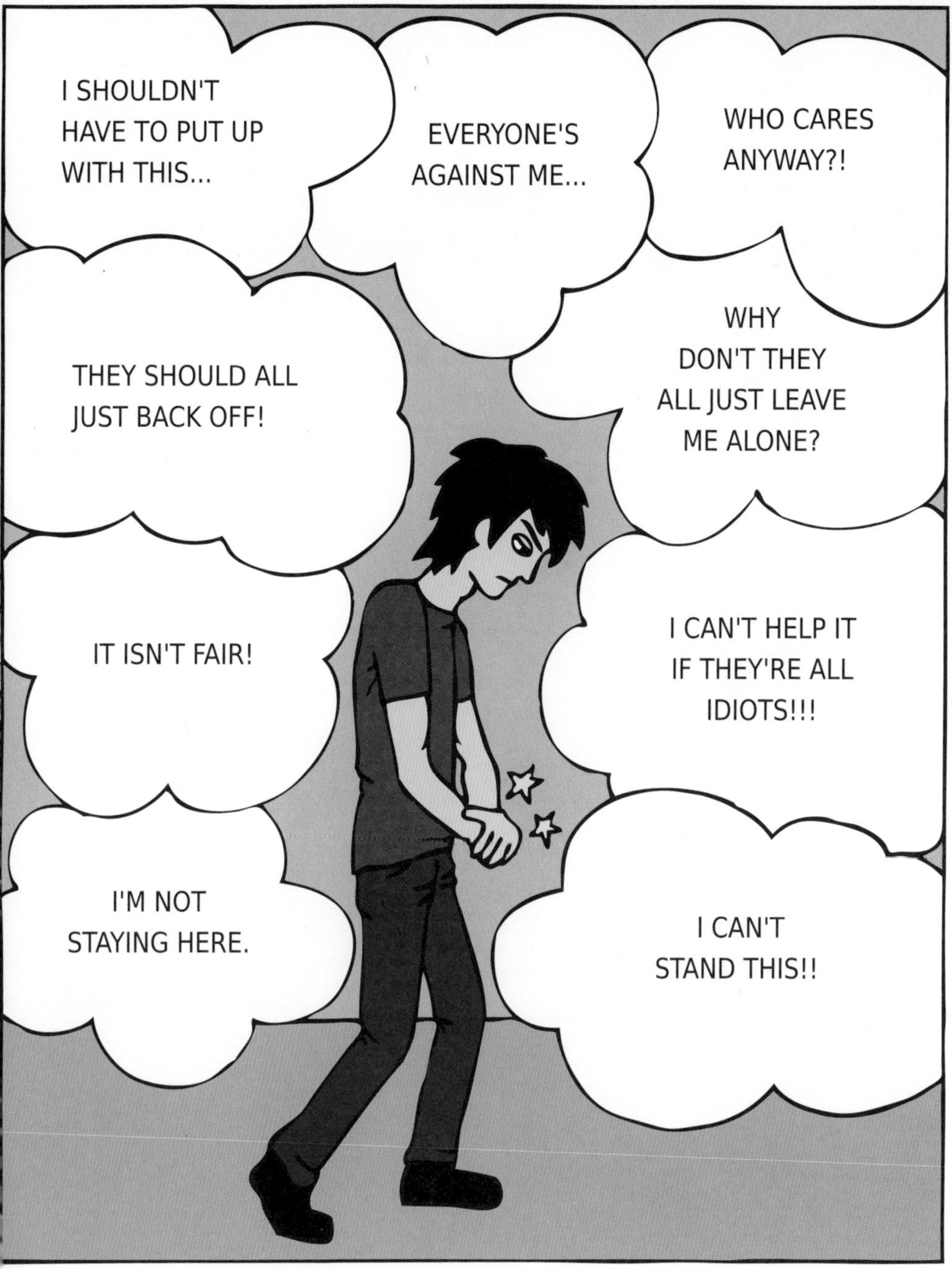
I SHOULDN'T HAVE TO PUT UP WITH THIS...
EVERYONE'S AGAINST ME...
WHO CARES ANYWAY?!
THEY SHOULD ALL JUST BACK OFF!
WHY DON'T THEY ALL JUST LEAVE ME ALONE?
IT ISN'T FAIR!
I CAN'T HELP IT IF THEY'RE ALL IDIOTS!!!
I'M NOT STAYING HERE.
I CAN'T STAND THIS!!

A FEW HOURS EARLIER...

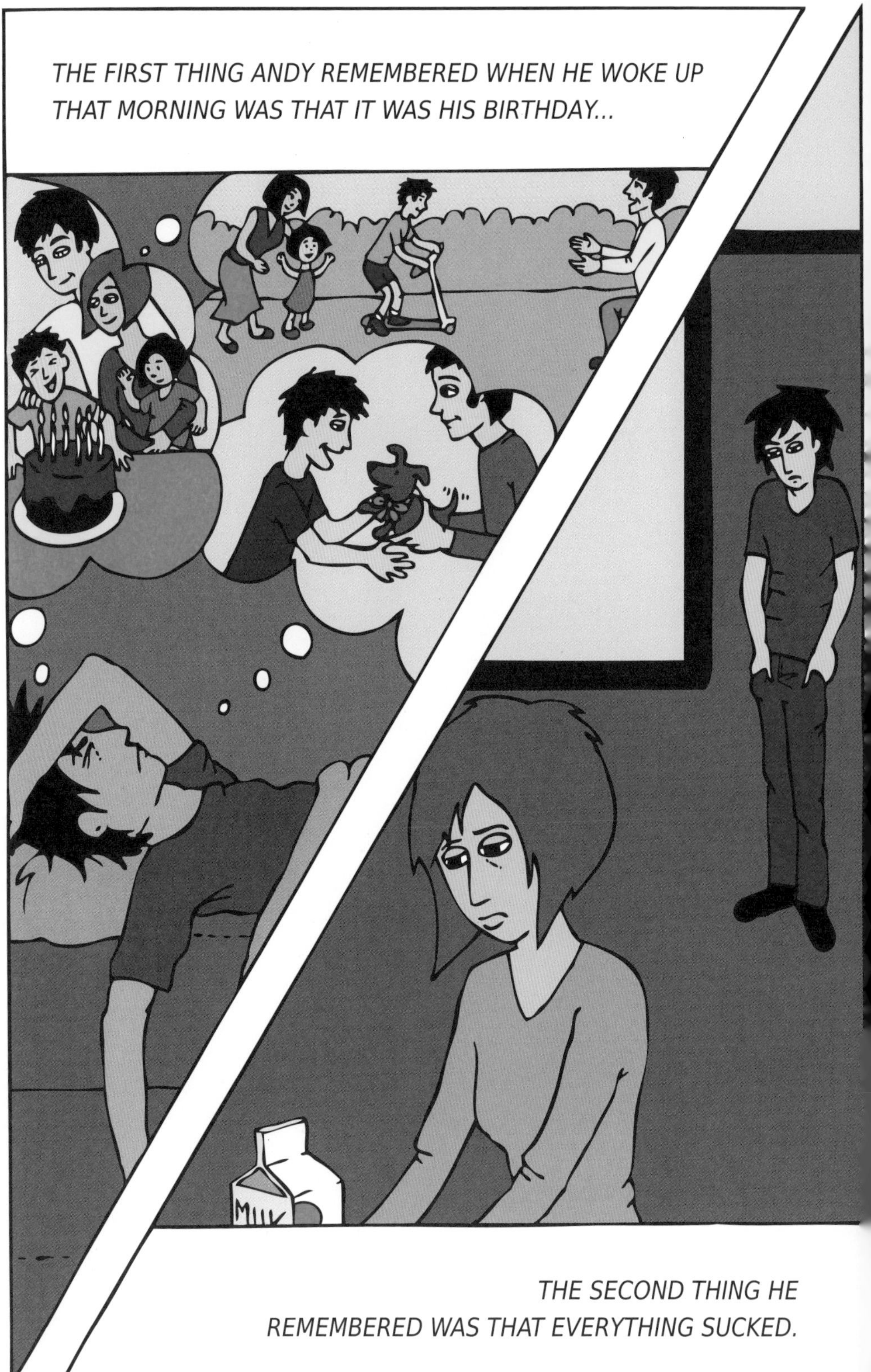
THE FIRST THING ANDY REMEMBERED WHEN HE WOKE UP THAT MORNING WAS THAT IT WAS HIS BIRTHDAY...
MILK
THE SECOND THING HE REMEMBERED WAS THAT EVERYTHING SUCKED.

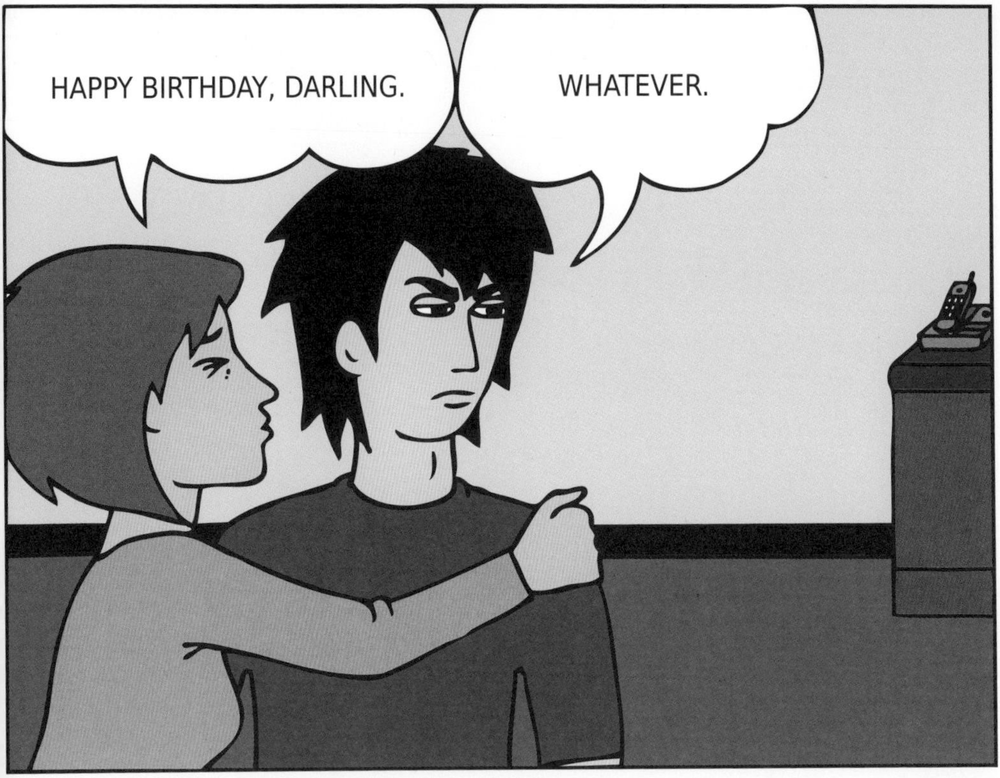
HAPPY BIRTHDAY, DARLING.
WHATEVER.

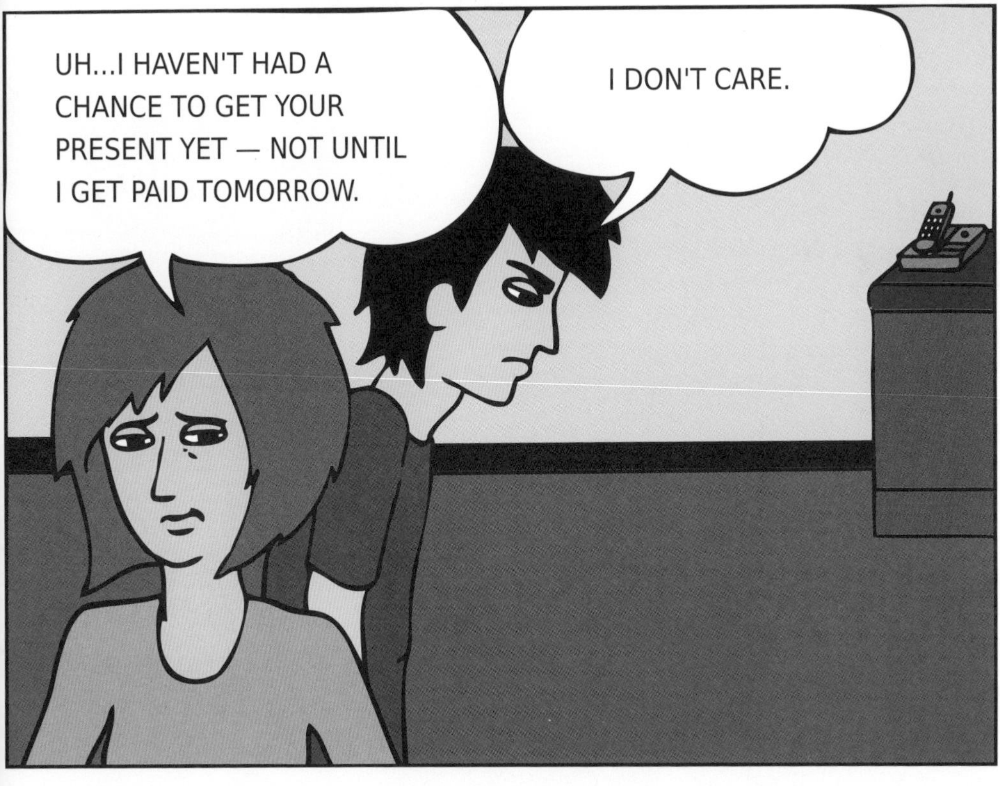
UH...I HAVEN'T HAD A CHANCE TO GET YOUR PRESENT YET — NOT UNTIL I GET PAID TOMORROW.
I DON'T CARE.

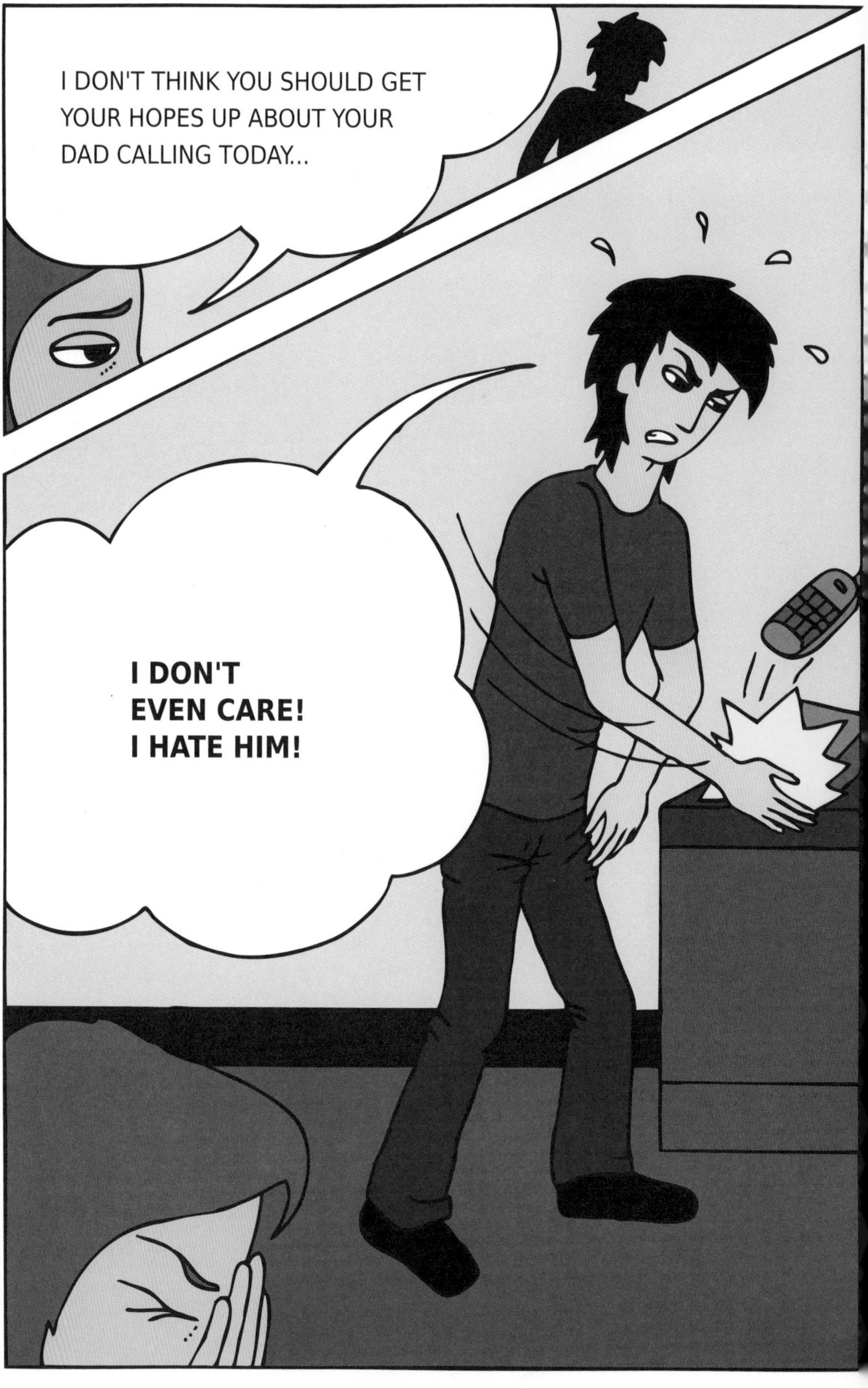
I DON'T THINK YOU SHOULD GET YOUR HOPES UP ABOUT YOUR DAD CALLING TODAY...
I DON'T EVEN CARE! I HATE HIM!

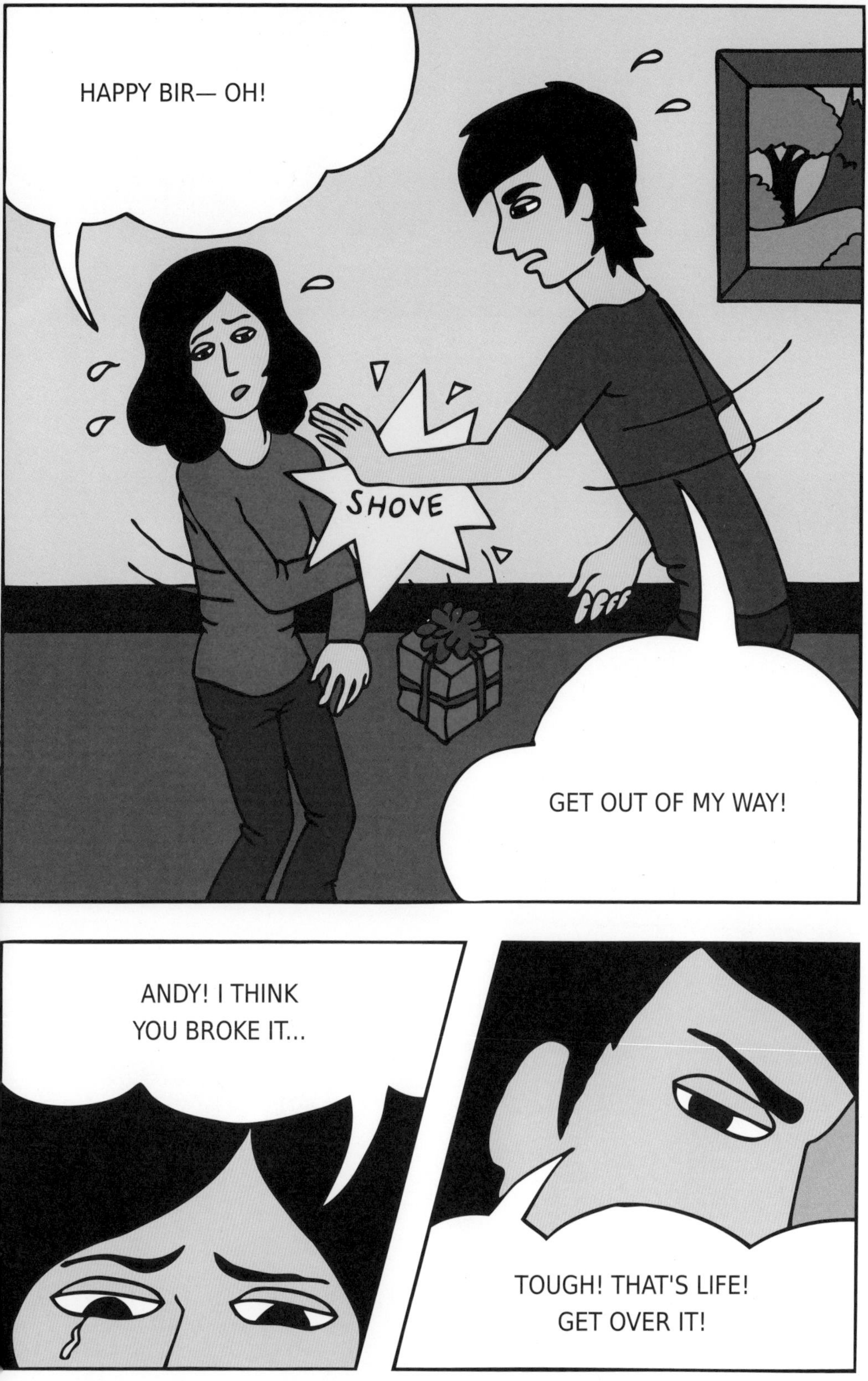
HAPPY BIR— OH!
SHOVE
GET OUT OF MY WAY!
ANDY! I THINK YOU BROKE IT...
TOUGH! THAT'S LIFE! GET OVER IT!

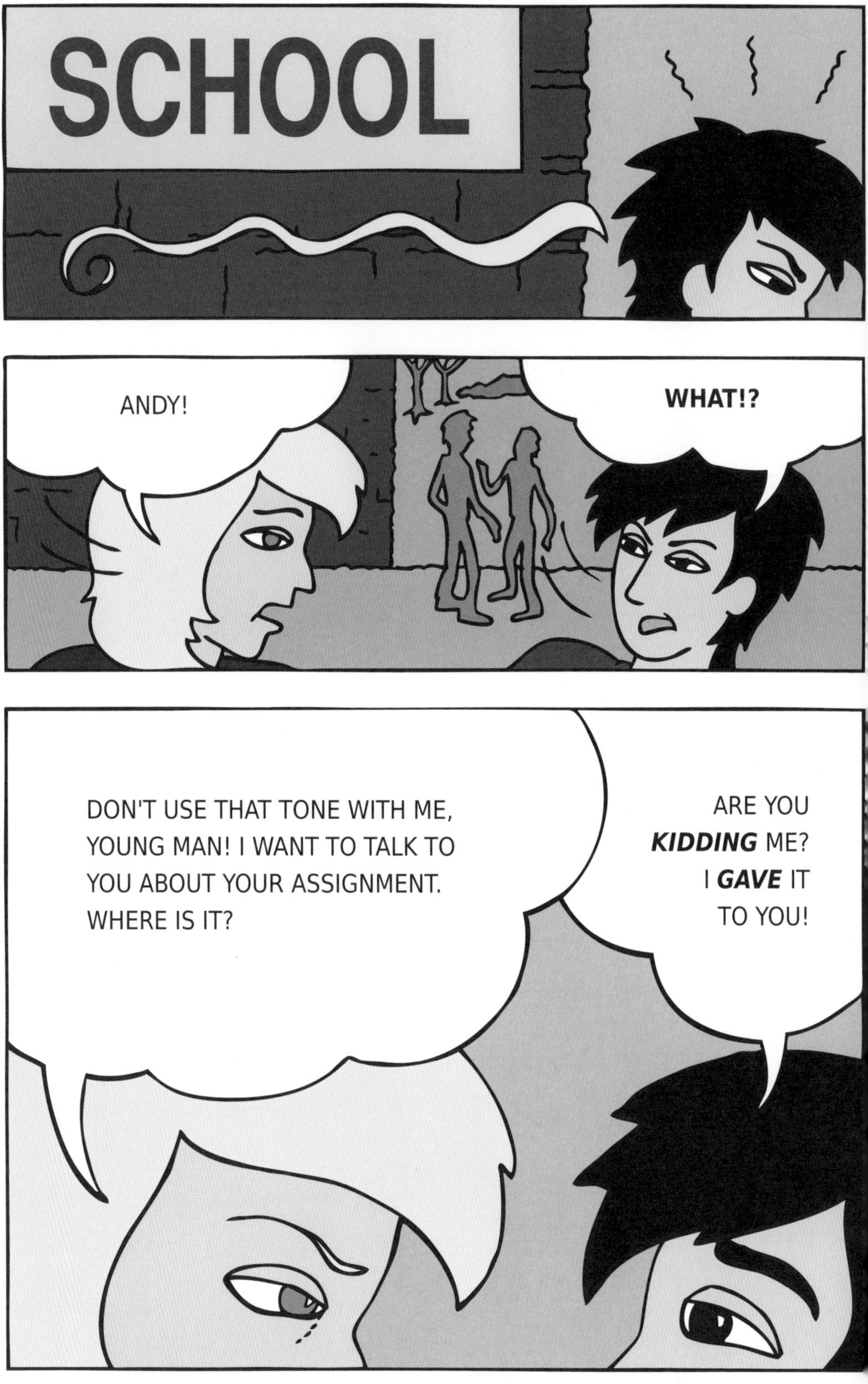
SCHOOL
ANDY!
WHAT!?
DON'T USE THAT TONE WITH ME, YOUNG MAN! I WANT TO TALK TO YOU ABOUT YOUR ASSIGNMENT. WHERE IS IT?
ARE YOU KIDDING ME? I GAVE IT TO YOU!

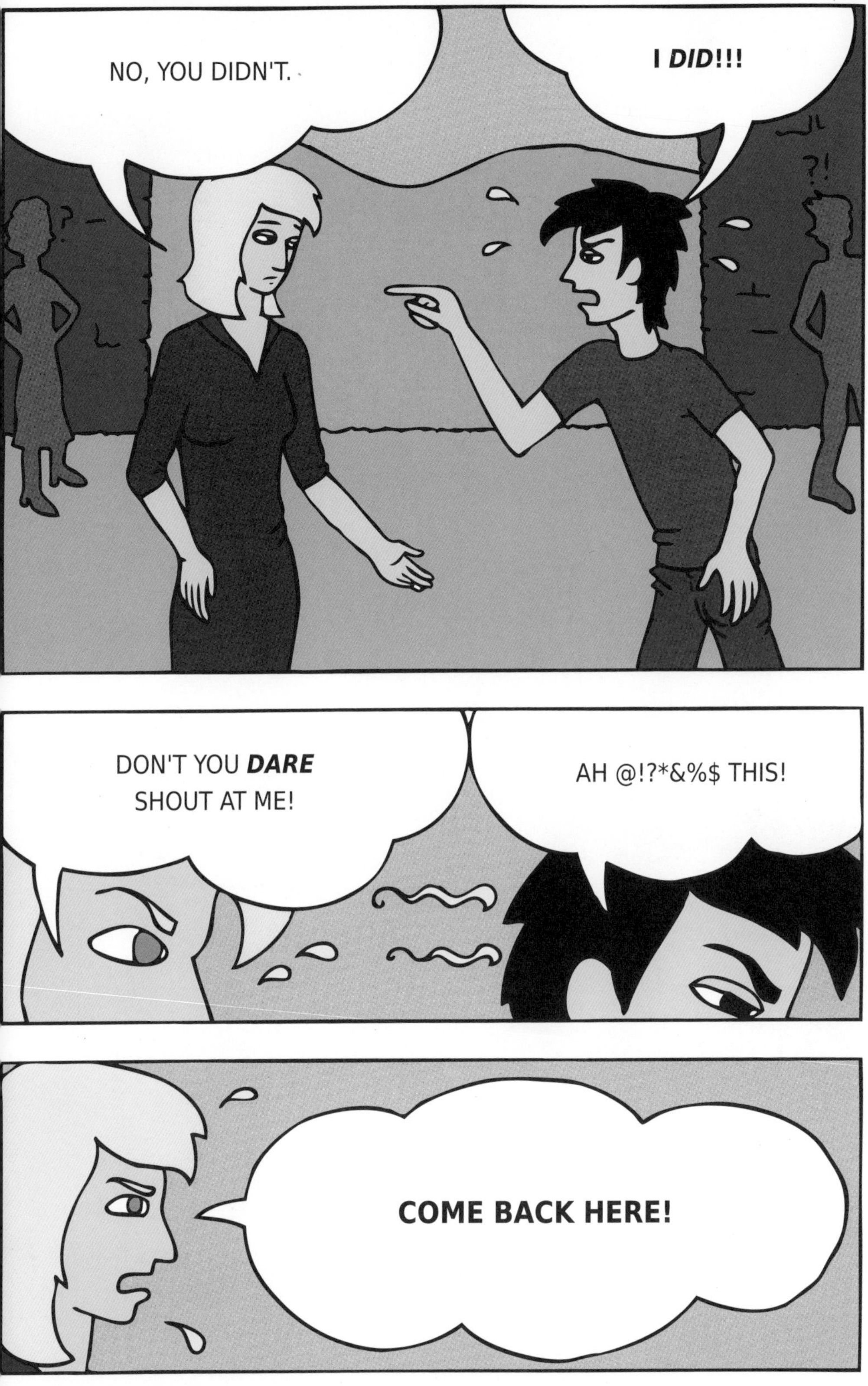
NO, YOU DIDN'T.
I ***DID***!!!
?!
?!
DON'T YOU ***DARE*** SHOUT AT ME!
AH @!?*&%$ THIS!
COME BACK HERE!

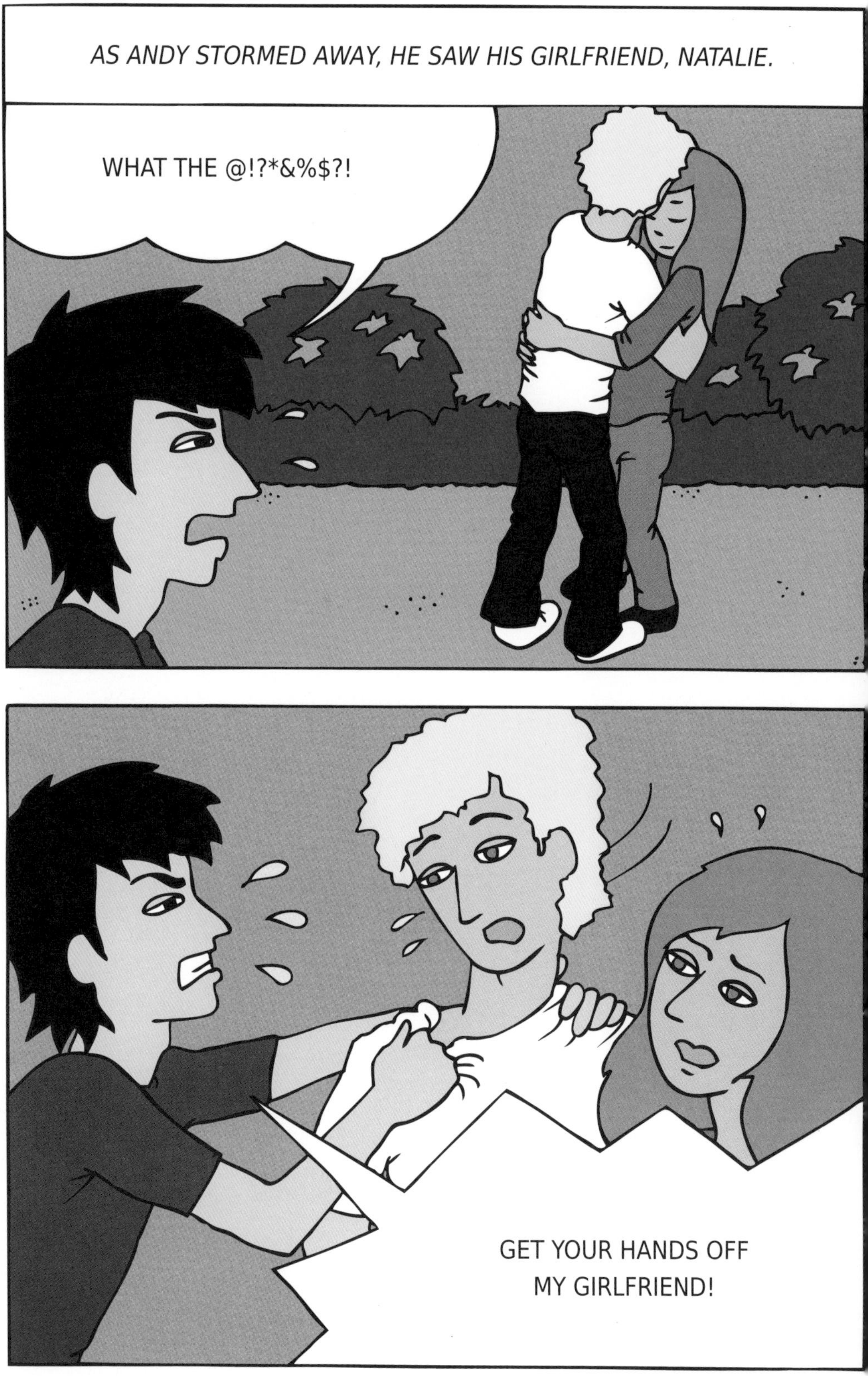
AS ANDY STORMED AWAY, HE SAW HIS GIRLFRIEND, NATALIE.
WHAT THE @!?*&%$?!
GET YOUR HANDS OFF MY GIRLFRIEND!

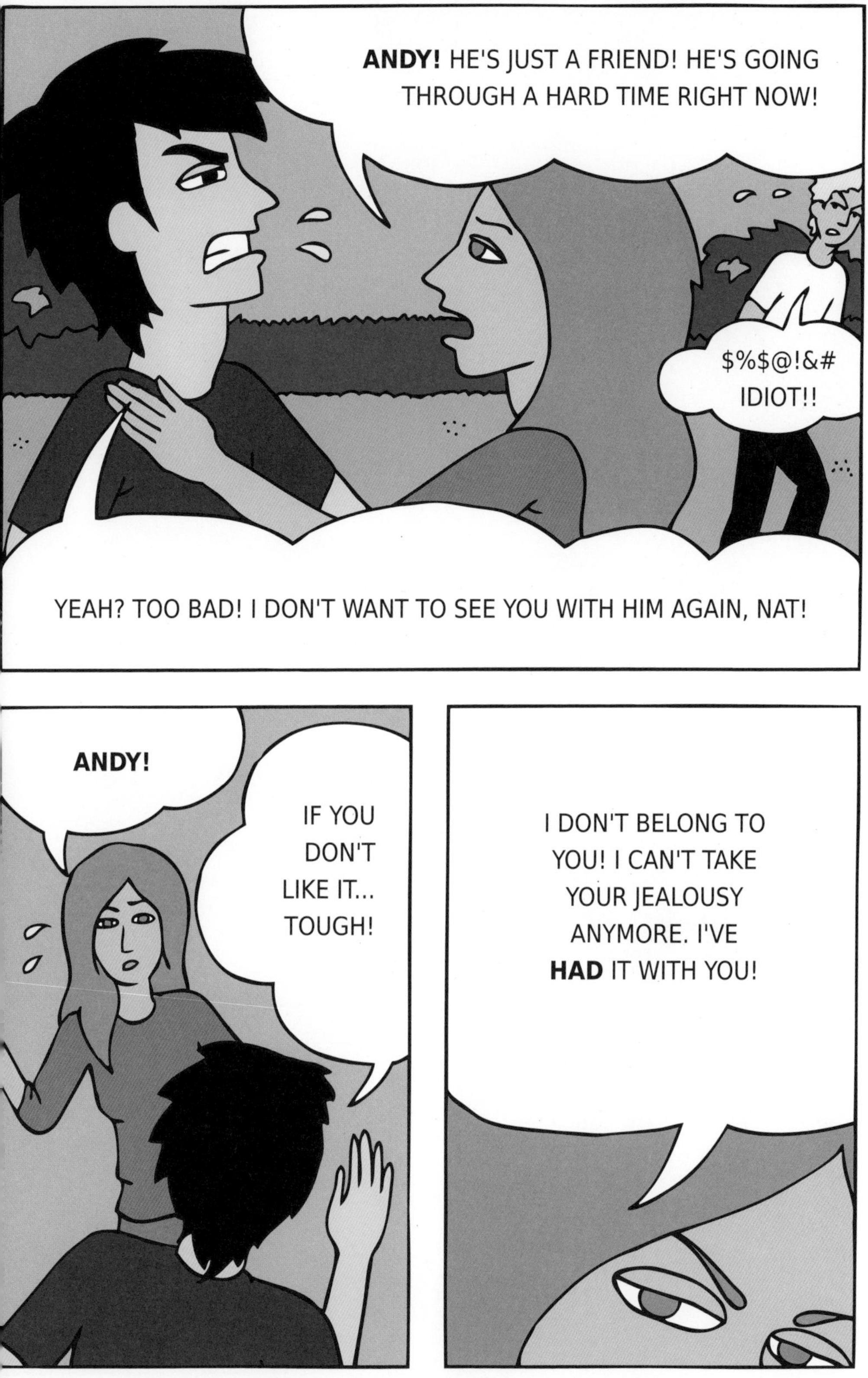
ANDY! HE'S JUST A FRIEND! HE'S GOING THROUGH A HARD TIME RIGHT NOW!
$%$@!&#
IDIOT!!
YEAH? TOO BAD! I DON'T WANT TO SEE YOU WITH HIM AGAIN, NAT!
ANDY!
IF YOU DON'T LIKE IT... TOUGH!
I DON'T BELONG TO YOU! I CAN'T TAKE YOUR JEALOUSY ANYMORE. I'VE **HAD** IT WITH YOU!

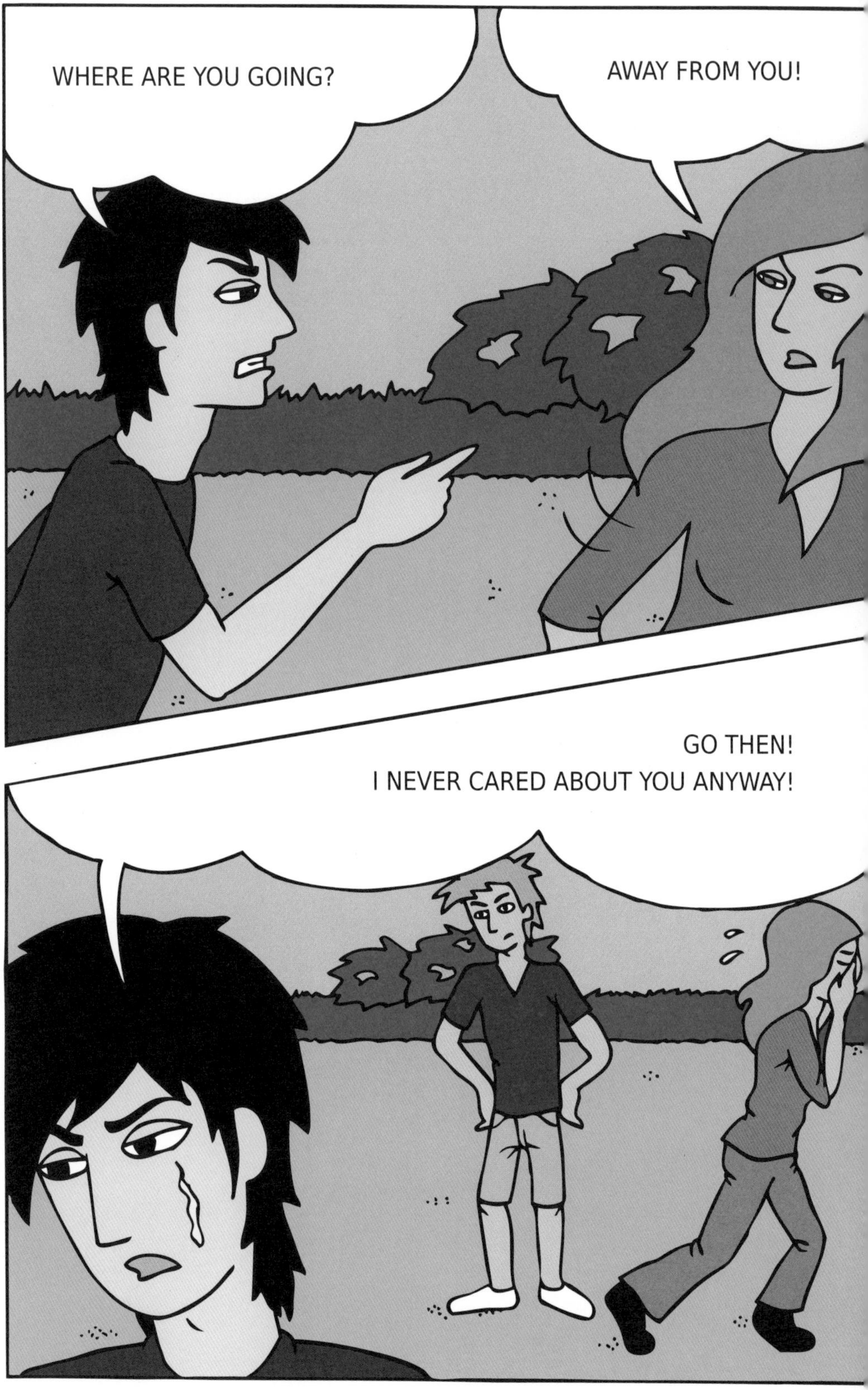
WHERE ARE YOU GOING?
AWAY FROM YOU!
GO THEN!
I NEVER CARED ABOUT YOU ANYWAY!

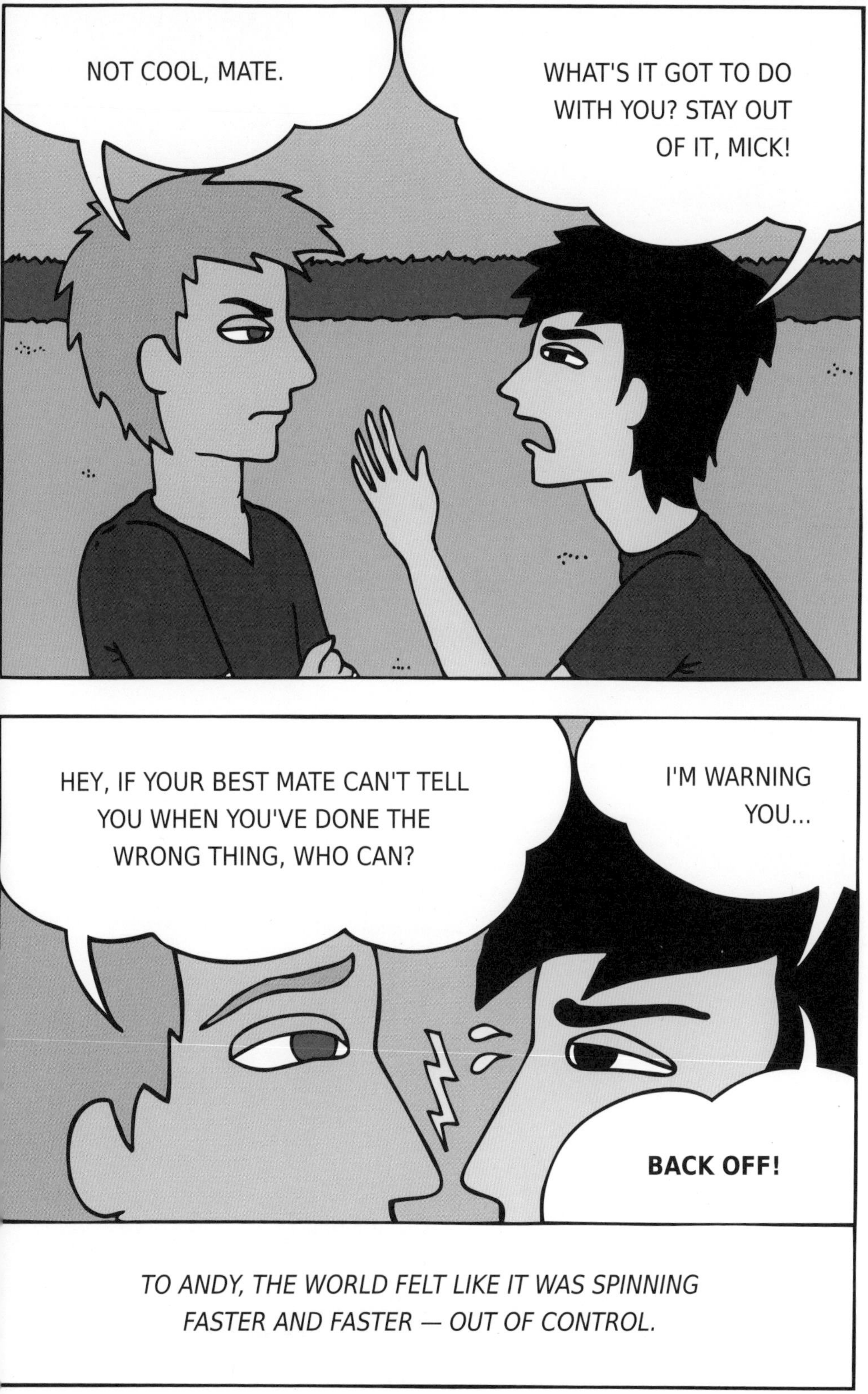
NOT COOL, MATE.
WHAT'S IT GOT TO DO WITH YOU? STAY OUT OF IT, MICK!
HEY, IF YOUR BEST MATE CAN'T TELL YOU WHEN YOU'VE DONE THE WRONG THING, WHO CAN?
I'M WARNING YOU...
BACK OFF!
TO ANDY, THE WORLD FELT LIKE IT WAS SPINNING FASTER AND FASTER — OUT OF CONTROL.

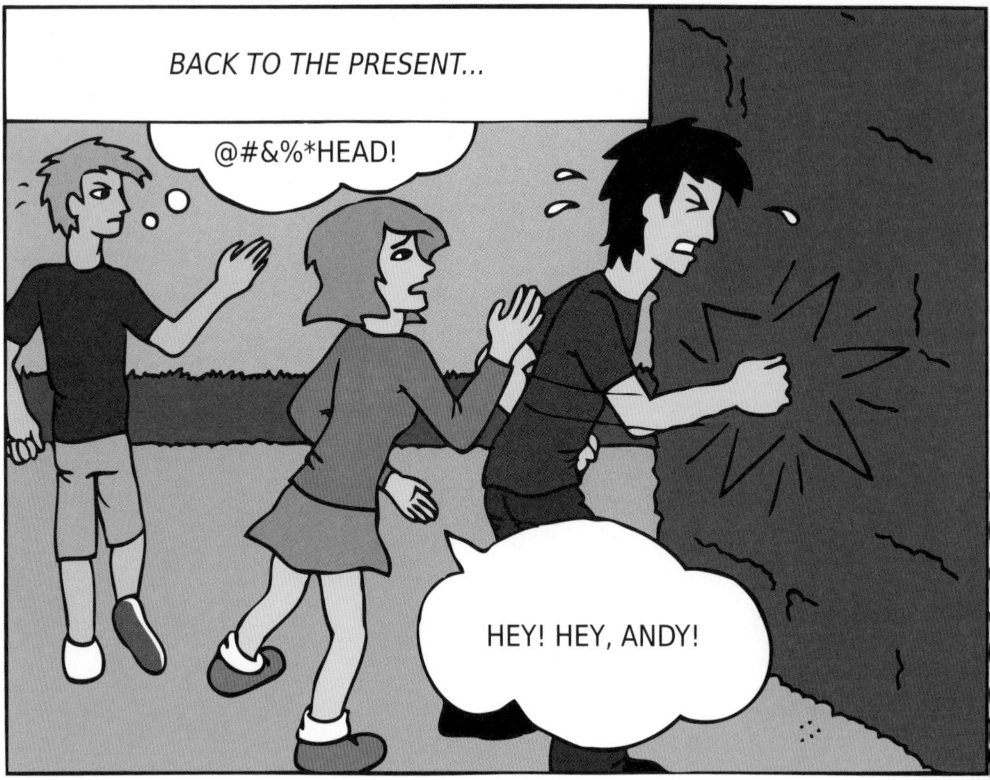
BACK TO THE PRESENT...
@#&%*HEAD!
HEY! HEY, ANDY!

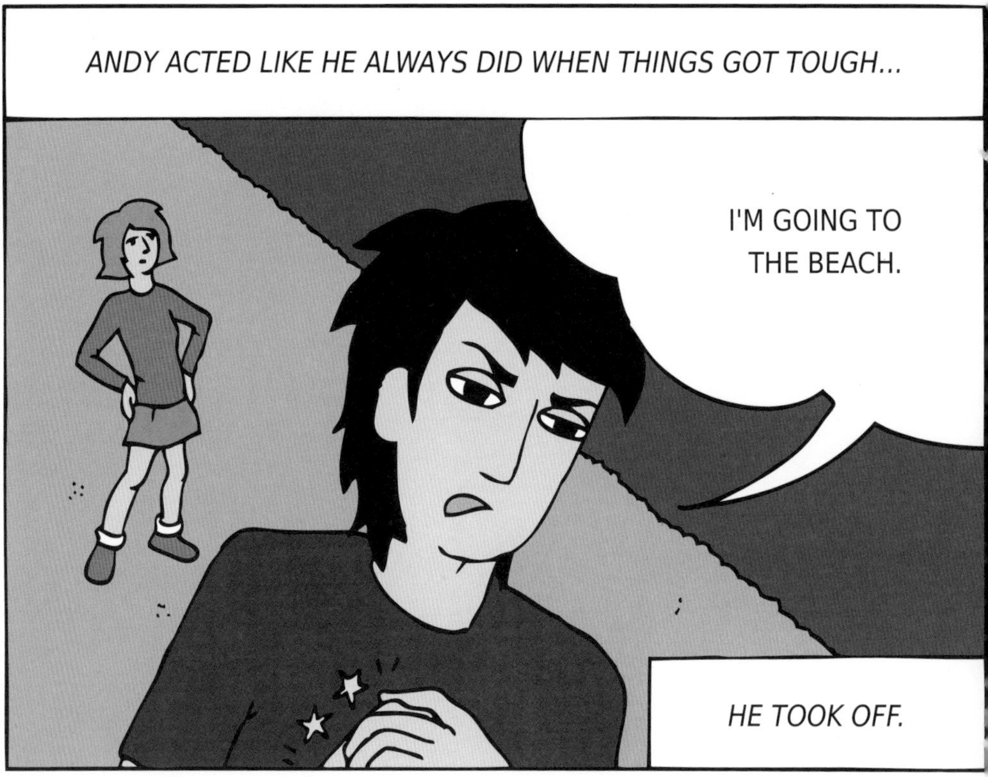
ANDY ACTED LIKE HE ALWAYS DID WHEN THINGS GOT TOUGH...
I'M GOING TO THE BEACH.
HE TOOK OFF.

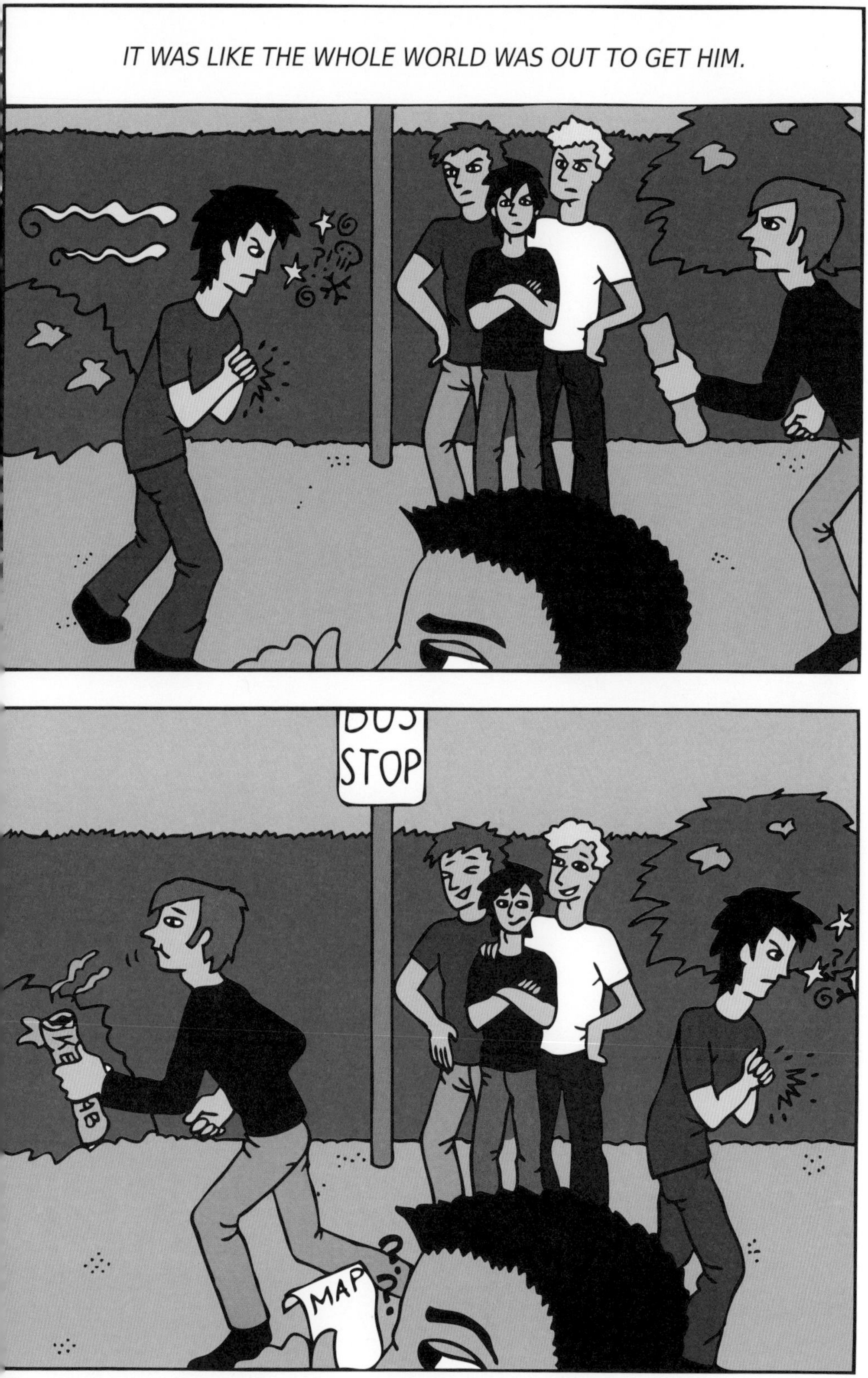
IT WAS LIKE THE WHOLE WORLD WAS OUT TO GET HIM.
STOP
MAP

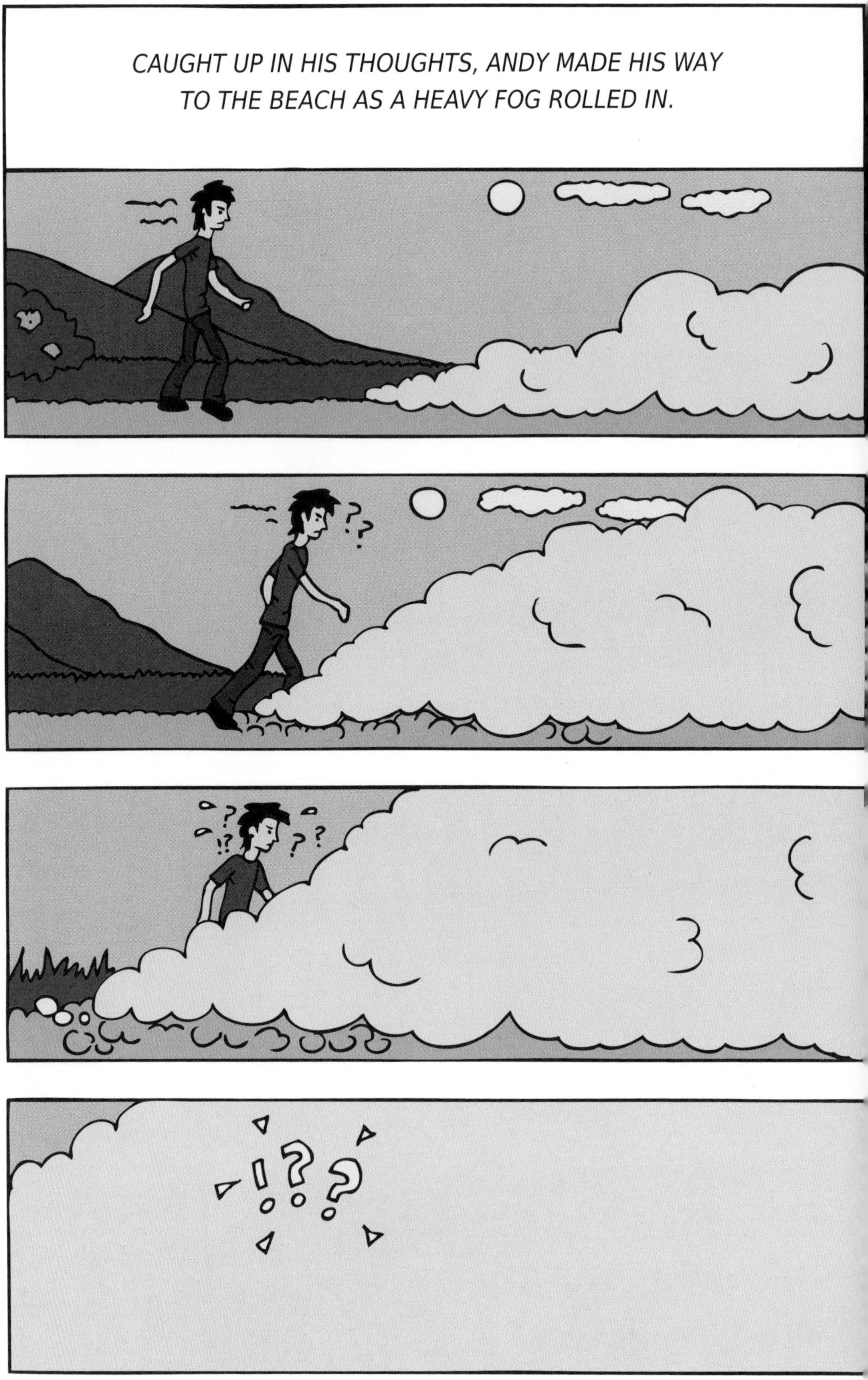
CAUGHT UP IN HIS THOUGHTS, ANDY MADE HIS WAY TO THE BEACH AS A HEAVY FOG ROLLED IN.

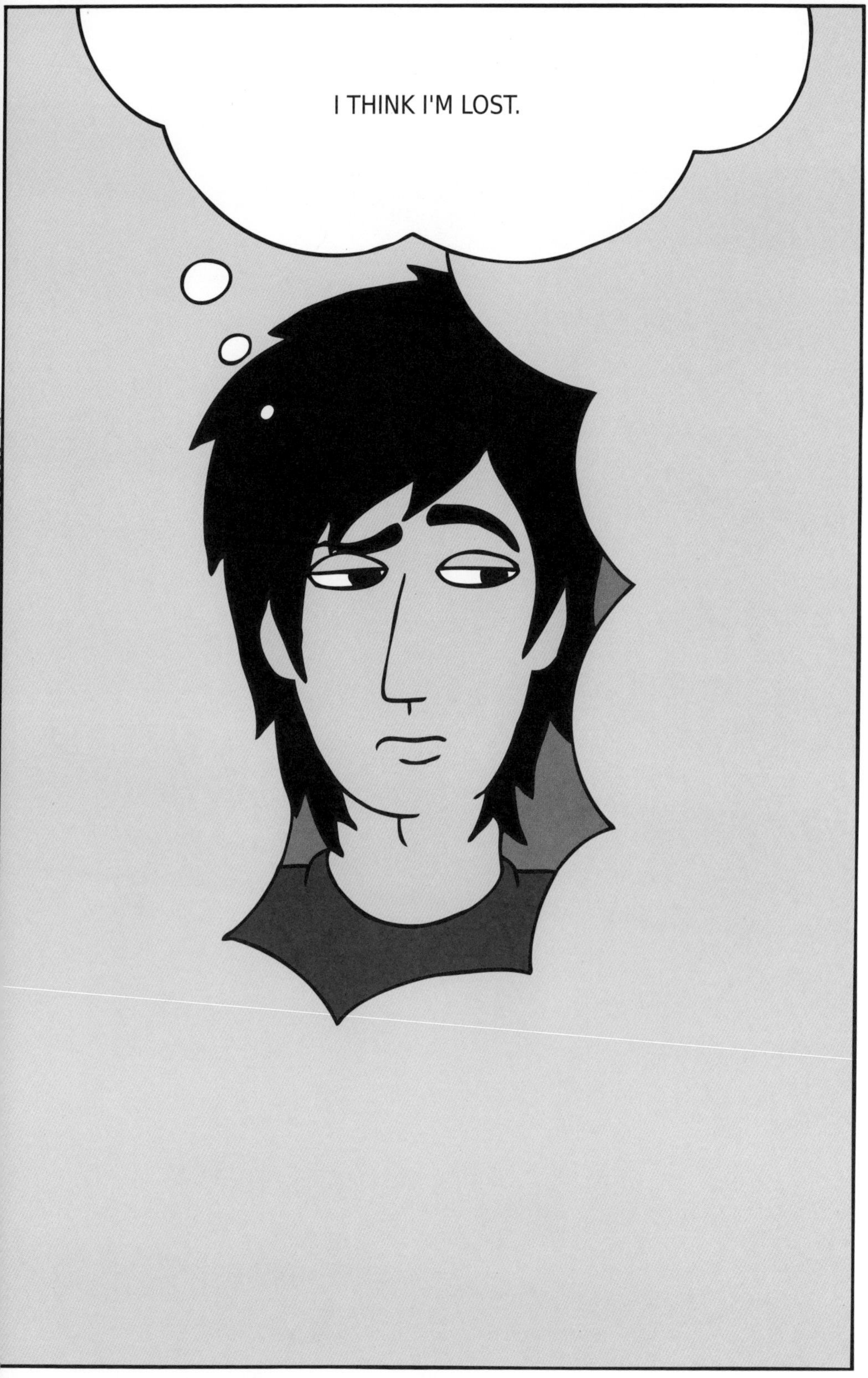
I THINK I'M LOST.

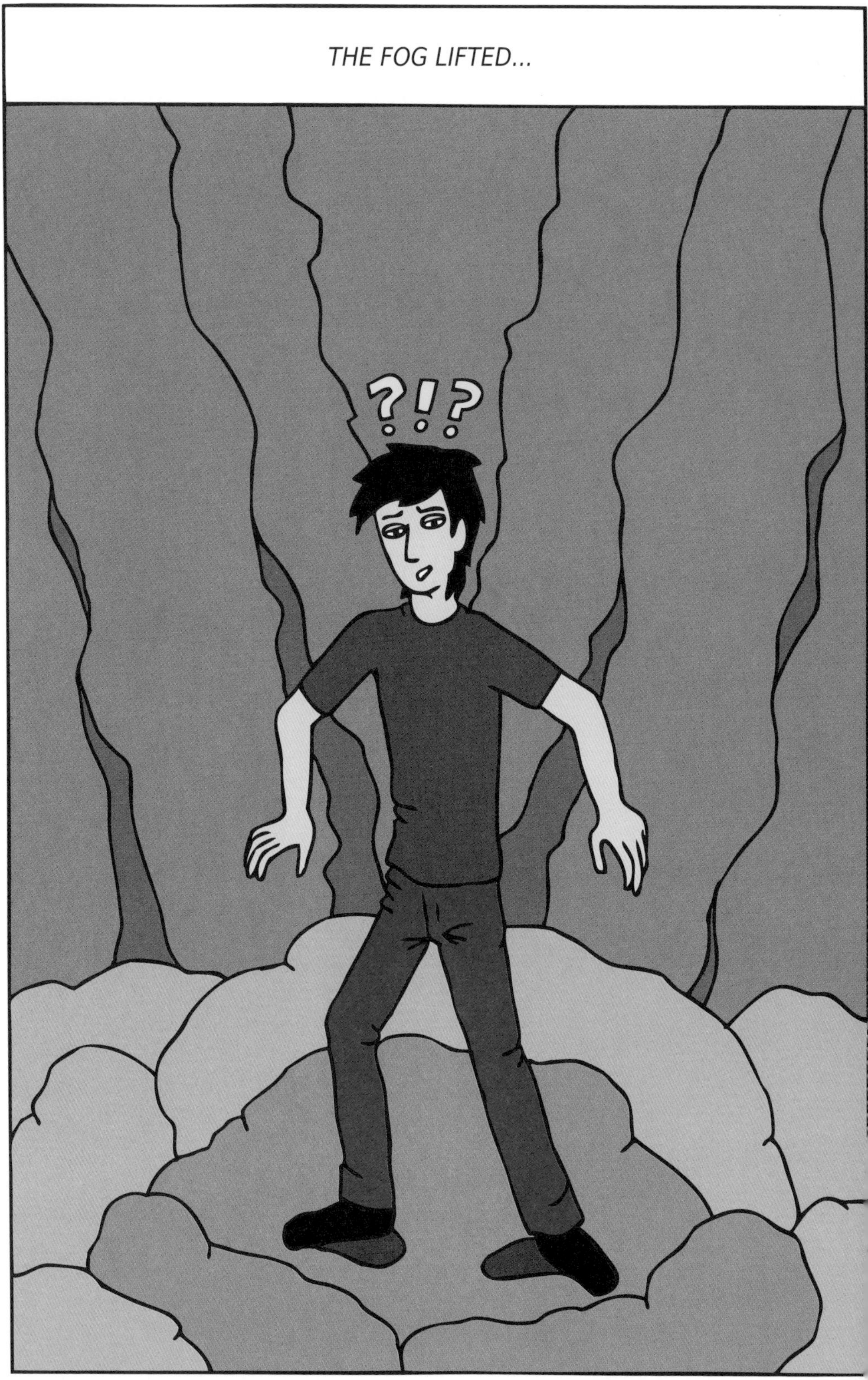
THE FOG LIFTED...
?!?

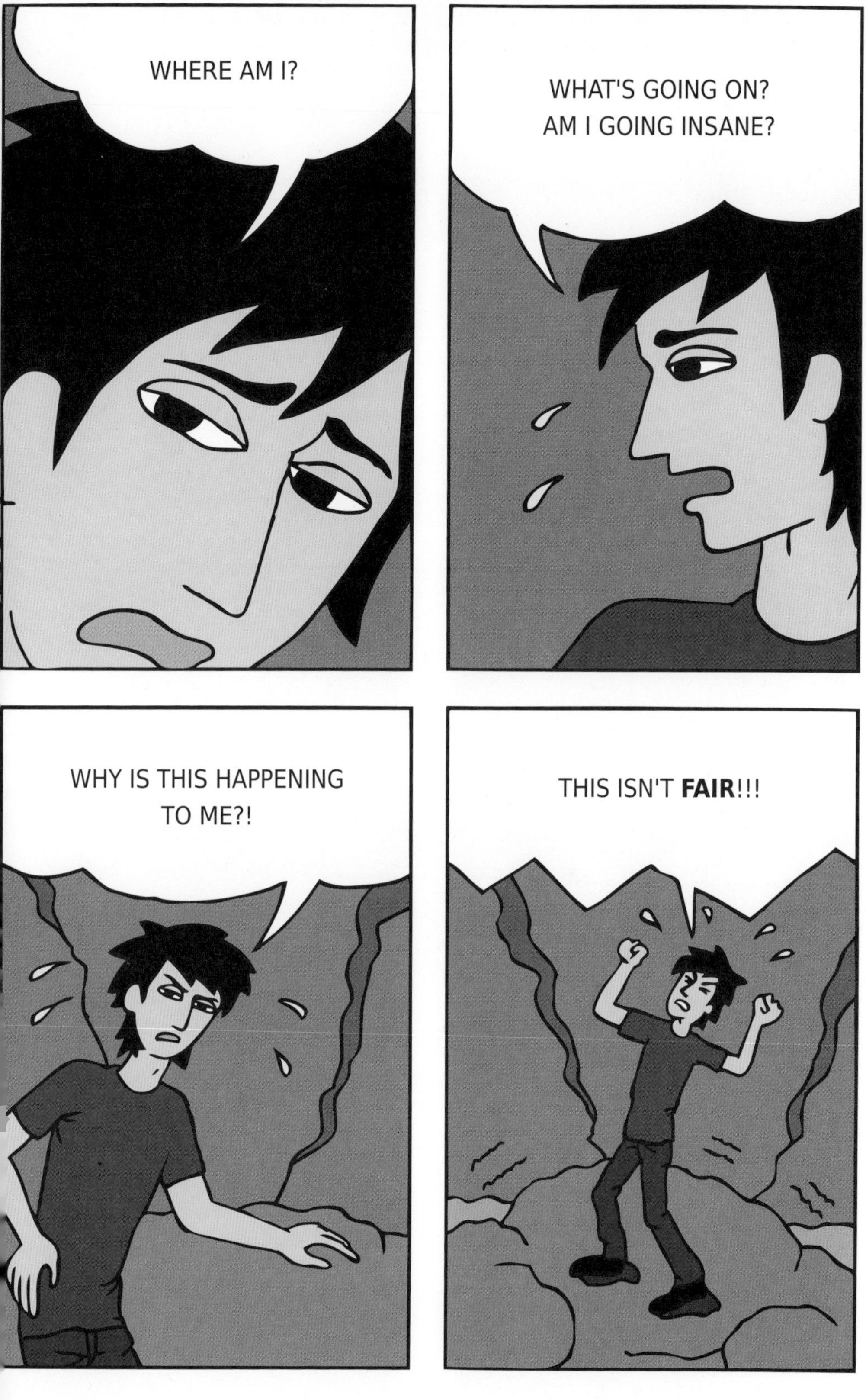
WHERE AM I?
WHAT'S GOING ON?
AM I GOING INSANE?
WHY IS THIS HAPPENING
TO ME?!
THIS ISN'T **FAIR**!!!

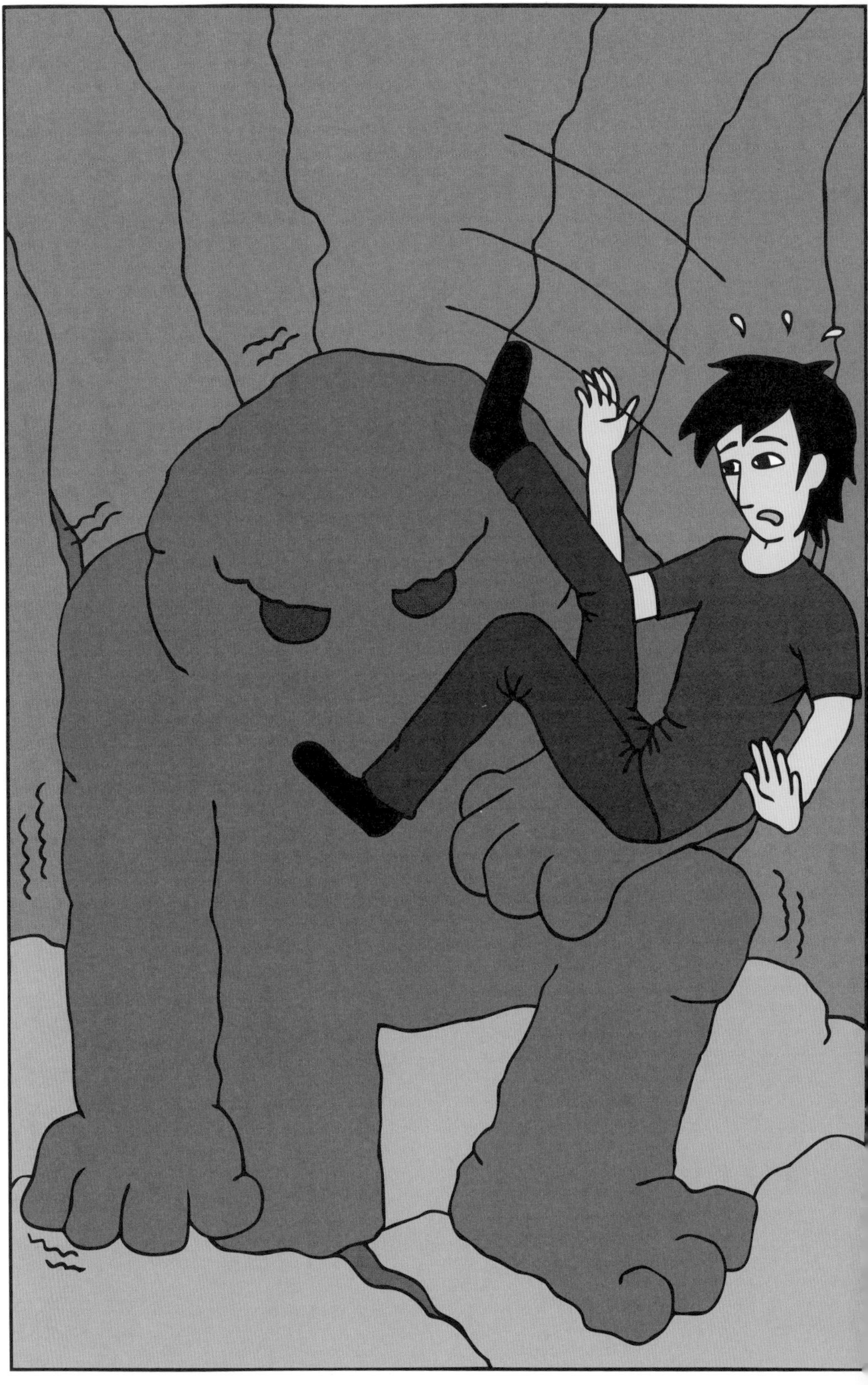

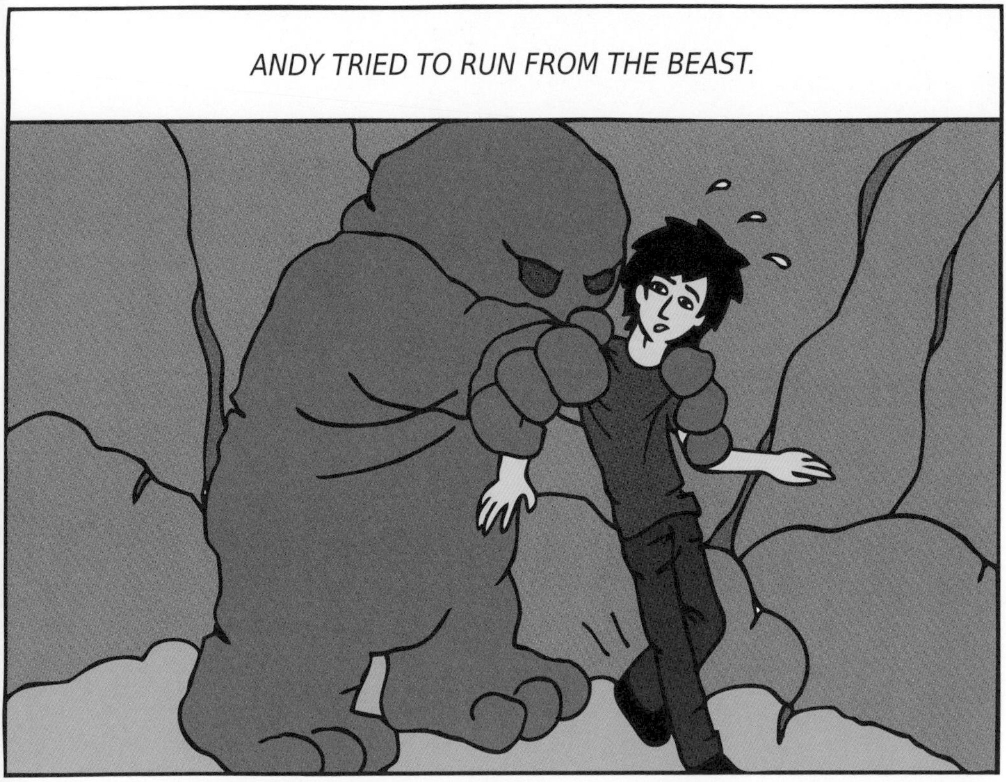
ANDY TRIED TO RUN FROM THE BEAST.

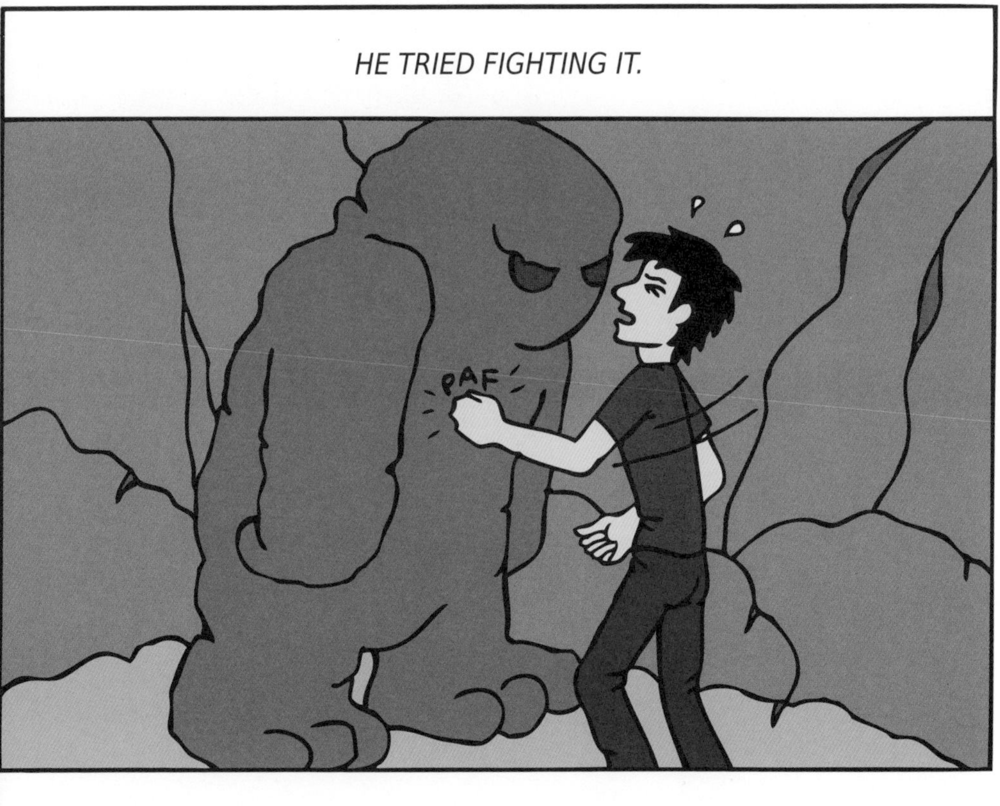
HE TRIED FIGHTING IT.
PAF

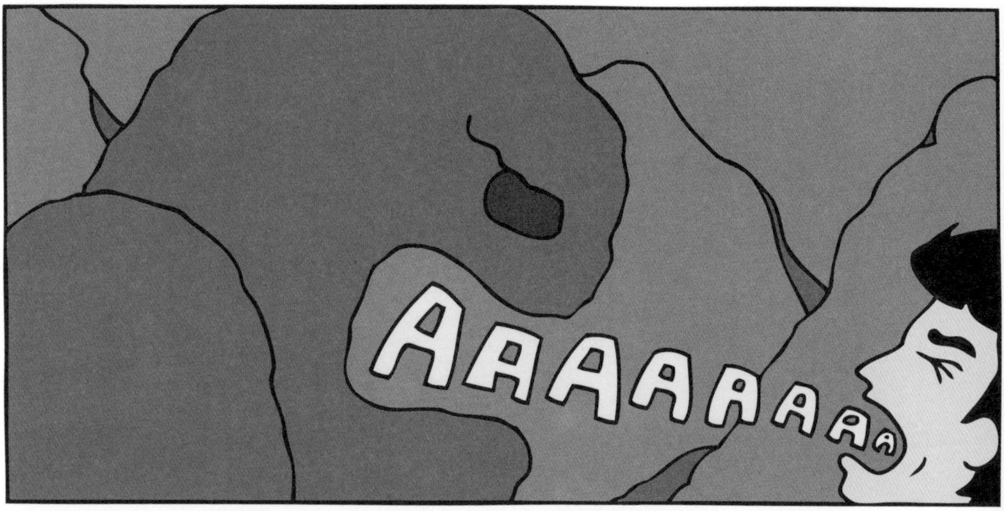
AAAAAAAAA

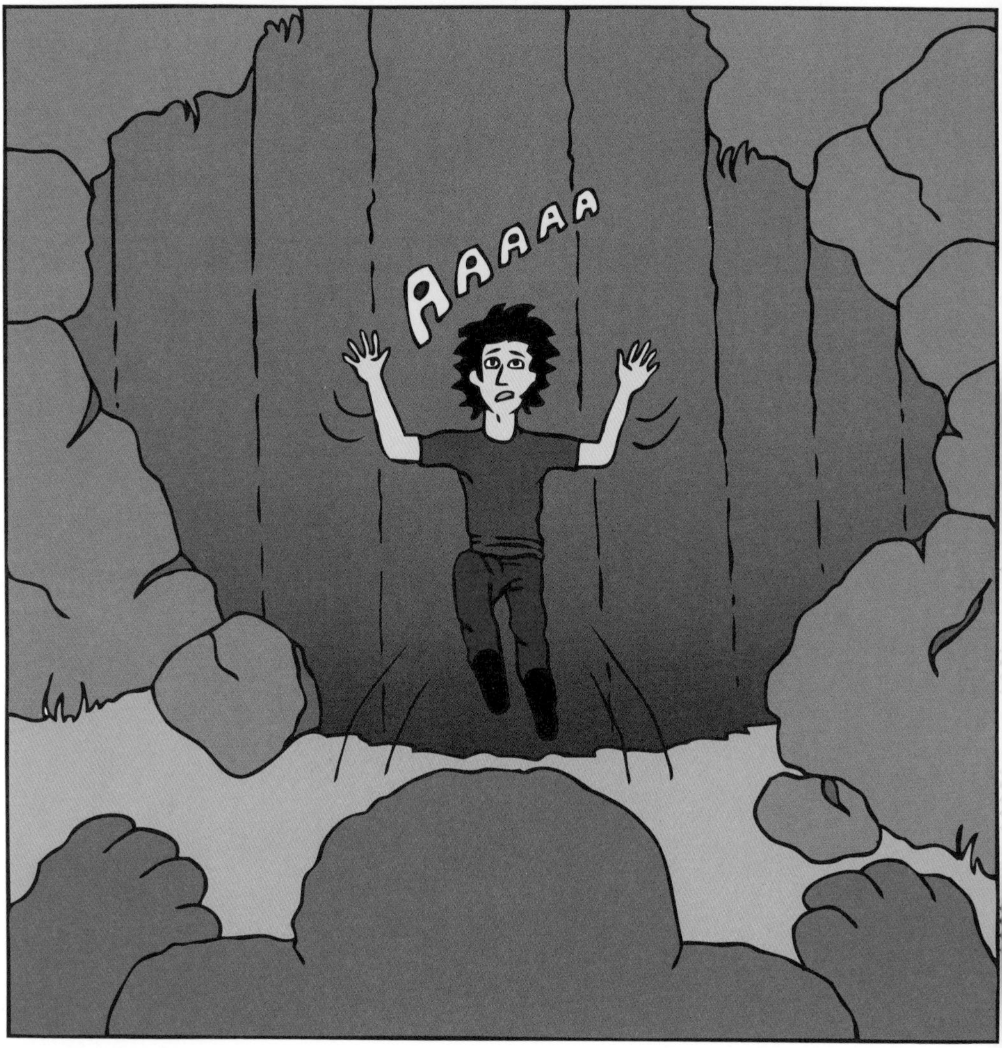
AAAAAA

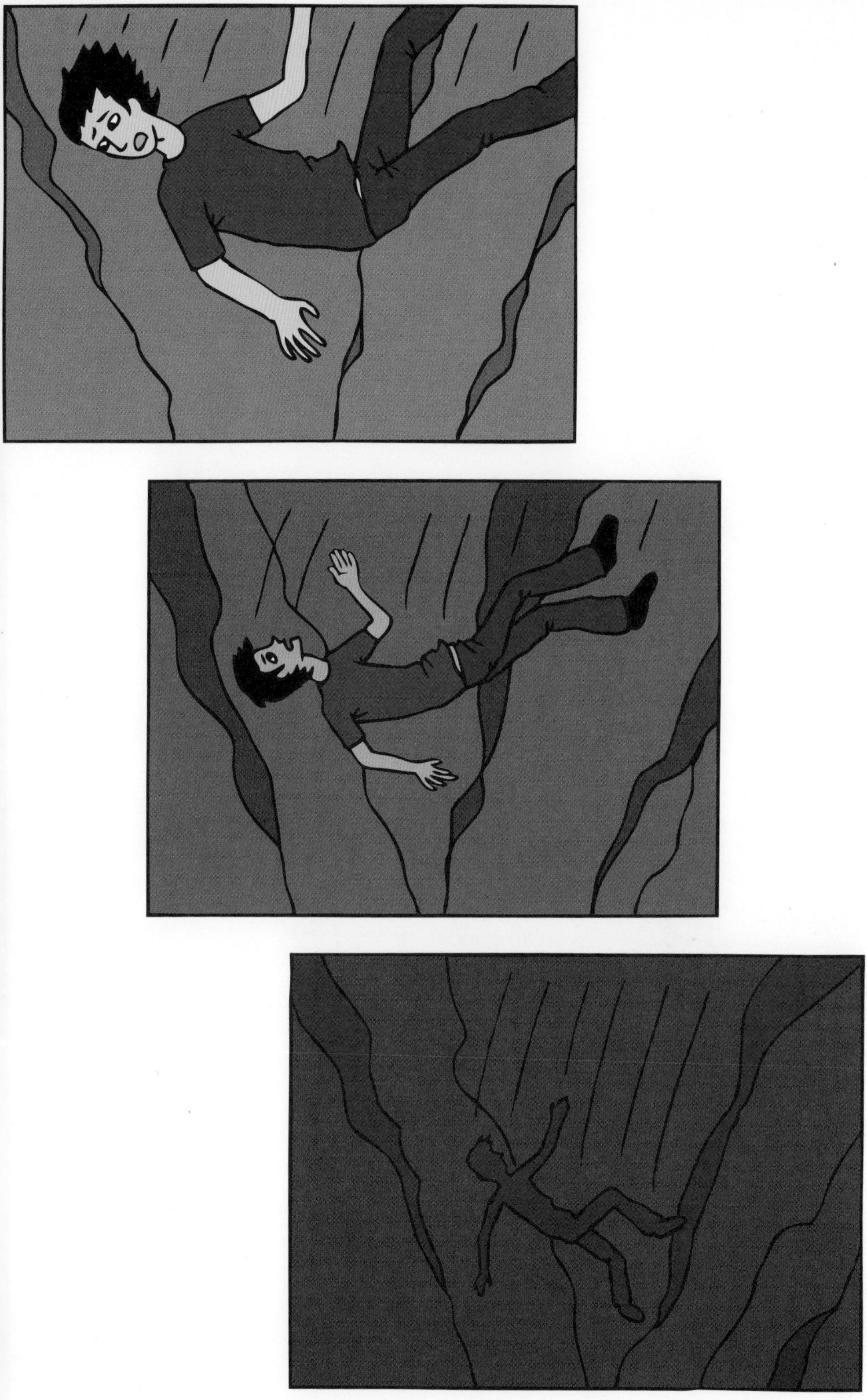

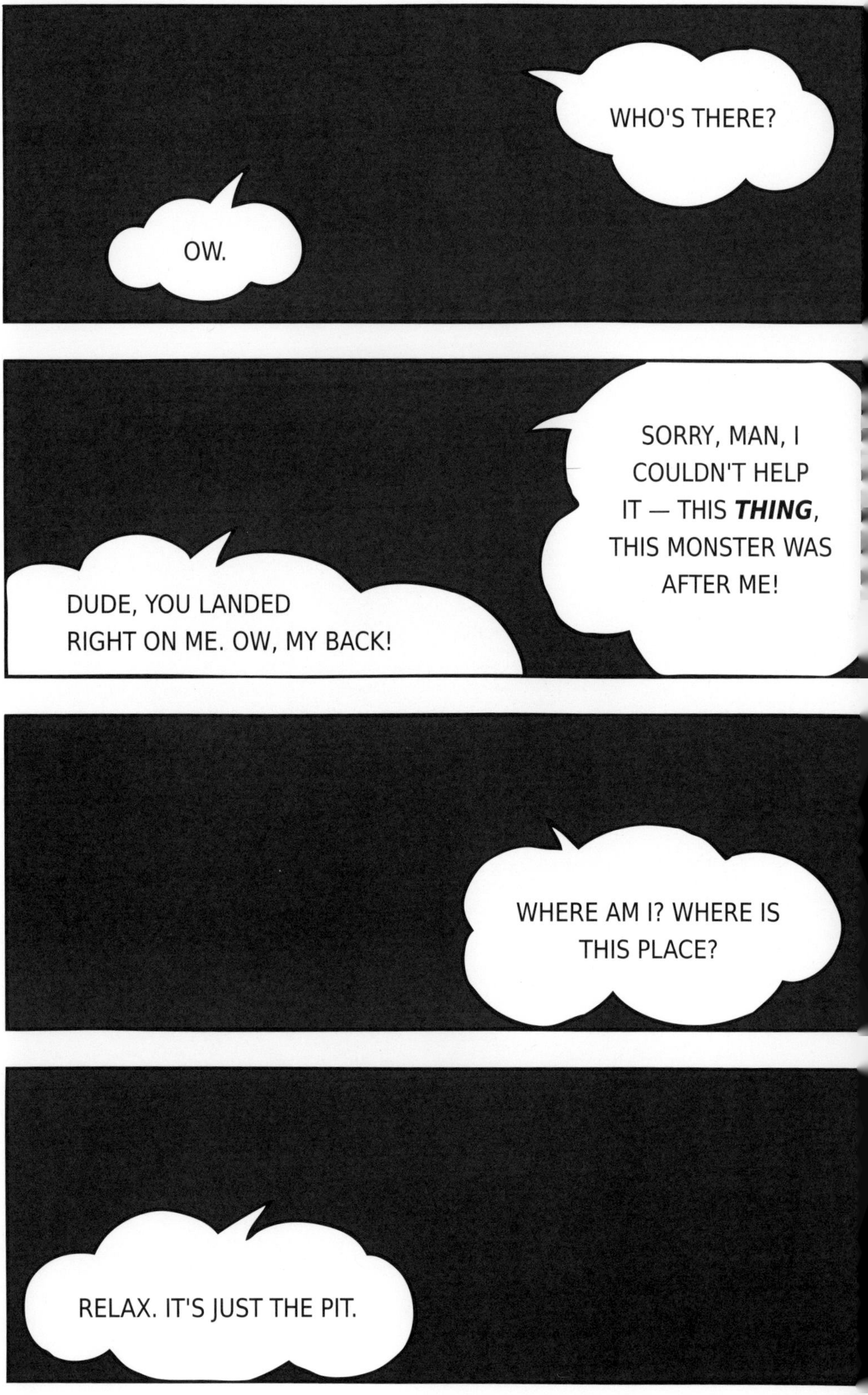
WHO'S THERE?
OW.
SORRY, MAN, I COULDN'T HELP IT — THIS ***THING***, THIS MONSTER WAS AFTER ME!
DUDE, YOU LANDED RIGHT ON ME. OW, MY BACK!
WHERE AM I? WHERE IS THIS PLACE?
RELAX. IT'S JUST THE PIT.

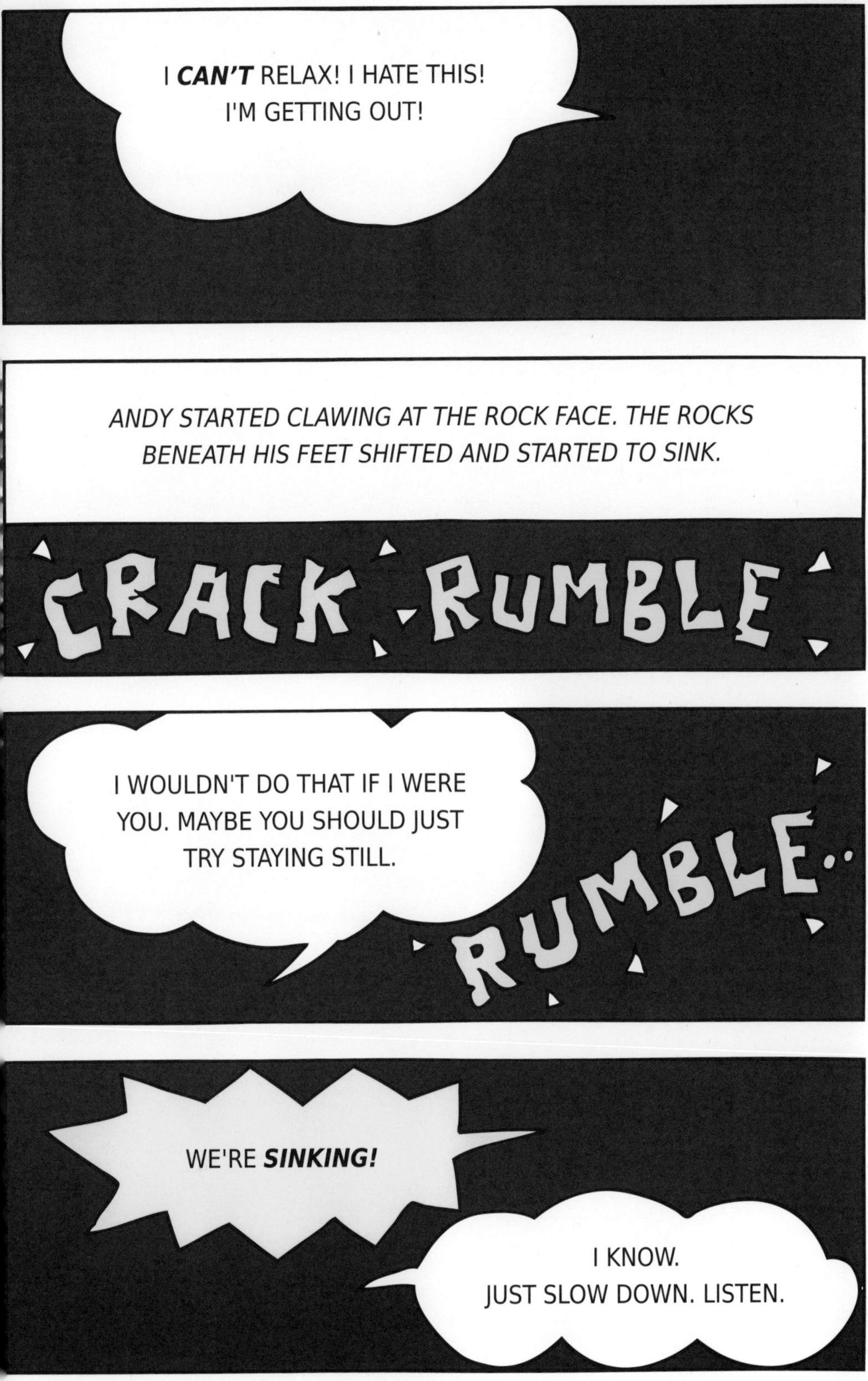
I **CAN'T** RELAX! I HATE THIS! I'M GETTING OUT!
ANDY STARTED CLAWING AT THE ROCK FACE. THE ROCKS BENEATH HIS FEET SHIFTED AND STARTED TO SINK.
CRACK RUMBLE
I WOULDN'T DO THAT IF I WERE YOU. MAYBE YOU SHOULD JUST TRY STAYING STILL.
RUMBLE..
WE'RE ***SINKING!***
I KNOW. JUST SLOW DOWN. LISTEN.

I CAN'T HEAR ANYTHING!
SURE YOU CAN.
FOR THE FIRST TIME IN A LONG WHILE, ANDY TOOK SOME ADVICE.
HE STOPPED, HE LISTENED, AND HE FOUND THAT...
HE ACTUALLY **COULD** HEAR SOME THINGS.
THE BEATING OF HIS HEART...
A DROP OF WATER.
AND THEN, IN THE DISTANCE...
ANDY SAW A PINPRICK OF LIGHT.

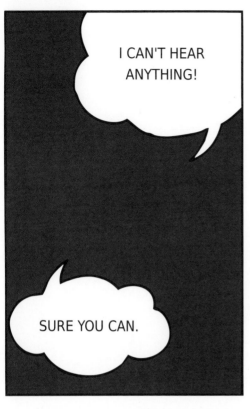

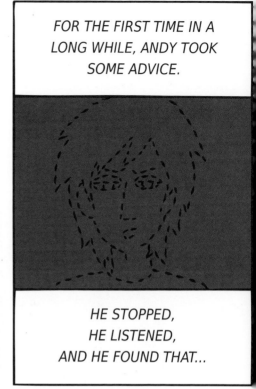

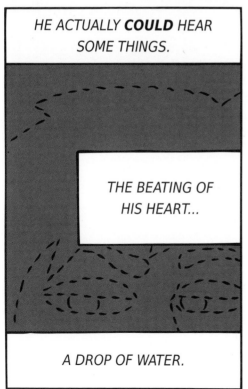

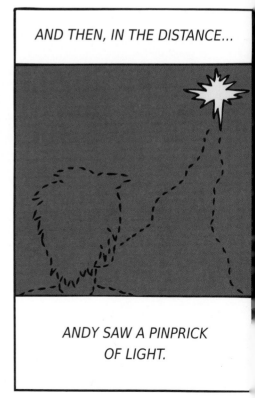

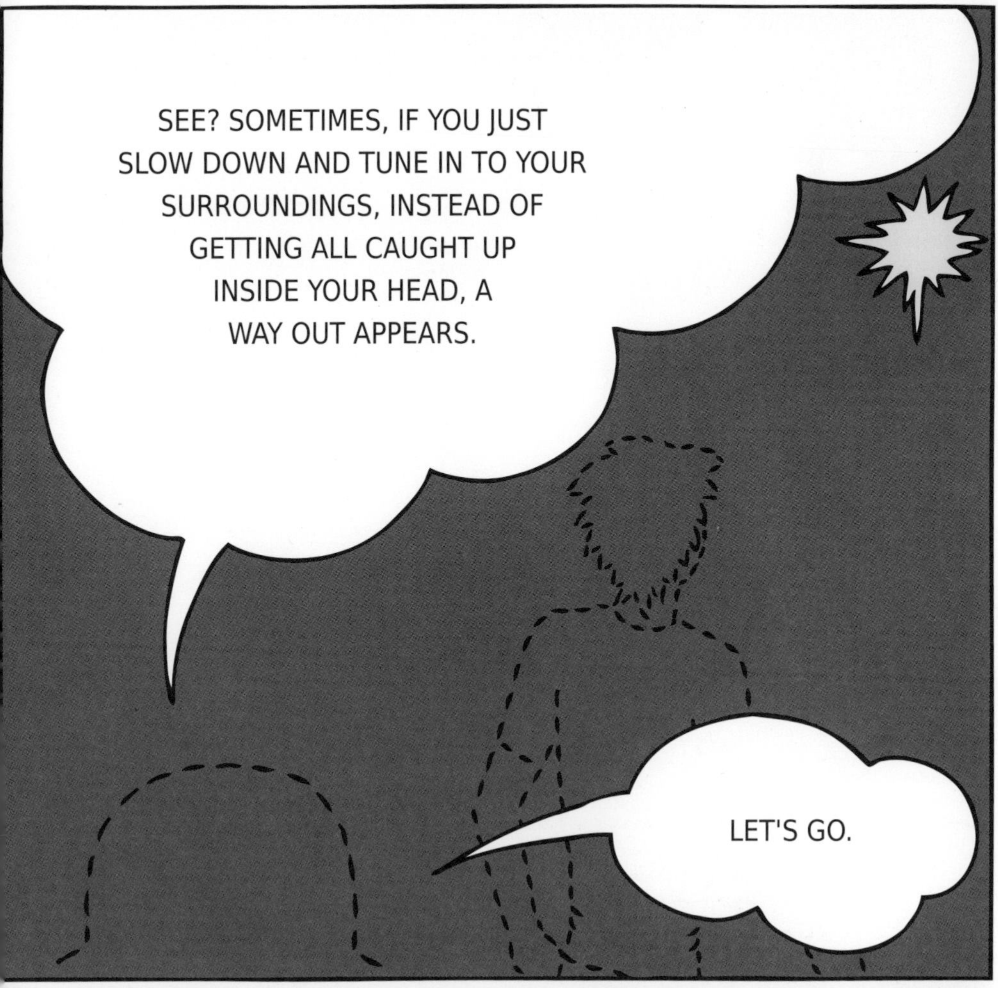
SEE? SOMETIMES, IF YOU JUST SLOW DOWN AND TUNE IN TO YOUR SURROUNDINGS, INSTEAD OF GETTING ALL CAUGHT UP INSIDE YOUR HEAD, A WAY OUT APPEARS.
LET'S GO.

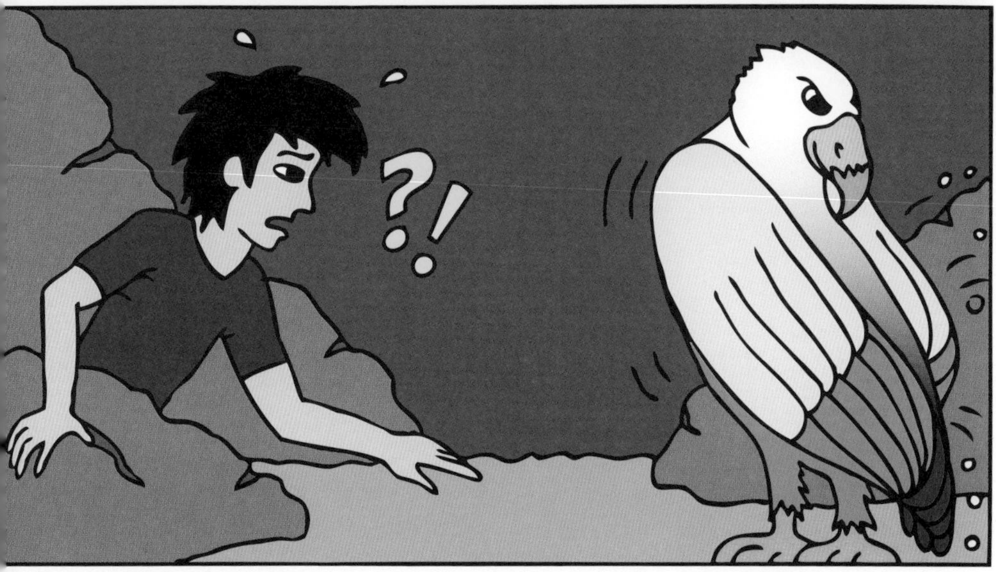
?!

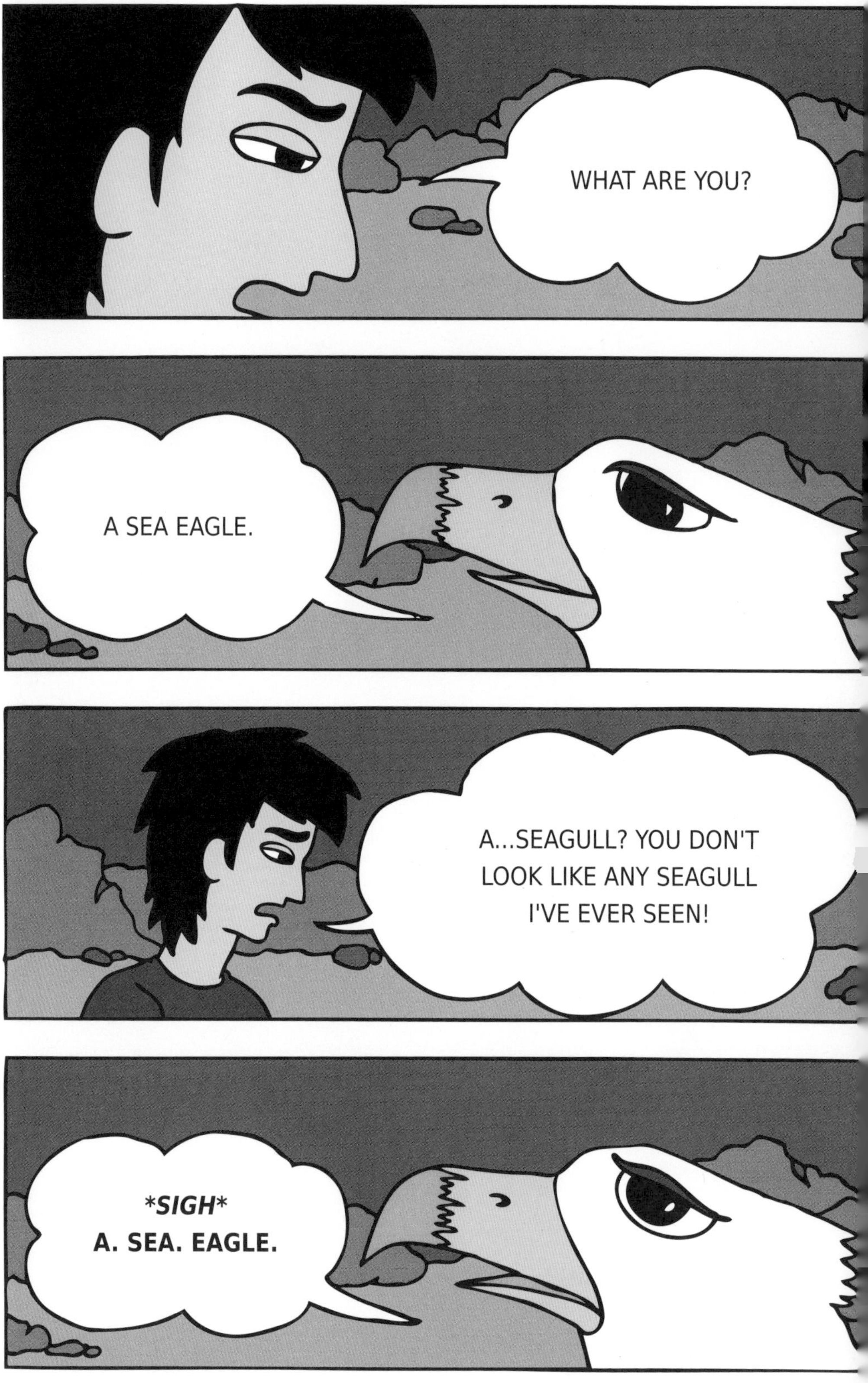
WHAT ARE YOU?
A SEA EAGLE.
A...SEAGULL? YOU DON'T LOOK LIKE ANY SEAGULL I'VE EVER SEEN!
SIGH A. SEA. EAGLE.

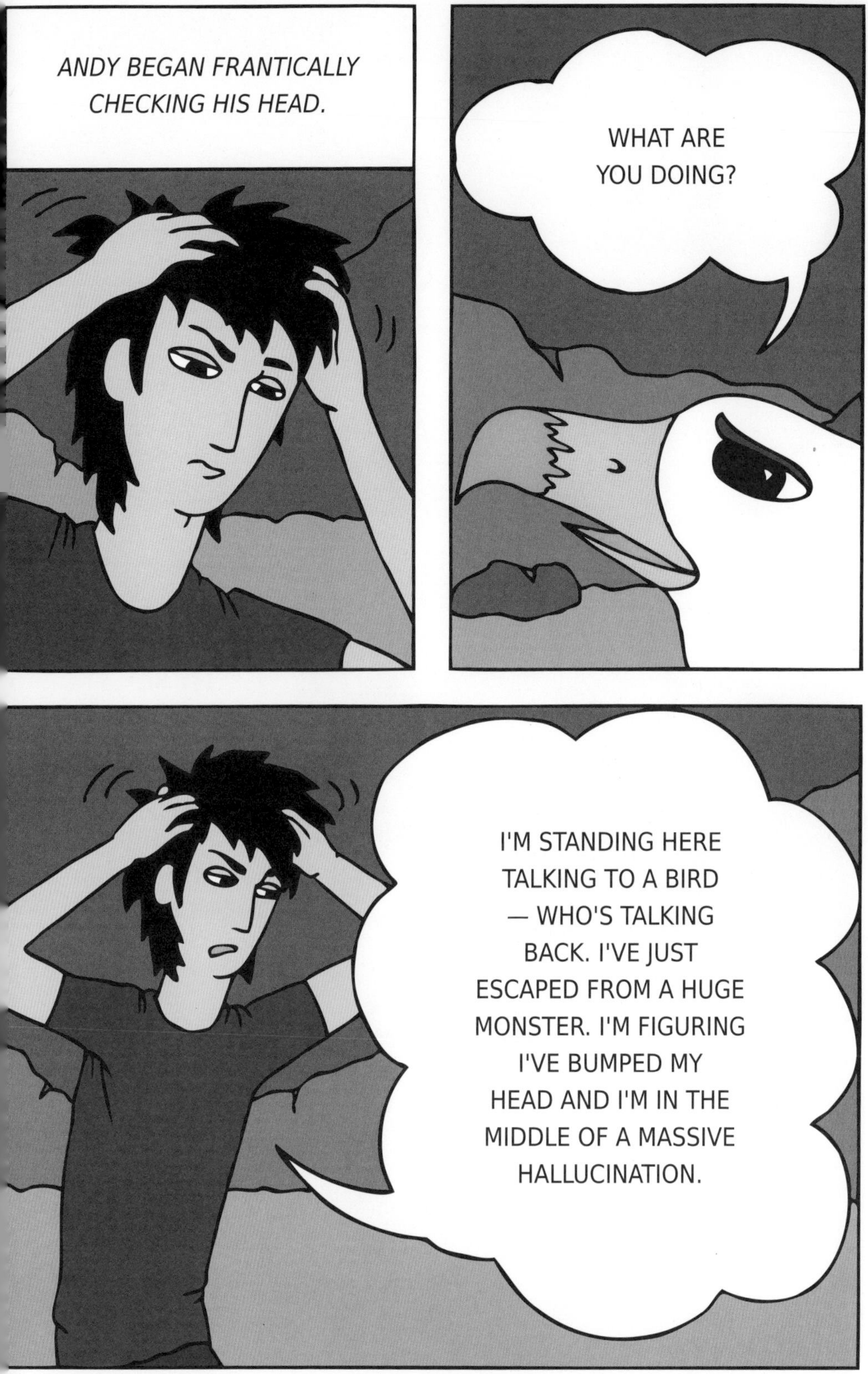
ANDY BEGAN FRANTICALLY CHECKING HIS HEAD.
WHAT ARE YOU DOING?
I'M STANDING HERE TALKING TO A BIRD — WHO'S TALKING BACK. I'VE JUST ESCAPED FROM A HUGE MONSTER. I'M FIGURING I'VE BUMPED MY HEAD AND I'M IN THE MIDDLE OF A MASSIVE HALLUCINATION.

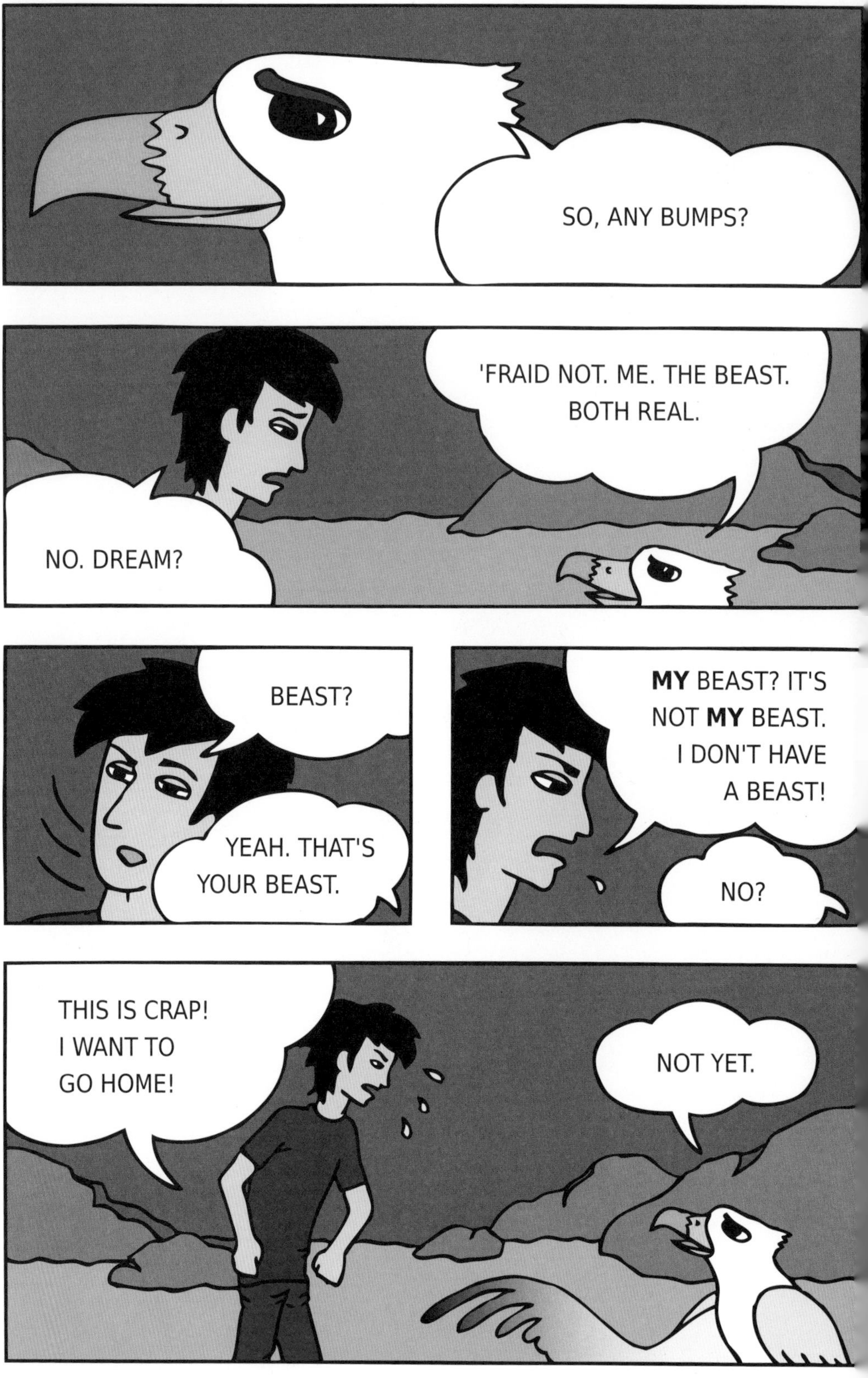
SO, ANY BUMPS?
NO. DREAM?
'FRAID NOT. ME. THE BEAST. BOTH REAL.
BEAST?
YEAH. THAT'S YOUR BEAST.
MY BEAST? IT'S NOT **MY** BEAST. I DON'T HAVE A BEAST!
NO?
THIS IS CRAP! I WANT TO GO HOME!
NOT YET.

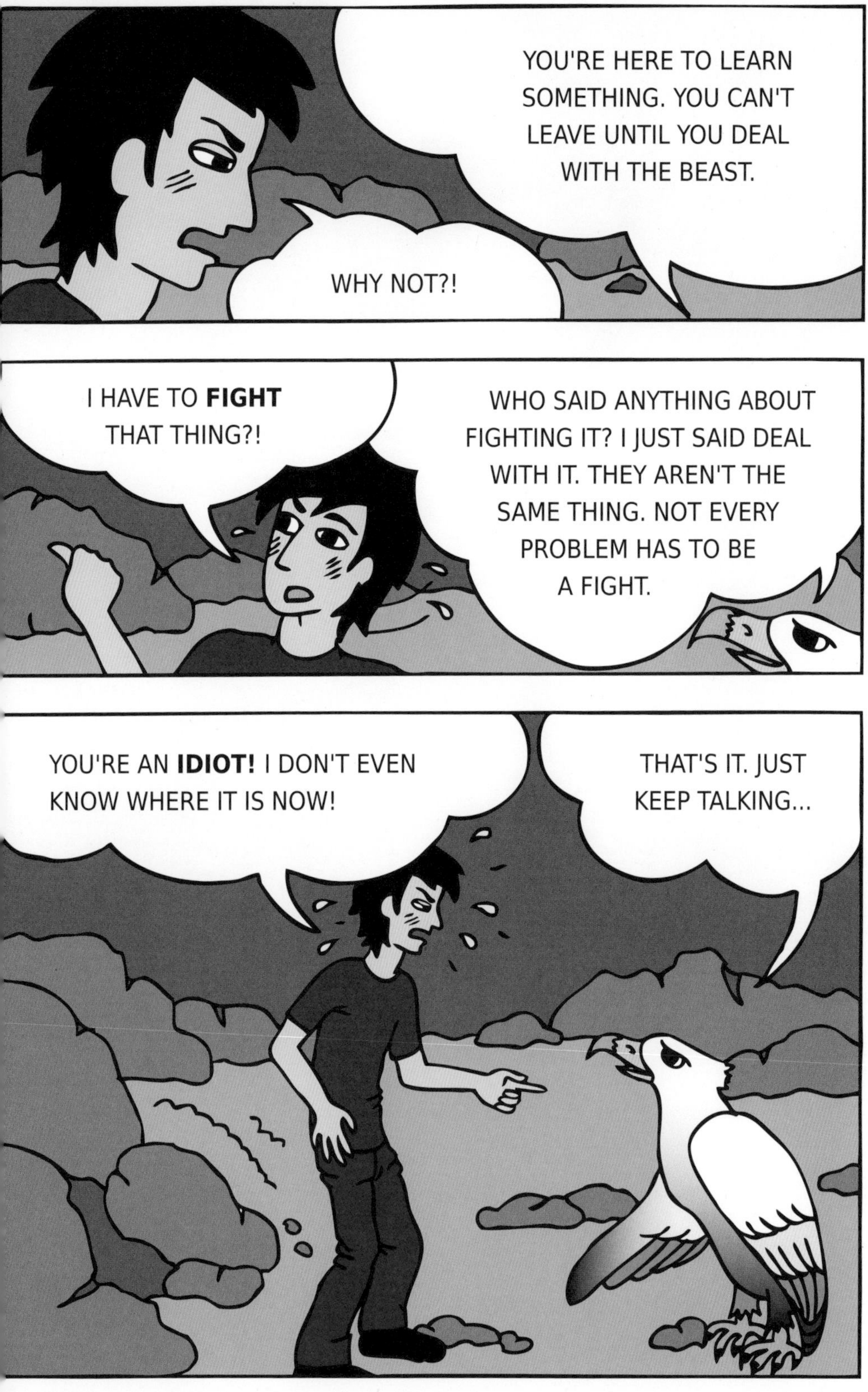
YOU'RE HERE TO LEARN SOMETHING. YOU CAN'T LEAVE UNTIL YOU DEAL WITH THE BEAST.
WHY NOT?!
I HAVE TO **FIGHT** THAT THING?!
WHO SAID ANYTHING ABOUT FIGHTING IT? I JUST SAID DEAL WITH IT. THEY AREN'T THE SAME THING. NOT EVERY PROBLEM HAS TO BE A FIGHT.
YOU'RE AN **IDIOT!** I DON'T EVEN KNOW WHERE IT IS NOW!
THAT'S IT. JUST KEEP TALKING...

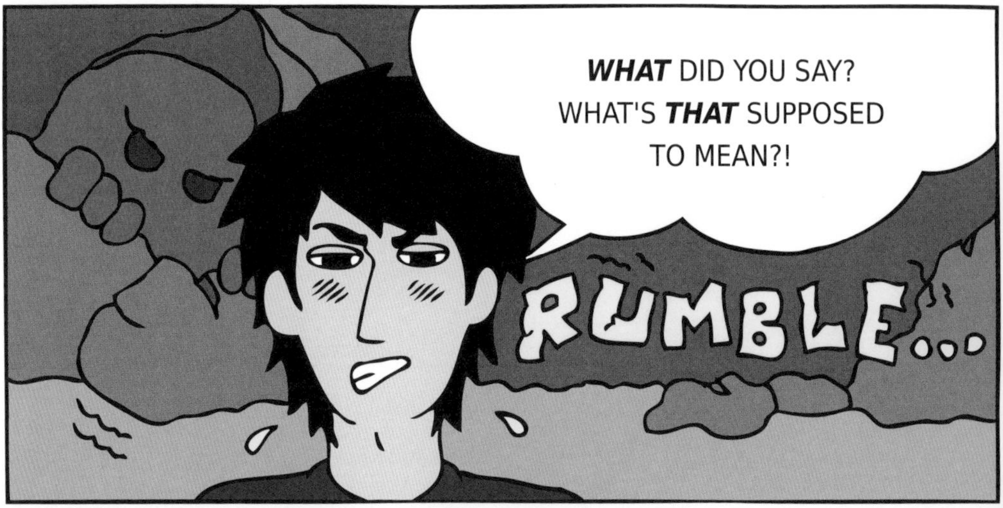
WHAT DID YOU SAY? WHAT'S **THAT** SUPPOSED TO MEAN?!
RUMBLE...

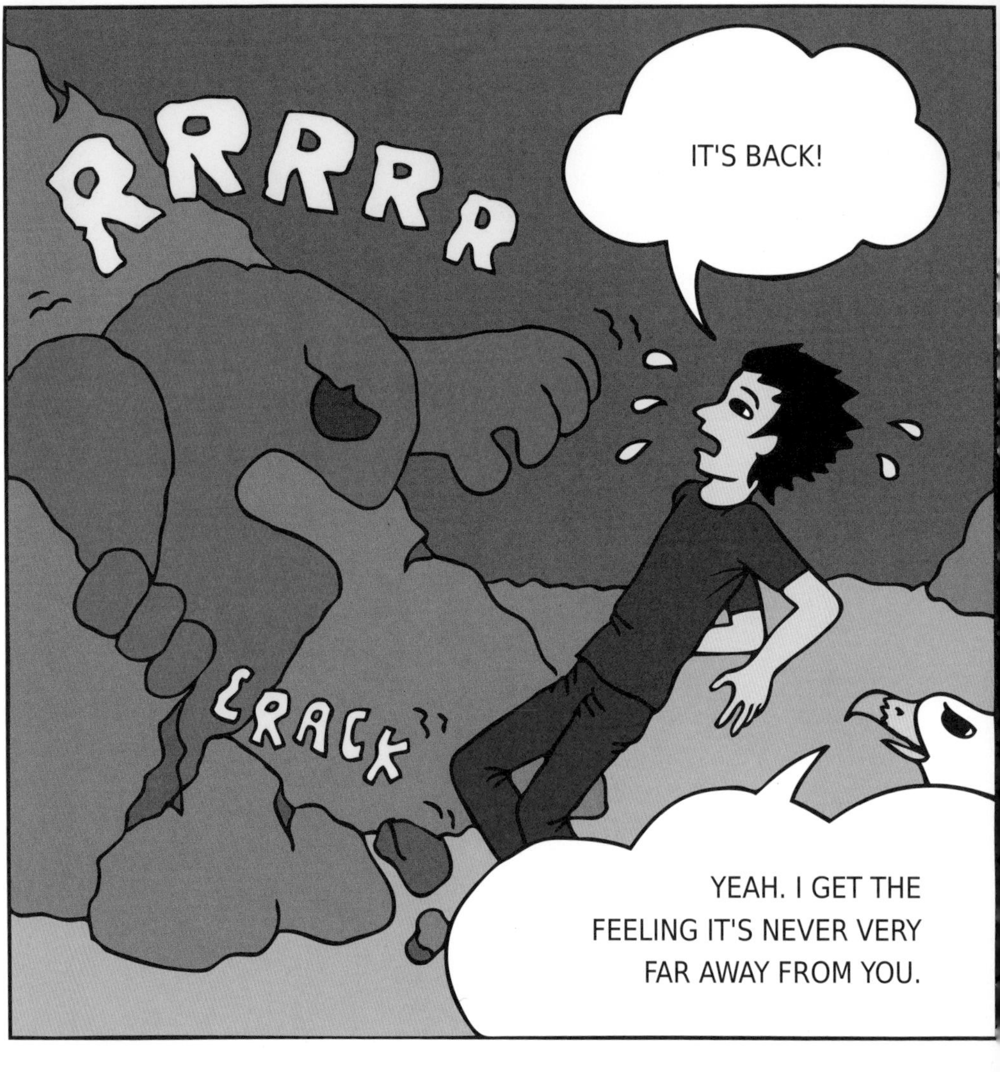
RRRRRR
IT'S BACK!
CRACK
YEAH. I GET THE FEELING IT'S NEVER VERY FAR AWAY FROM YOU.

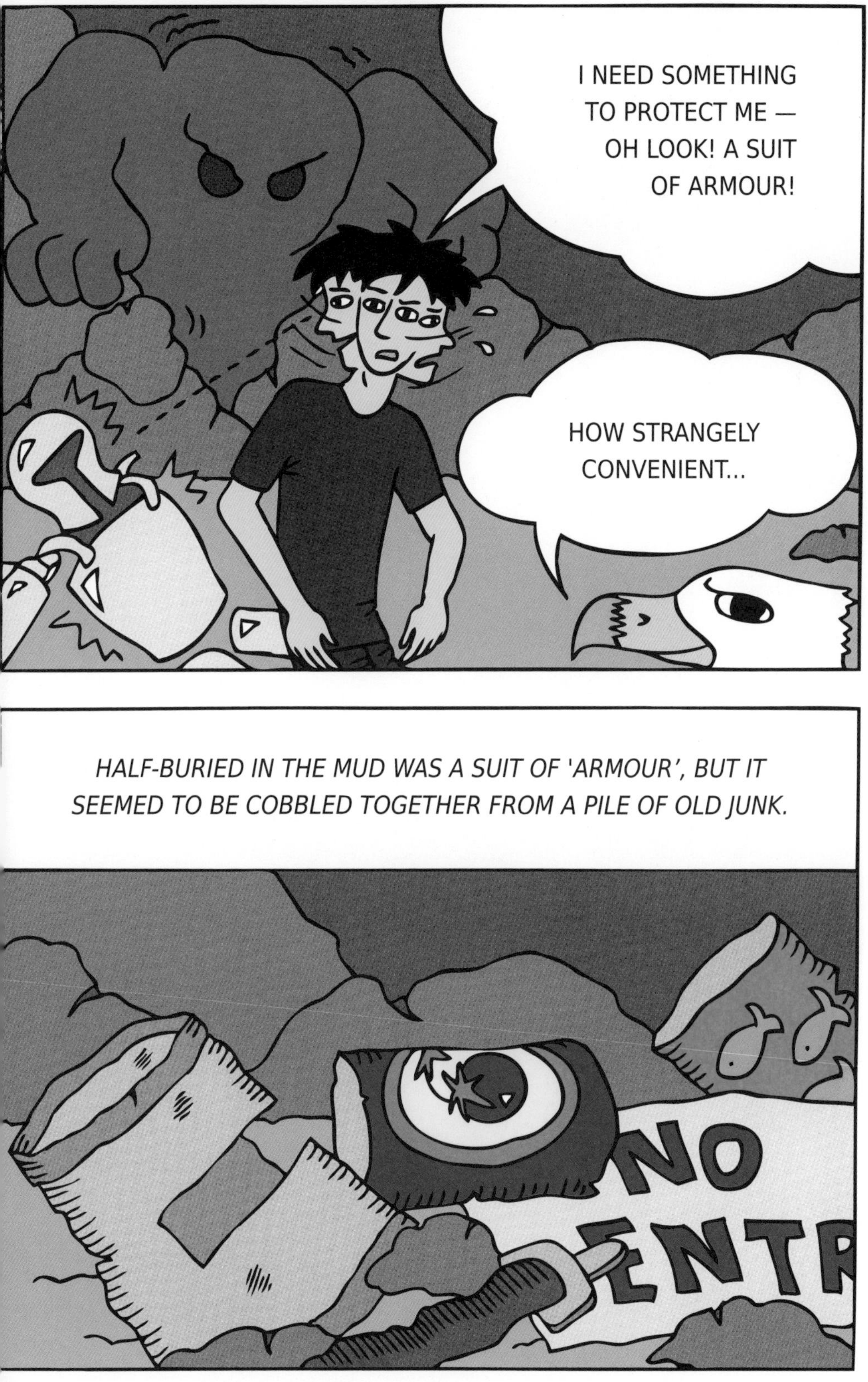
I NEED SOMETHING TO PROTECT ME — OH LOOK! A SUIT OF ARMOUR!
HOW STRANGELY CONVENIENT...
HALF-BURIED IN THE MUD WAS A SUIT OF 'ARMOUR', BUT IT SEEMED TO BE COBBLED TOGETHER FROM A PILE OF OLD JUNK.
NO
ENTR

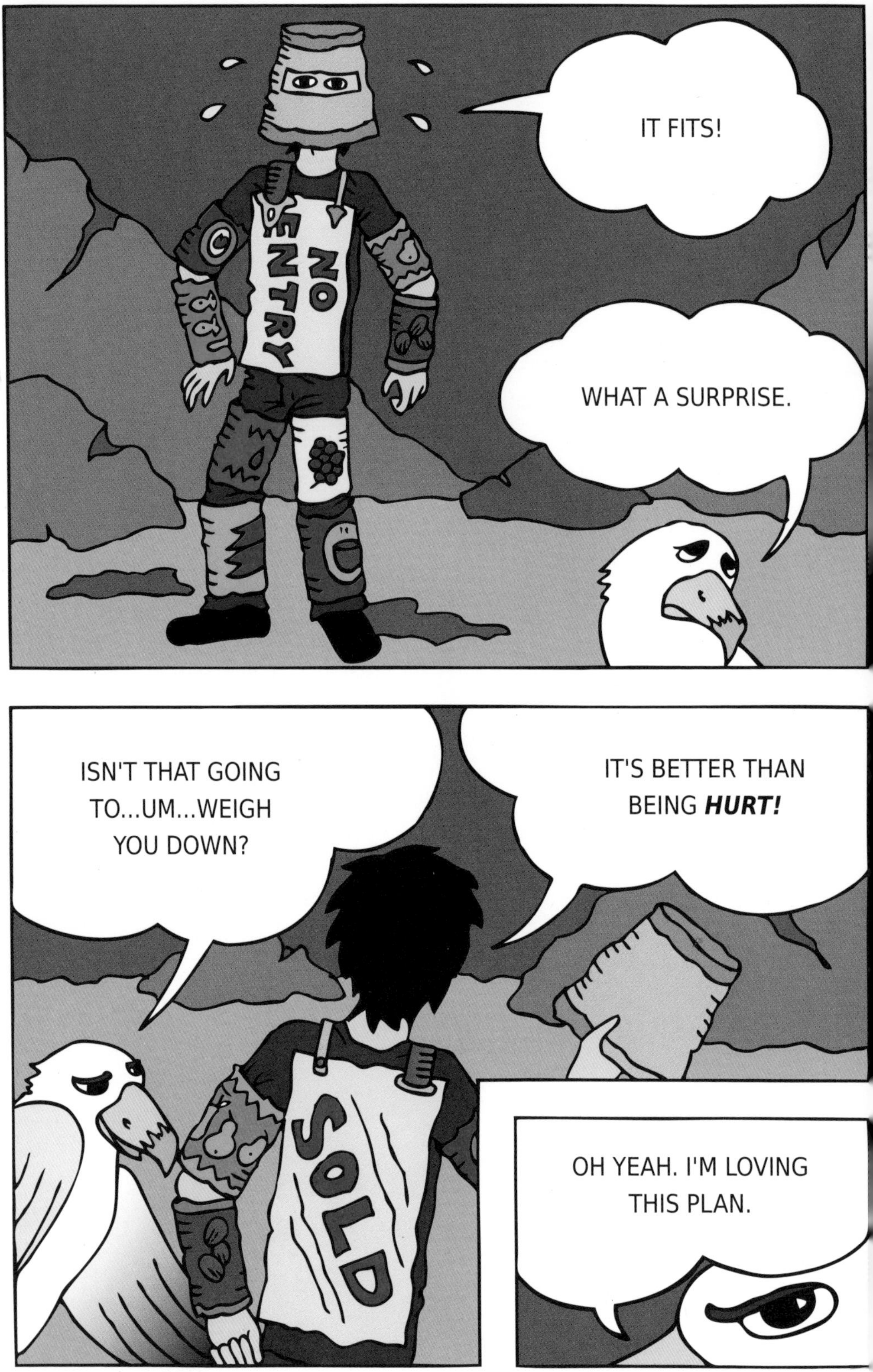
IT FITS!
WHAT A SURPRISE.
NO ENTRY
ISN'T THAT GOING TO...UM...WEIGH YOU DOWN?
IT'S BETTER THAN BEING ***HURT!***
SOLD
OH YEAH. I'M LOVING THIS PLAN.

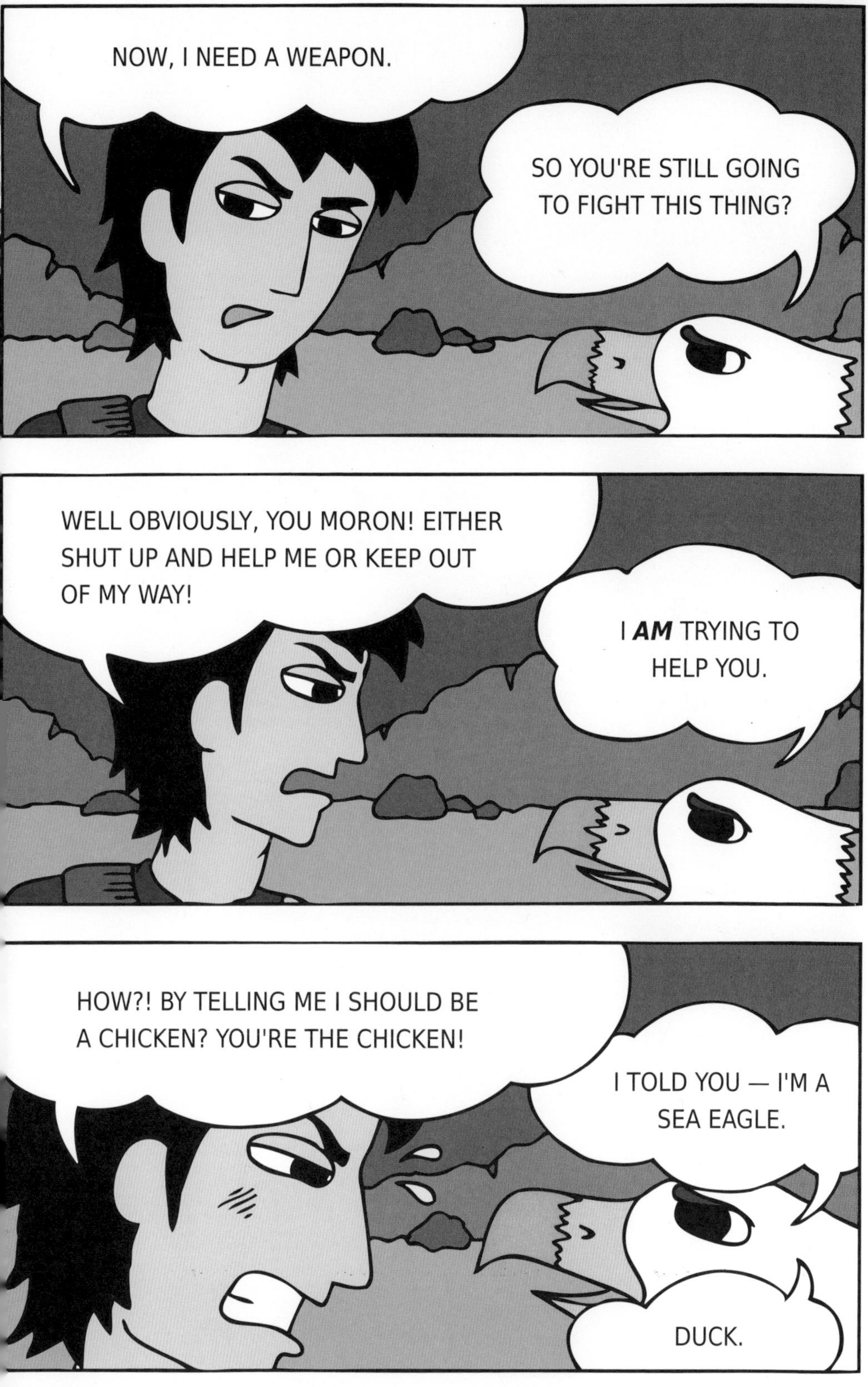
NOW, I NEED A WEAPON.
SO YOU'RE STILL GOING TO FIGHT THIS THING?
WELL OBVIOUSLY, YOU MORON! EITHER SHUT UP AND HELP ME OR KEEP OUT OF MY WAY!
I ***AM*** TRYING TO HELP YOU.
HOW?! BY TELLING ME I SHOULD BE A CHICKEN? YOU'RE THE CHICKEN!
I TOLD YOU — I'M A SEA EAGLE.
DUCK.

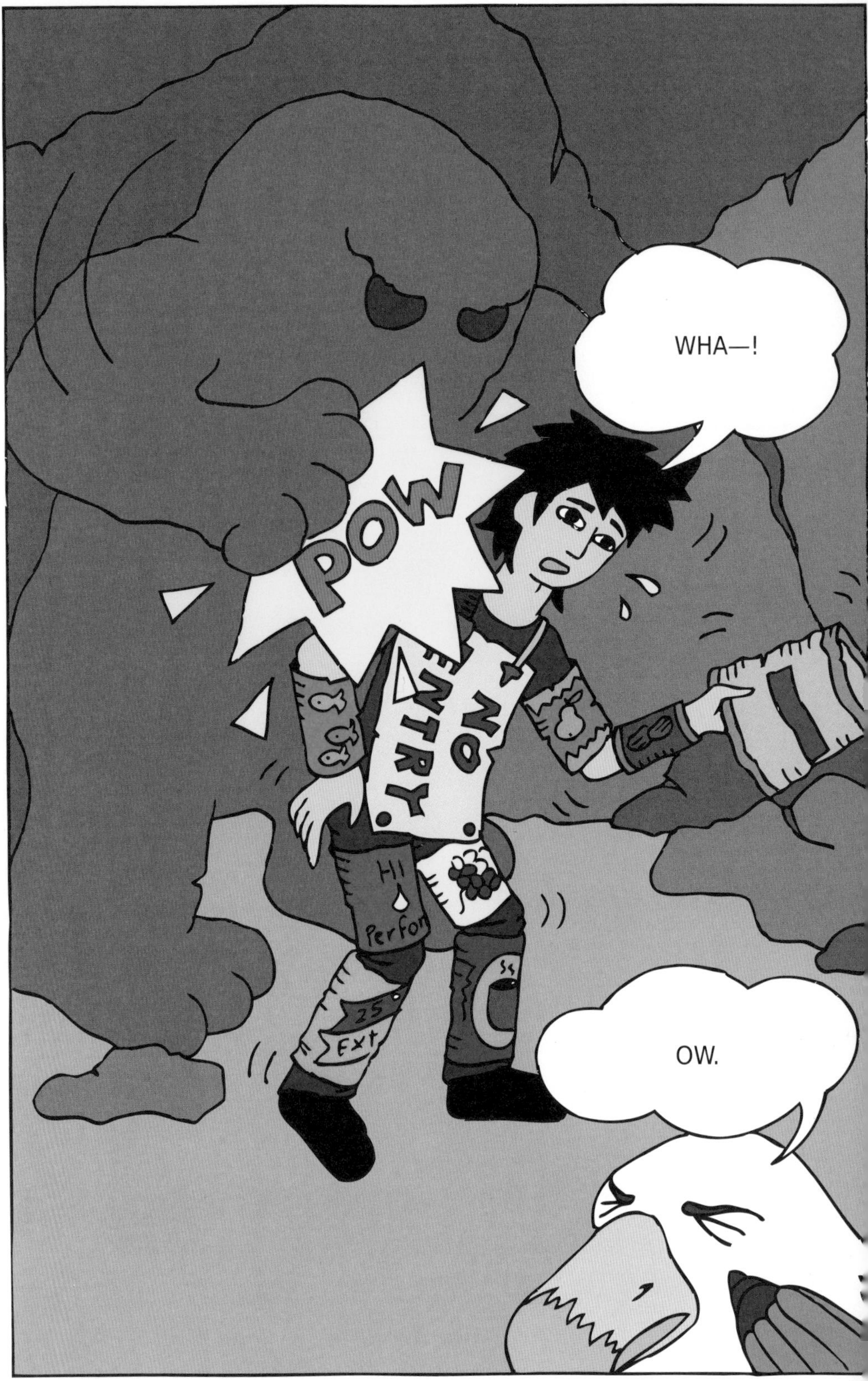
WHA—!
POW
NO ENTRY
HI Perfor
25 Ext
OW.

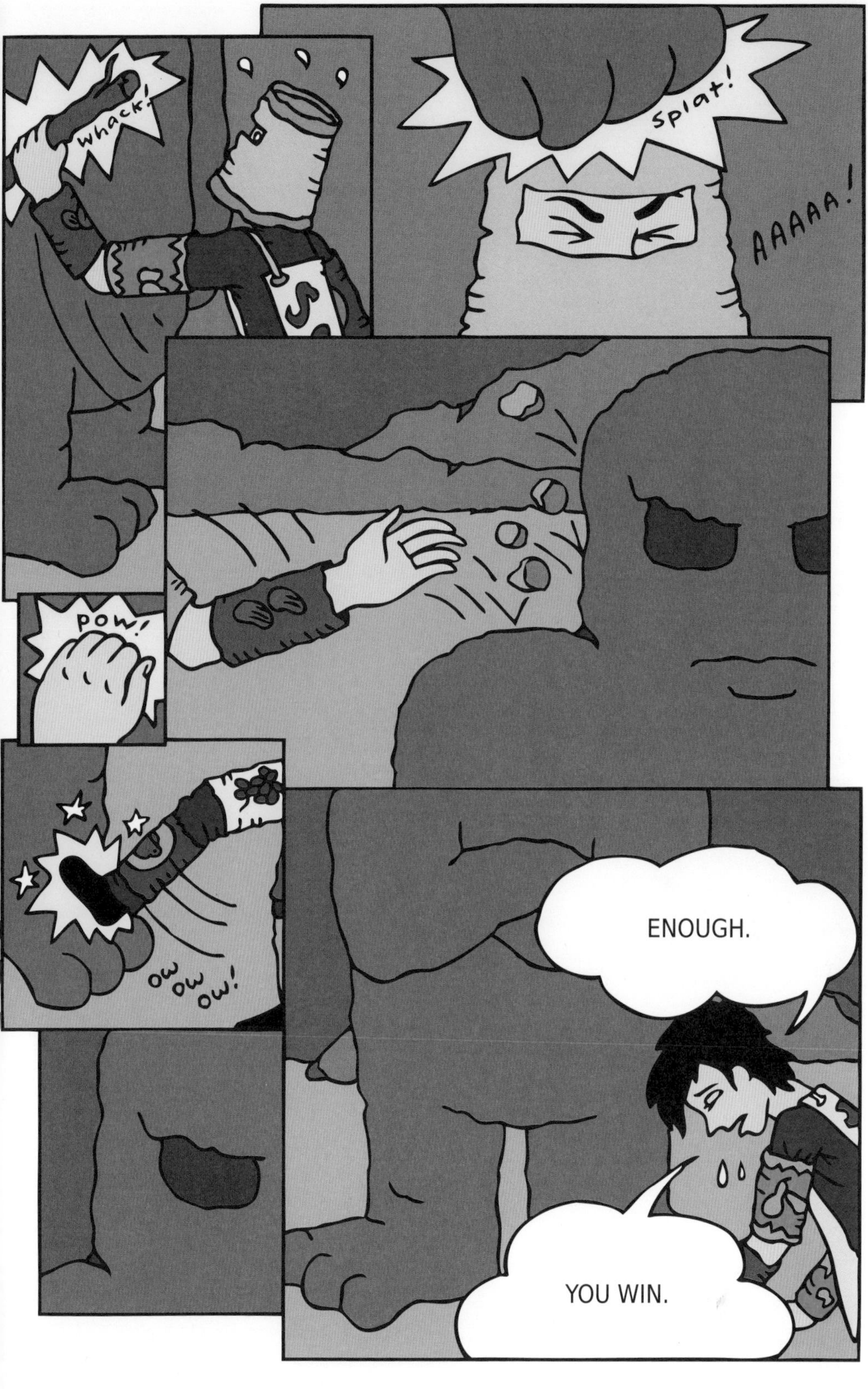
whack!
Splat!
AAAAA!
POW!
OW OW OW!
ENOUGH.
YOU WIN.

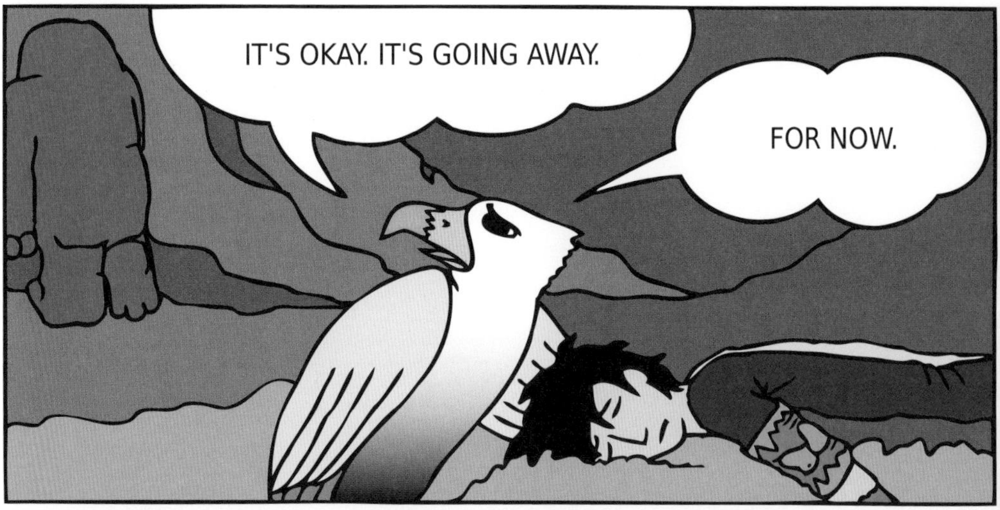
IT'S OKAY. IT'S GOING AWAY.
FOR NOW.

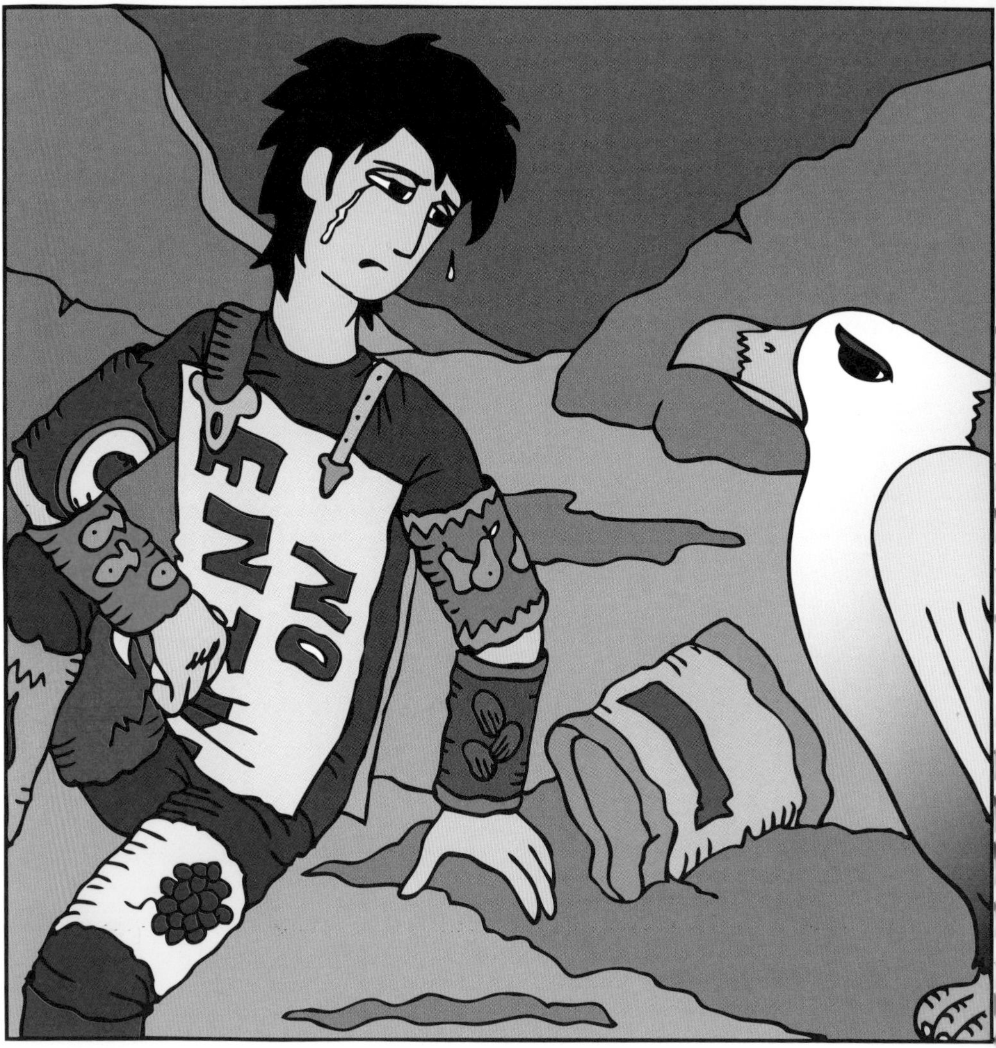
ENNOI

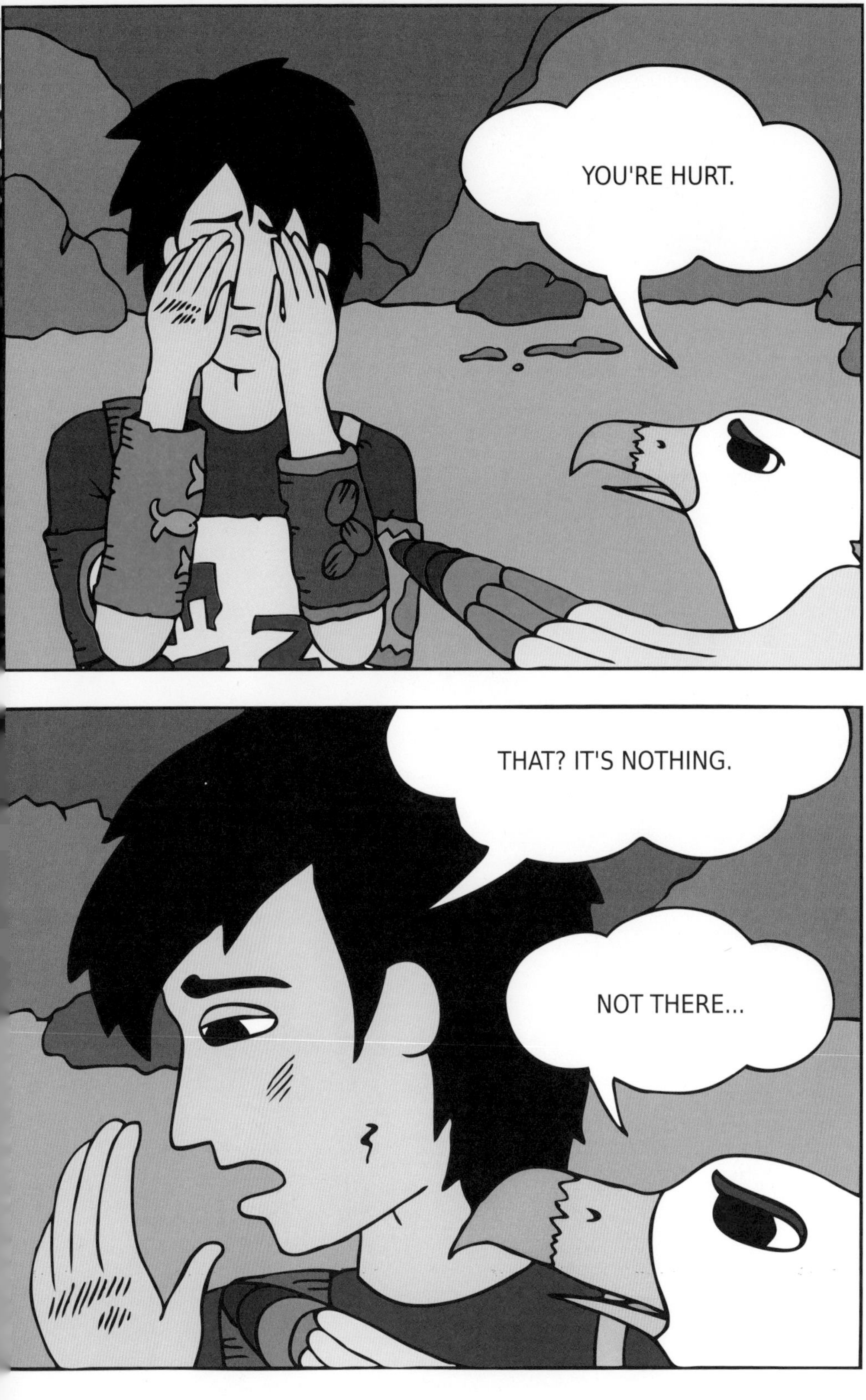
YOU'RE HURT.
THAT? IT'S NOTHING.
NOT THERE...

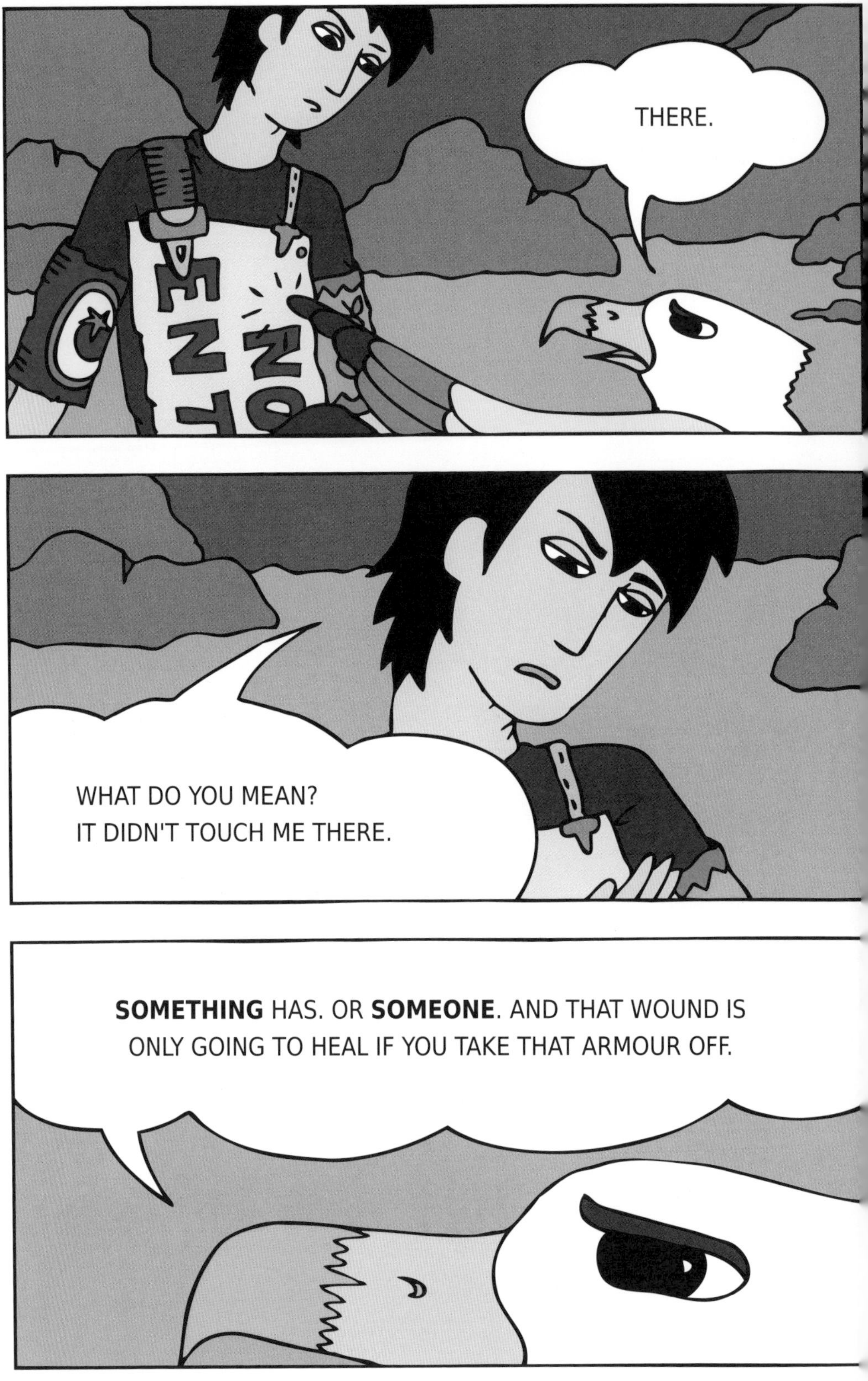
THERE.
WHAT DO YOU MEAN? IT DIDN'T TOUCH ME THERE.
SOMETHING HAS. OR **SOMEONE**. AND THAT WOUND IS ONLY GOING TO HEAL IF YOU TAKE THAT ARMOUR OFF.

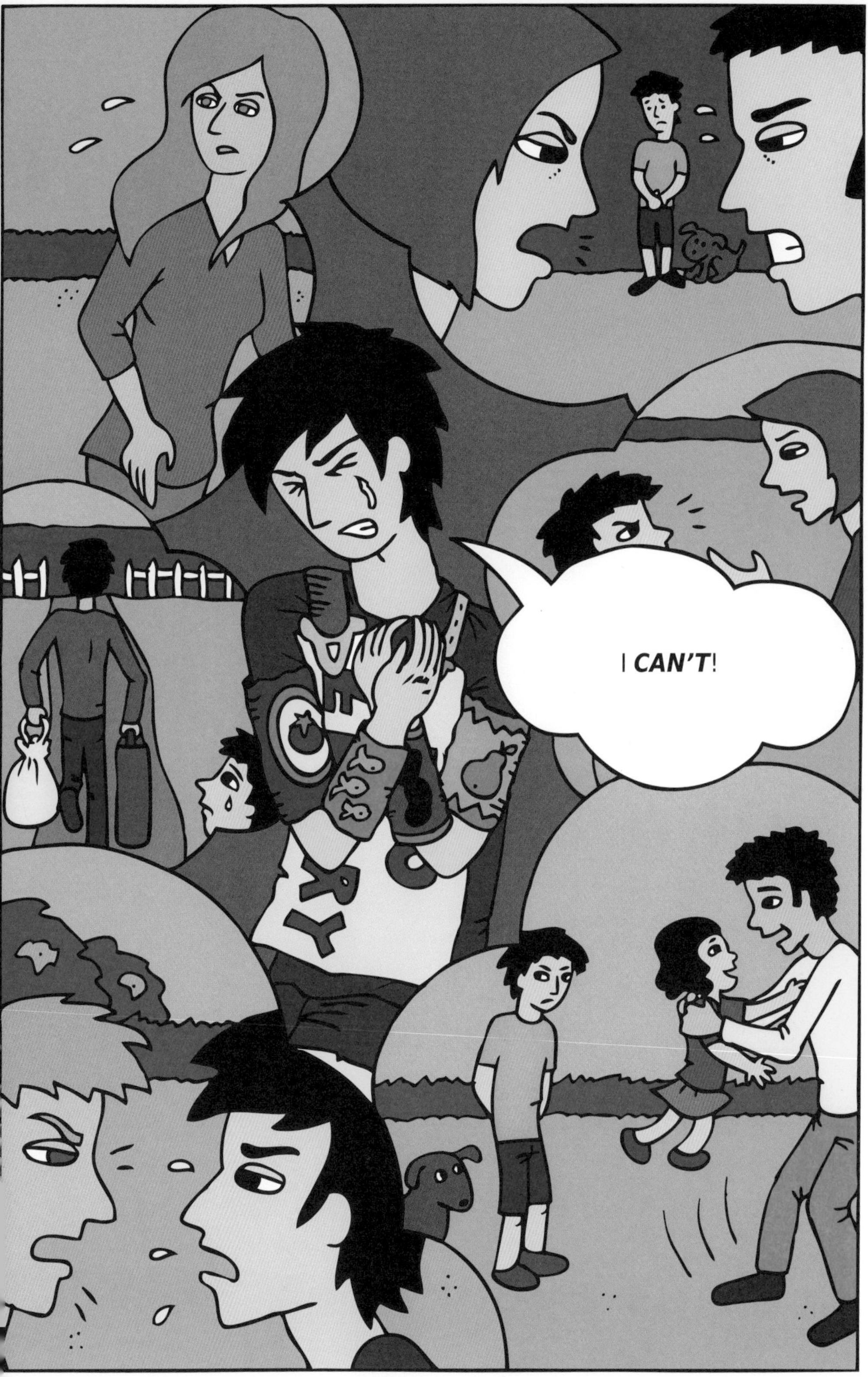
I **CAN'T**!

IT SEEMS LIKE THAT ARMOUR IS PROTECTING YOU, BUT IT'S ALSO HOLDING A LOT OF STUFF IN. THAT'S WHAT ANGER IS LIKE — IT COVERS THE FEELINGS UNDERNEATH. ANGER OFTEN SEEMS 'EASIER' TO DEAL WITH THAN THOSE OTHER FEELINGS...

BUT WHEN WE ALLOW ANGER TO DRIVE WHAT WE SAY AND DO, IT'S LIKE THE BEAST — IT CAN DO A LOT OF DAMAGE TO OURSELVES AND OTHERS.

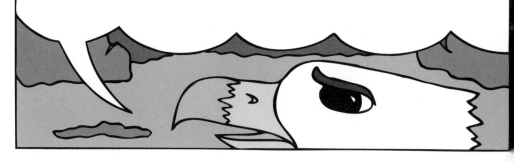

THIS ARMOUR LOOKS PRETTY OLD, TOO...LIKE YOU'VE BEEN USING IT FOR A LONG TIME.

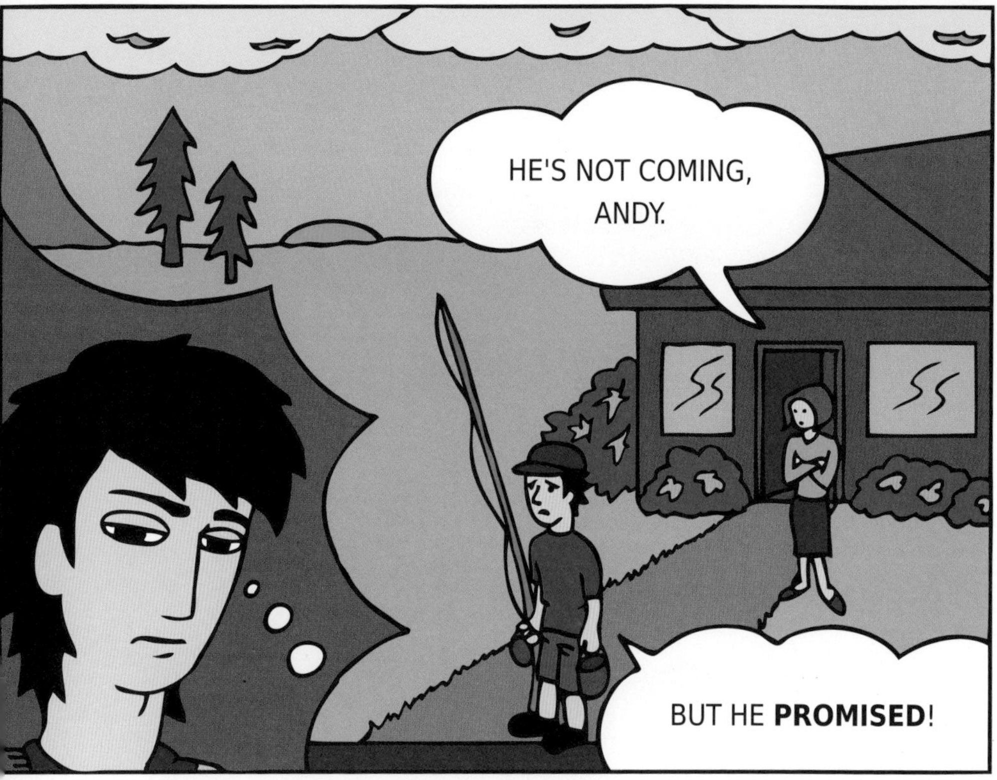
HE'S NOT COMING, ANDY.
BUT HE **PROMISED**!

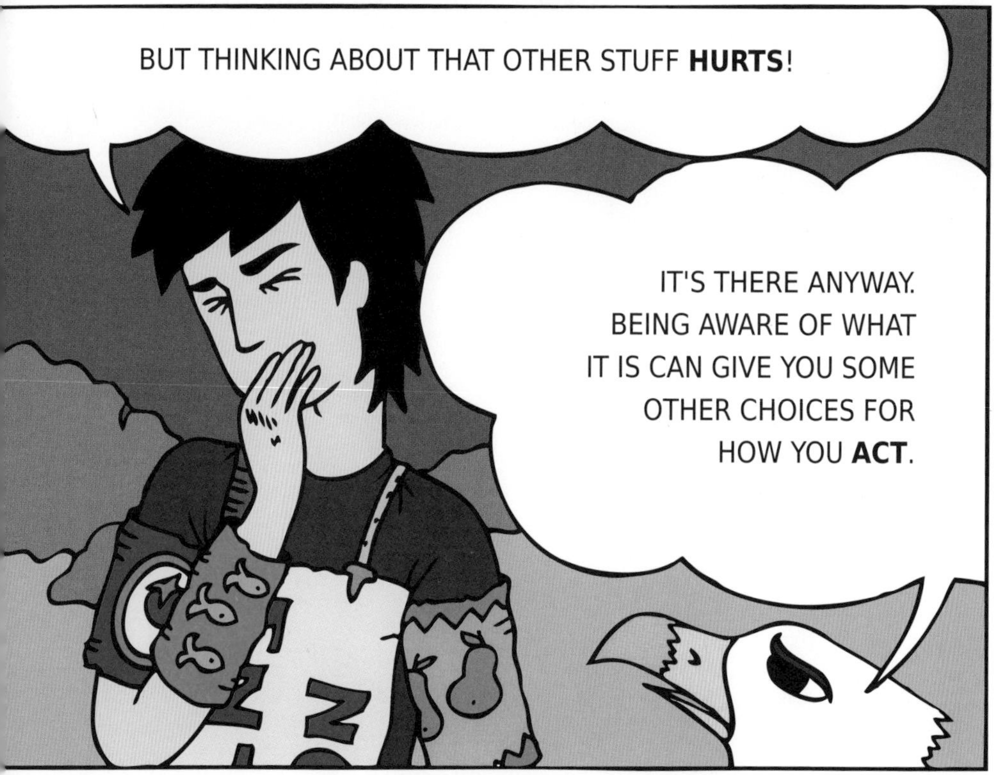
BUT THINKING ABOUT THAT OTHER STUFF **HURTS**!
IT'S THERE ANYWAY. BEING AWARE OF WHAT IT IS CAN GIVE YOU SOME OTHER CHOICES FOR HOW YOU **ACT**.

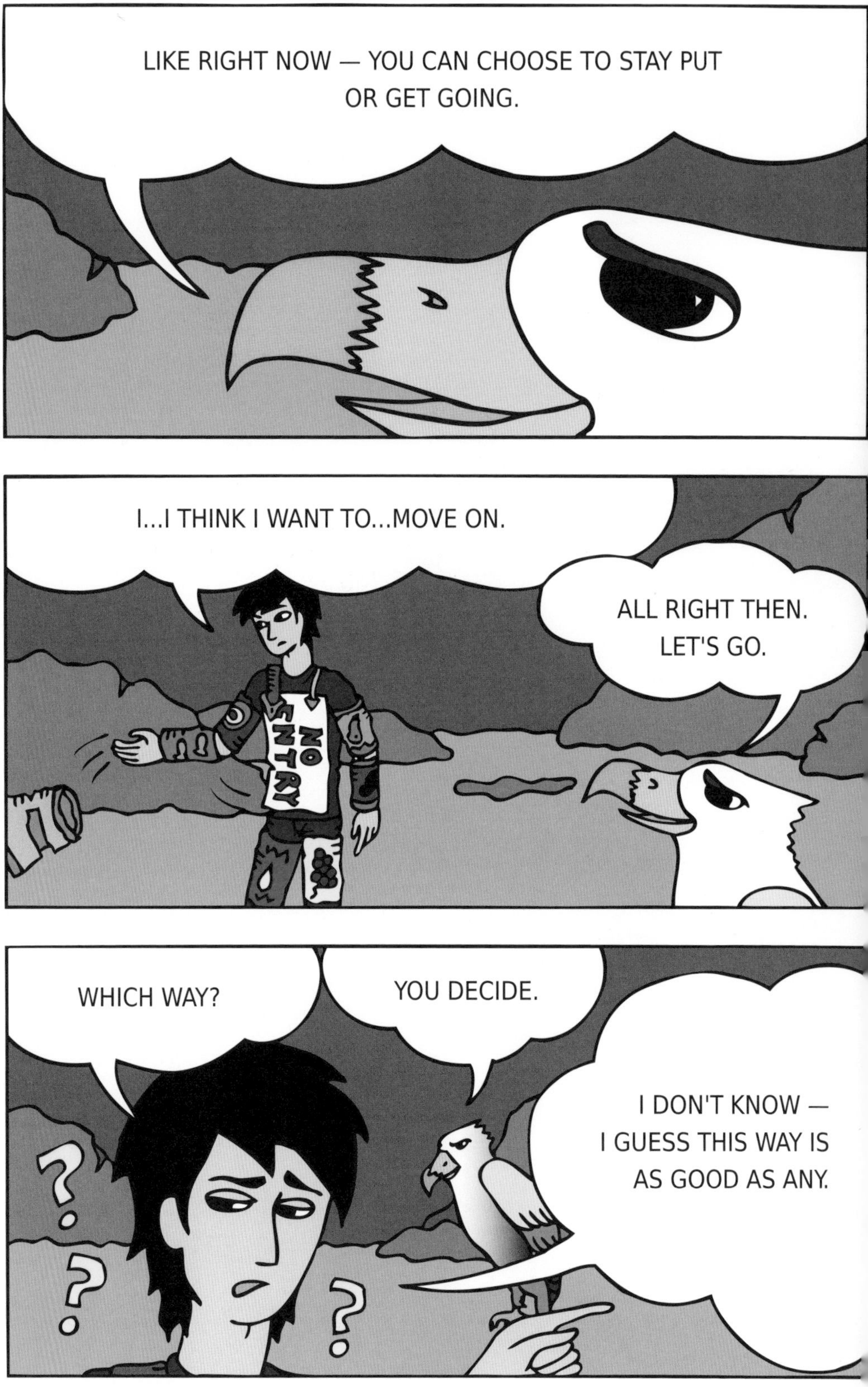
LIKE RIGHT NOW — YOU CAN CHOOSE TO STAY PUT OR GET GOING.
I...I THINK I WANT TO...MOVE ON.
NO ENTRY
ALL RIGHT THEN. LET'S GO.
WHICH WAY?
YOU DECIDE.
I DON'T KNOW — I GUESS THIS WAY IS AS GOOD AS ANY.

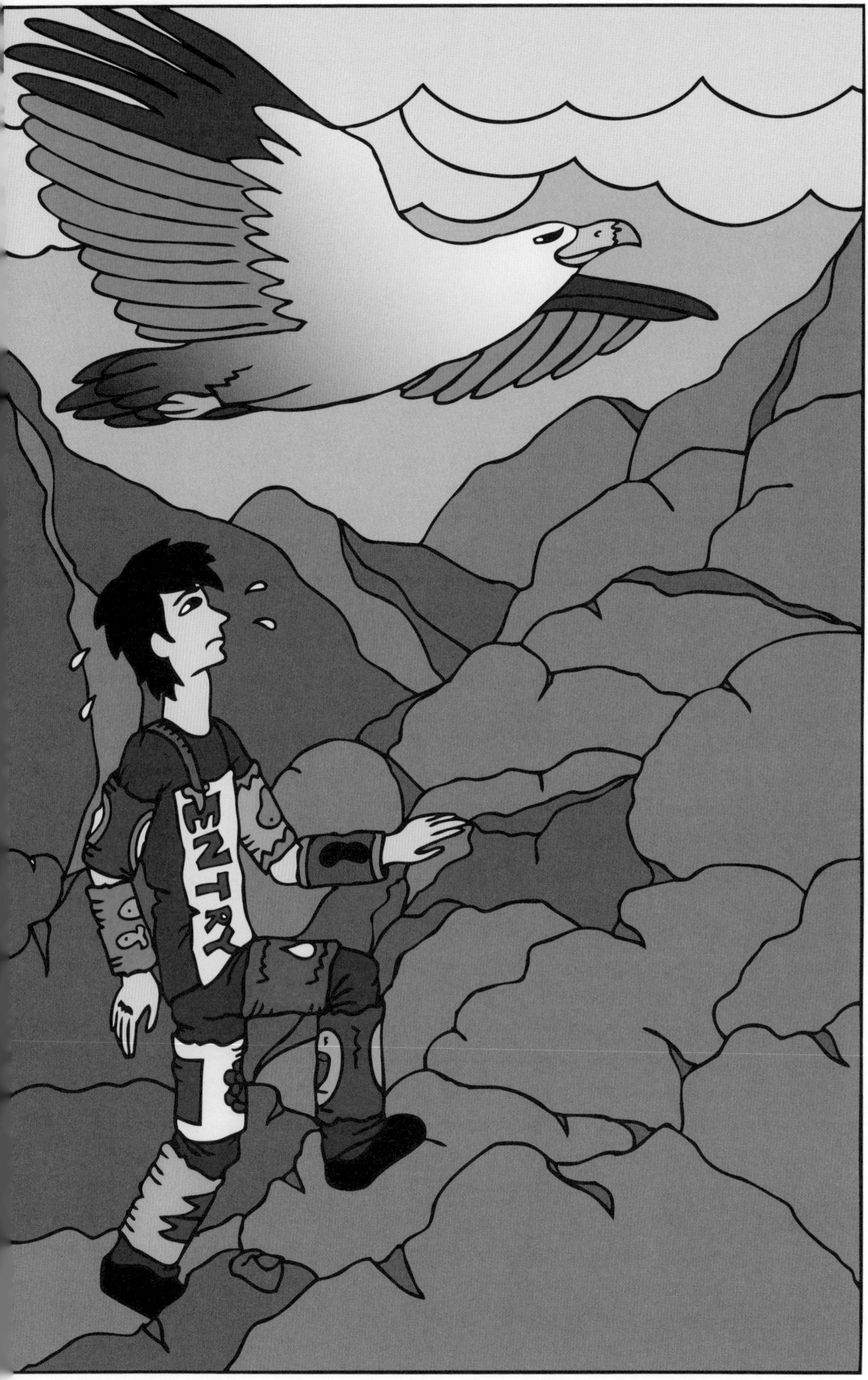
ENTRY

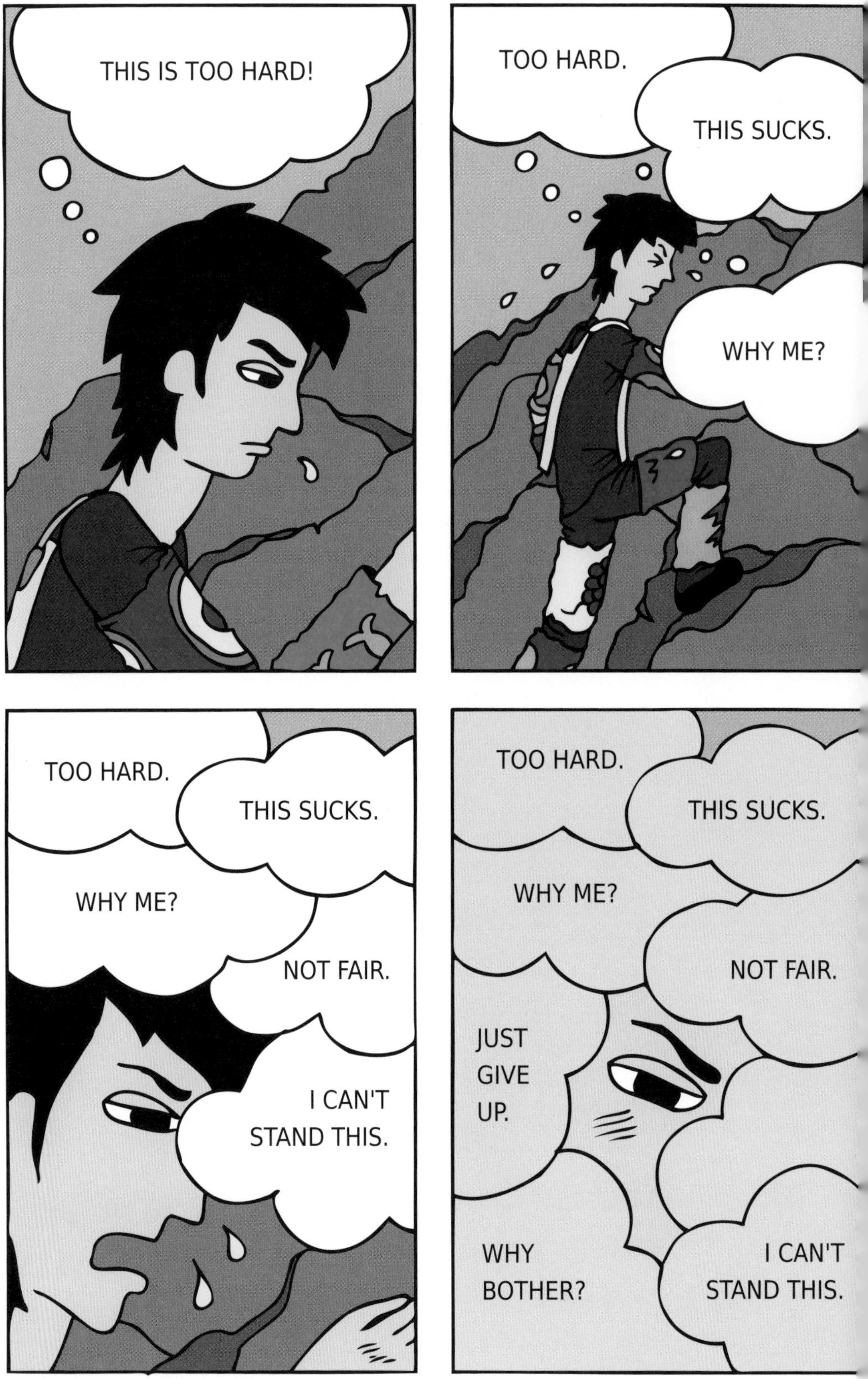
THIS IS TOO HARD!
TOO HARD.
THIS SUCKS.
WHY ME?
TOO HARD.
THIS SUCKS.
WHY ME?
NOT FAIR.
I CAN'T STAND THIS.
TOO HARD.
THIS SUCKS.
WHY ME?
NOT FAIR.
JUST GIVE UP.
WHY BOTHER?
I CAN'T STAND THIS.

WELL NOW I CAN'T EVEN SEE WHERE I'M GOING!!

IT'S YOUR THOUGHTS. THEY'RE CLOUDING YOUR VISION.

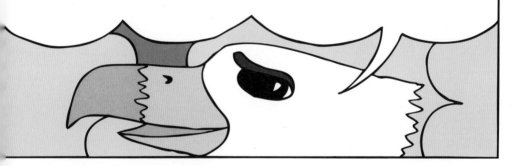

THOSE THOUGHTS ARE GETTING IN THE WAY — IT MAKES IT HARDER FOR YOU TO SEE IF YOU NEED TO CHANGE WHAT YOU ARE DOING OR PERSEVERE.

YOU MIGHT BE ON TOTALLY THE WRONG TRACK AND NEED TO CHANGE DIRECTION.

OR YOU MIGHT ALMOST BE THERE, IF YOU JUST KEEP GOING.

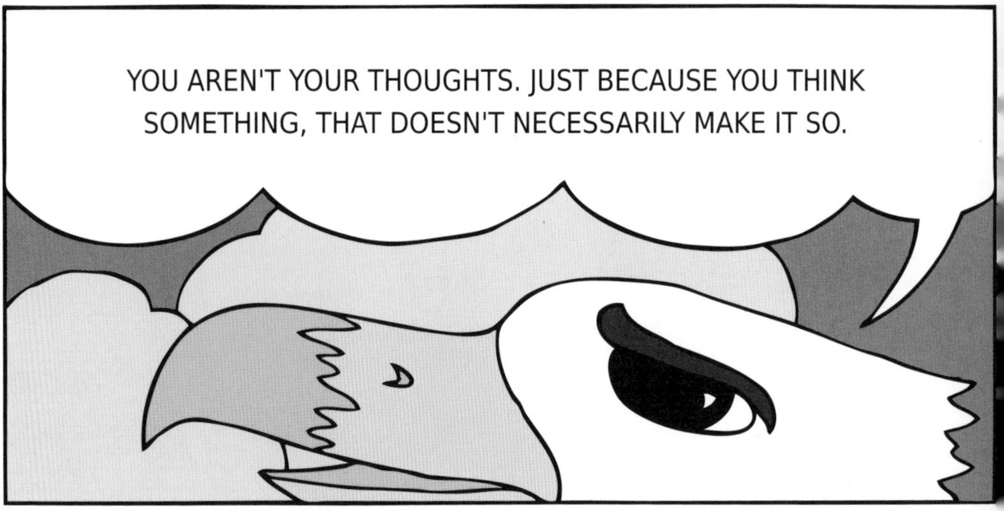
YOU AREN'T YOUR THOUGHTS. JUST BECAUSE YOU THINK SOMETHING, THAT DOESN'T NECESSARILY MAKE IT SO.

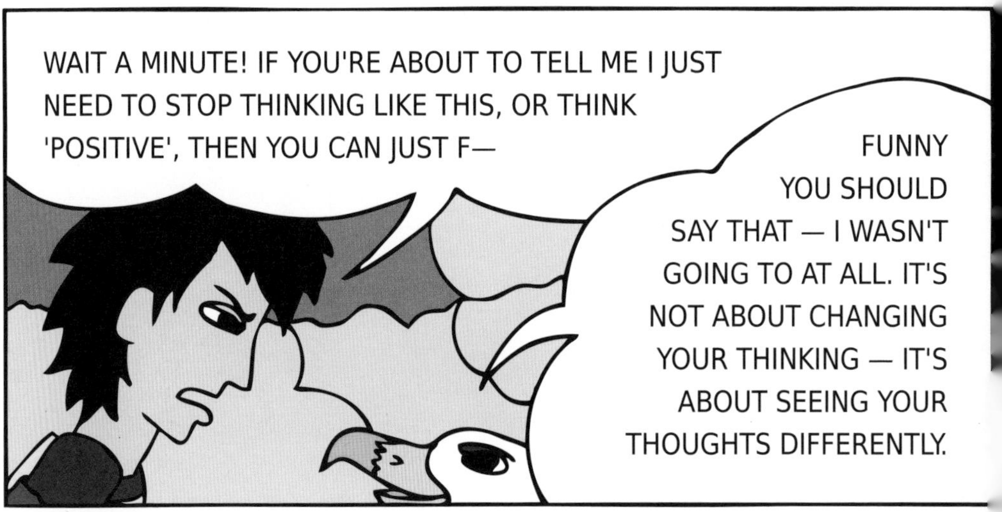
WAIT A MINUTE! IF YOU'RE ABOUT TO TELL ME I JUST NEED TO STOP THINKING LIKE THIS, OR THINK 'POSITIVE', THEN YOU CAN JUST F—
FUNNY YOU SHOULD SAY THAT — I WASN'T GOING TO AT ALL. IT'S NOT ABOUT CHANGING YOUR THINKING — IT'S ABOUT SEEING YOUR THOUGHTS DIFFERENTLY.

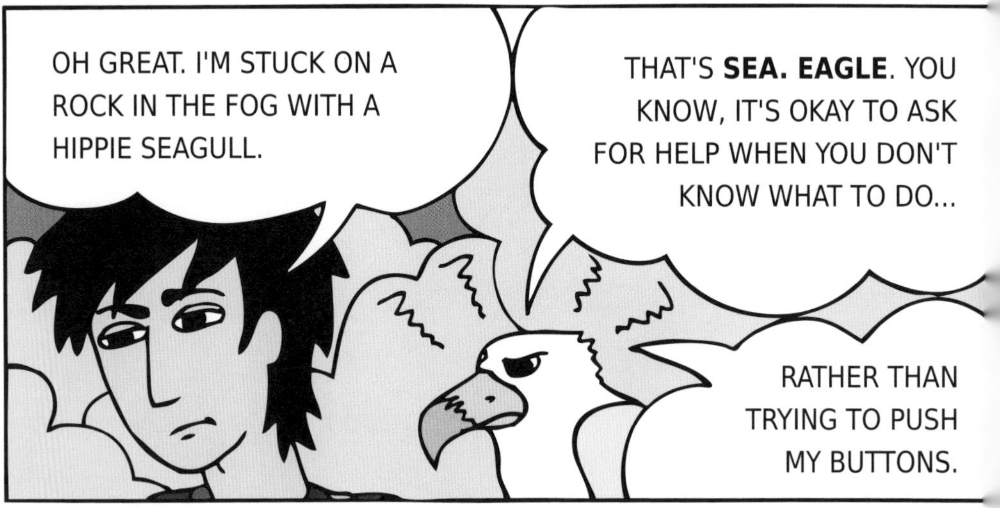
OH GREAT. I'M STUCK ON A ROCK IN THE FOG WITH A HIPPIE SEAGULL.
THAT'S **SEA. EAGLE**. YOU KNOW, IT'S OKAY TO ASK FOR HELP WHEN YOU DON'T KNOW WHAT TO DO...
RATHER THAN TRYING TO PUSH MY BUTTONS.

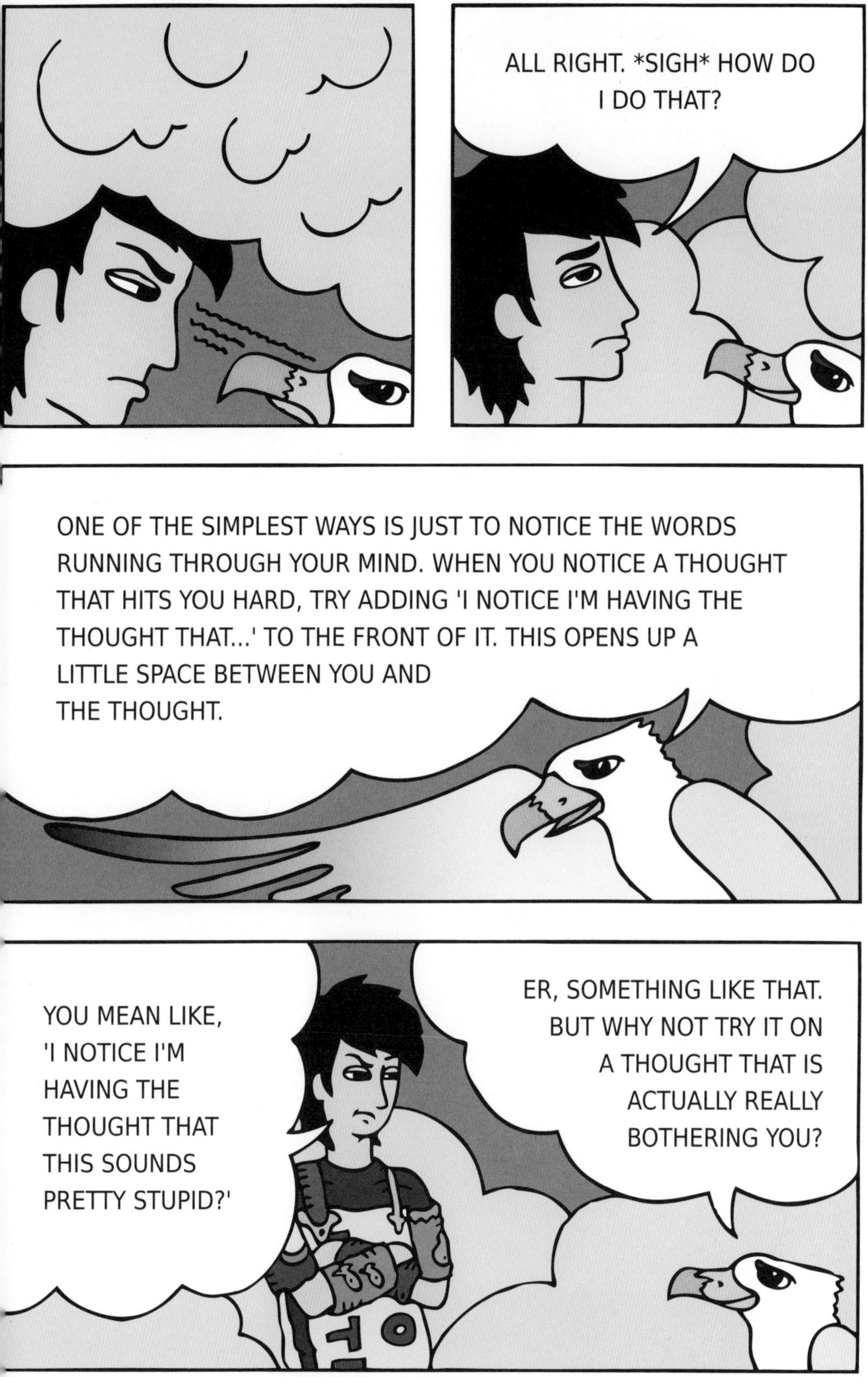
ALL RIGHT. *SIGH* HOW DO I DO THAT?
ONE OF THE SIMPLEST WAYS IS JUST TO NOTICE THE WORDS RUNNING THROUGH YOUR MIND. WHEN YOU NOTICE A THOUGHT THAT HITS YOU HARD, TRY ADDING 'I NOTICE I'M HAVING THE THOUGHT THAT...' TO THE FRONT OF IT. THIS OPENS UP A LITTLE SPACE BETWEEN YOU AND THE THOUGHT.
YOU MEAN LIKE, 'I NOTICE I'M HAVING THE THOUGHT THAT THIS SOUNDS PRETTY STUPID?'
ER, SOMETHING LIKE THAT. BUT WHY NOT TRY IT ON A THOUGHT THAT IS ACTUALLY REALLY BOTHERING YOU?

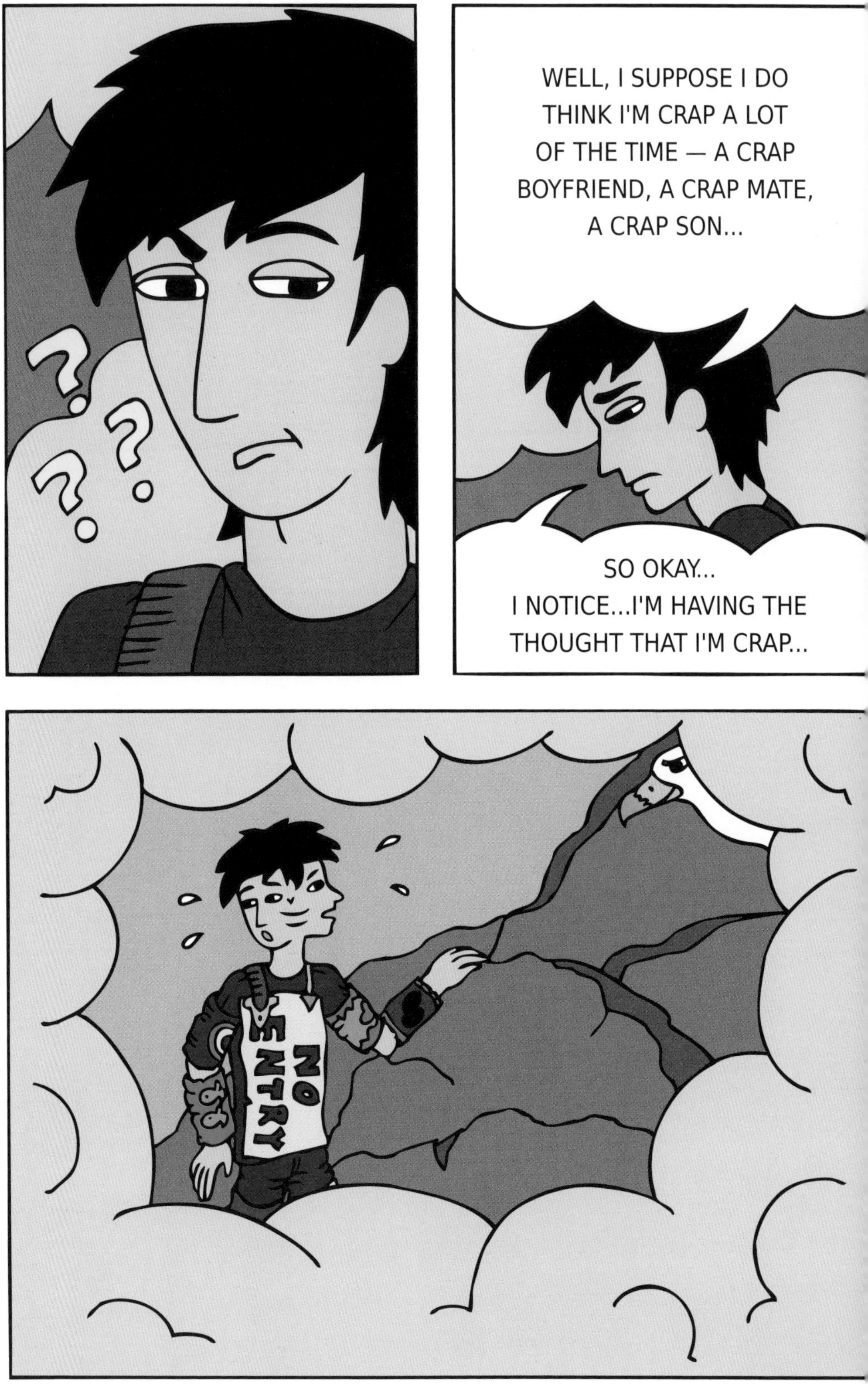
WELL, I SUPPOSE I DO THINK I'M CRAP A LOT OF THE TIME — A CRAP BOYFRIEND, A CRAP MATE, A CRAP SON...
SO OKAY... I NOTICE...I'M HAVING THE THOUGHT THAT I'M CRAP...
NO ENTRY

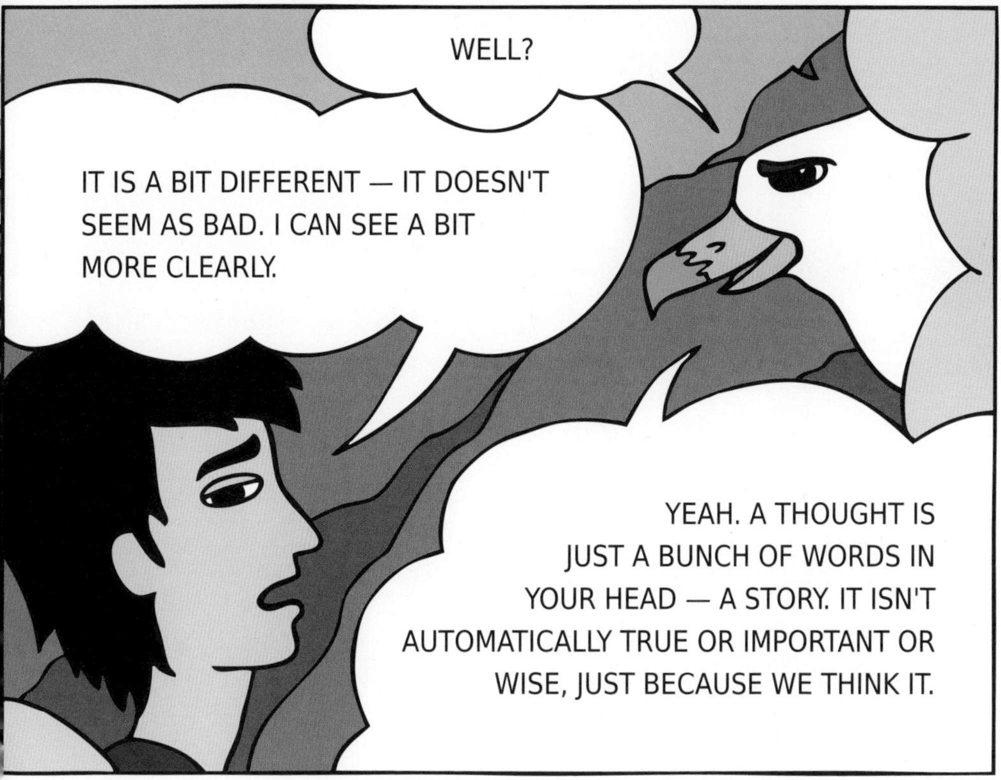
WELL?
IT IS A BIT DIFFERENT — IT DOESN'T SEEM AS BAD. I CAN SEE A BIT MORE CLEARLY.
YEAH. A THOUGHT IS JUST A BUNCH OF WORDS IN YOUR HEAD — A STORY. IT ISN'T AUTOMATICALLY TRUE OR IMPORTANT OR WISE, JUST BECAUSE WE THINK IT.

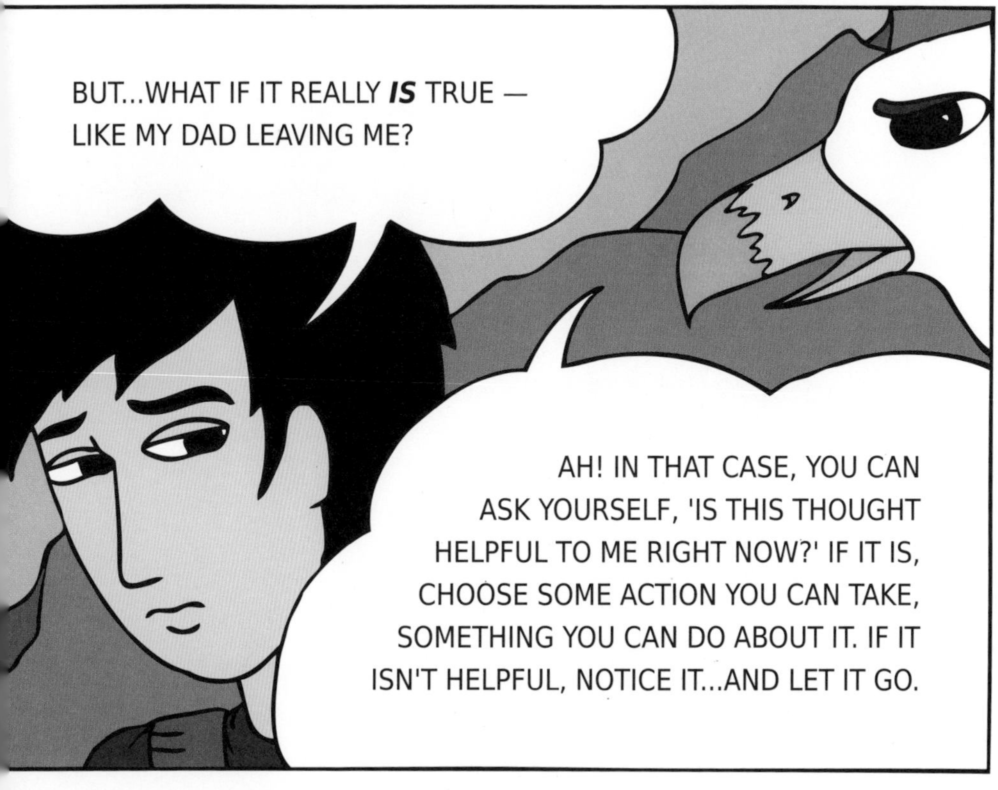
BUT...WHAT IF IT REALLY ***IS*** TRUE — LIKE MY DAD LEAVING ME?
AH! IN THAT CASE, YOU CAN ASK YOURSELF, 'IS THIS THOUGHT HELPFUL TO ME RIGHT NOW?' IF IT IS, CHOOSE SOME ACTION YOU CAN TAKE, SOMETHING YOU CAN DO ABOUT IT. IF IT ISN'T HELPFUL, NOTICE IT...AND LET IT GO.

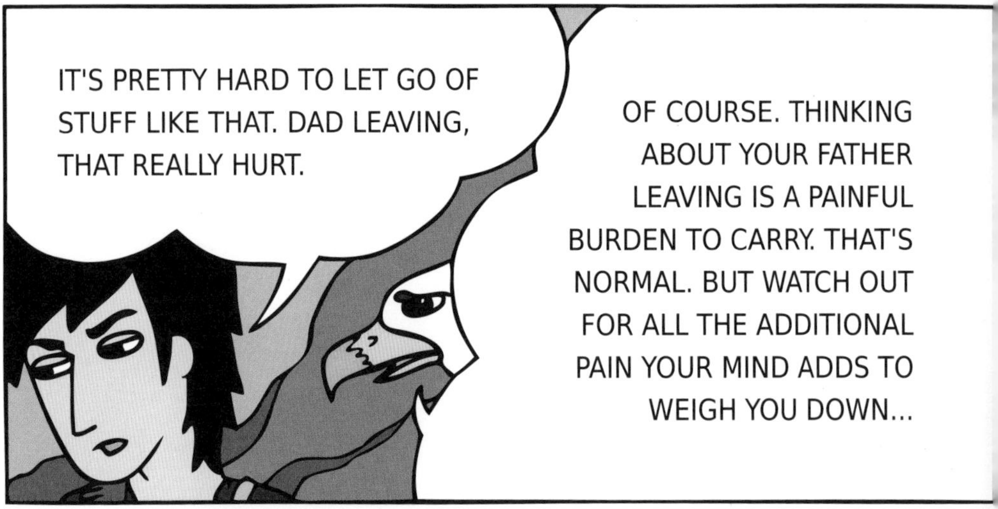
IT'S PRETTY HARD TO LET GO OF STUFF LIKE THAT. DAD LEAVING, THAT REALLY HURT.
OF COURSE. THINKING ABOUT YOUR FATHER LEAVING IS A PAINFUL BURDEN TO CARRY. THAT'S NORMAL. BUT WATCH OUT FOR ALL THE ADDITIONAL PAIN YOUR MIND ADDS TO WEIGH YOU DOWN...

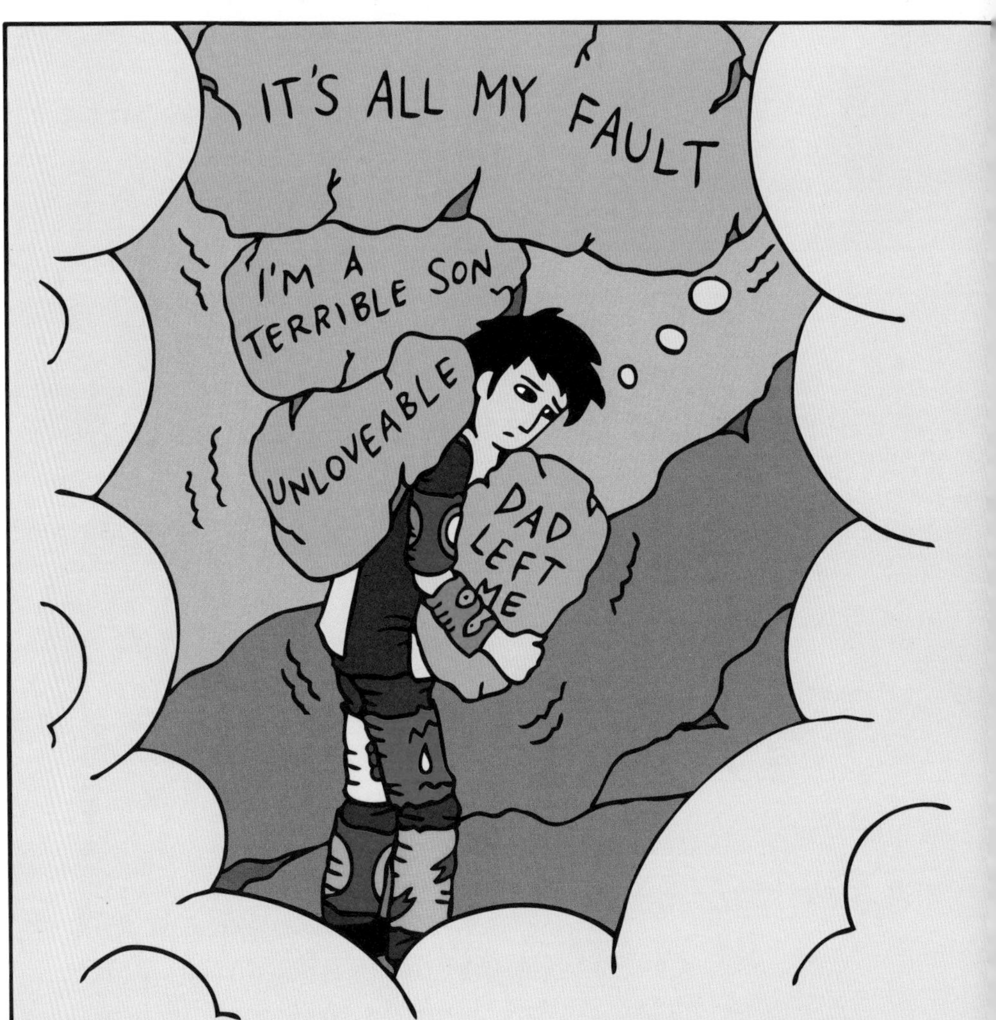
IT'S ALL MY FAULT
I'M A TERRIBLE SON
UNLOVEABLE
DAD LEFT ME

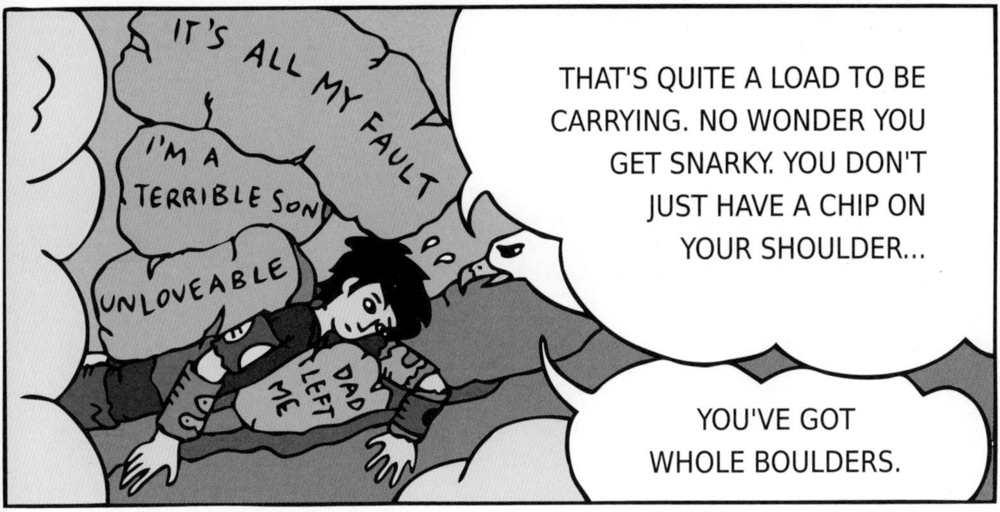
IT'S ALL MY FAULT
I'M A TERRIBLE SON
UNLOVEABLE
DAD LEFT ME
THAT'S QUITE A LOAD TO BE CARRYING. NO WONDER YOU GET SNARKY. YOU DON'T JUST HAVE A CHIP ON YOUR SHOULDER...
YOU'VE GOT WHOLE BOULDERS.

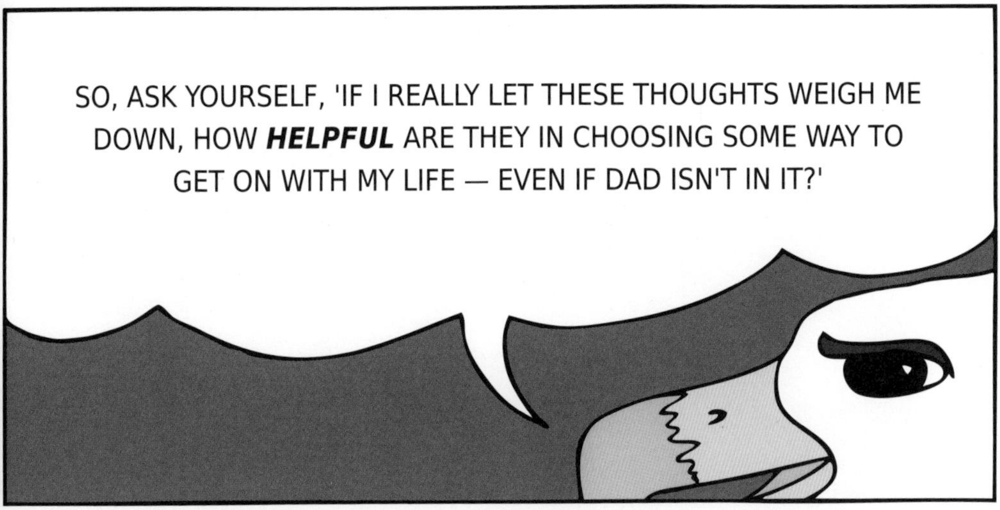
SO, ASK YOURSELF, 'IF I REALLY LET THESE THOUGHTS WEIGH ME DOWN, HOW ***HELPFUL*** ARE THEY IN CHOOSING SOME WAY TO GET ON WITH MY LIFE — EVEN IF DAD ISN'T IN IT?'

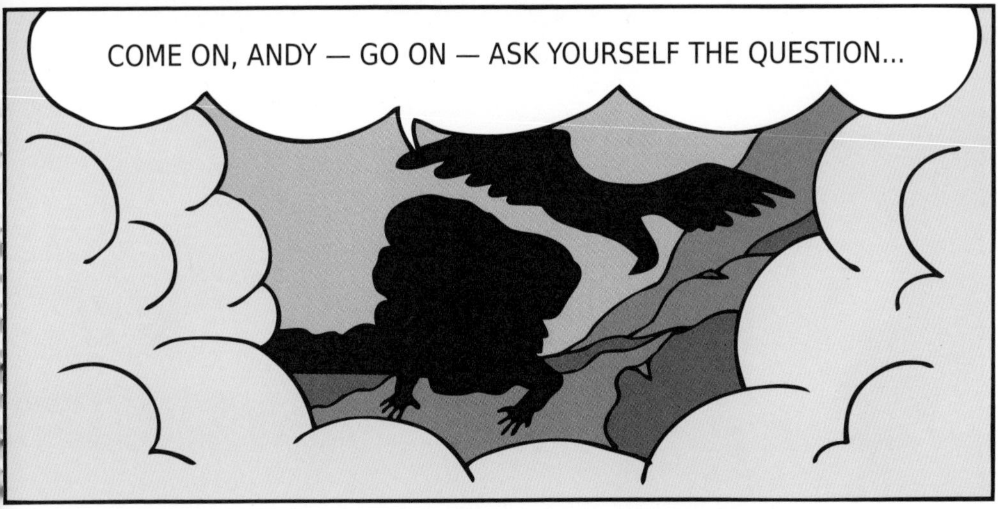
COME ON, ANDY — GO ON — ASK YOURSELF THE QUESTION...

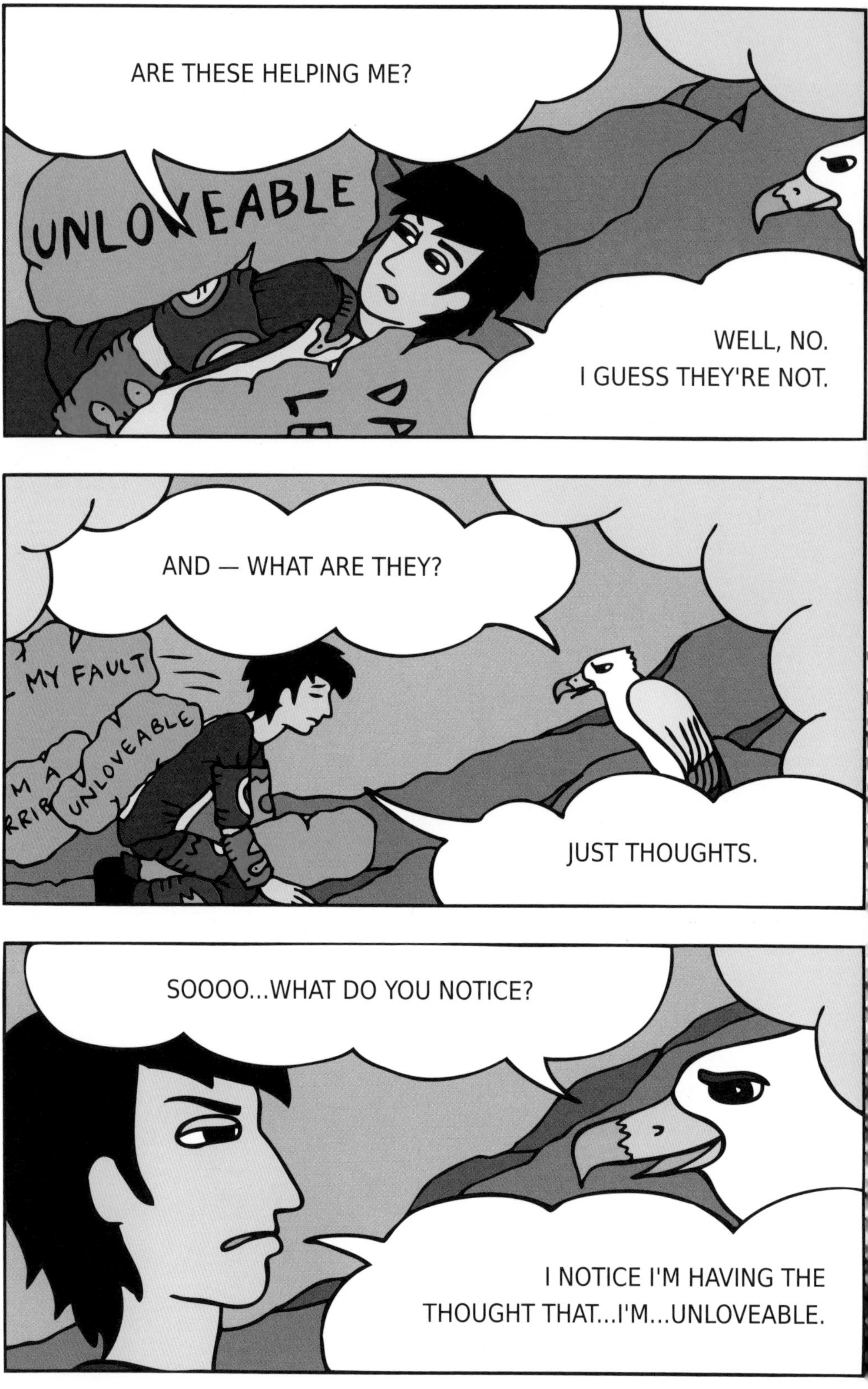
ARE THESE HELPING ME?
UNLOVEABLE
WELL, NO.
I GUESS THEY'RE NOT.
AND — WHAT ARE THEY?
MY FAULT
UNLOVEABLE
JUST THOUGHTS.
SOOOO...WHAT DO YOU NOTICE?
I NOTICE I'M HAVING THE
THOUGHT THAT...I'M...UNLOVEABLE.

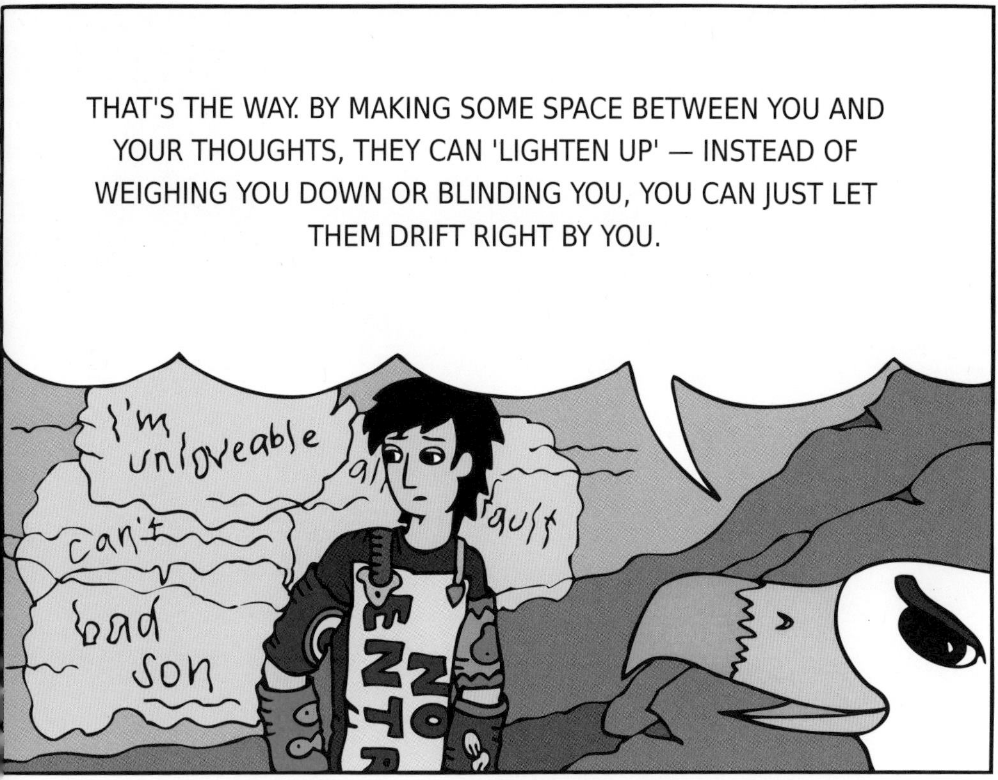
THAT'S THE WAY. BY MAKING SOME SPACE BETWEEN YOU AND YOUR THOUGHTS, THEY CAN 'LIGHTEN UP' — INSTEAD OF WEIGHING YOU DOWN OR BLINDING YOU, YOU CAN JUST LET THEM DRIFT RIGHT BY YOU.
I'm unloveable
can't
bad son
fault
NO ENTRY

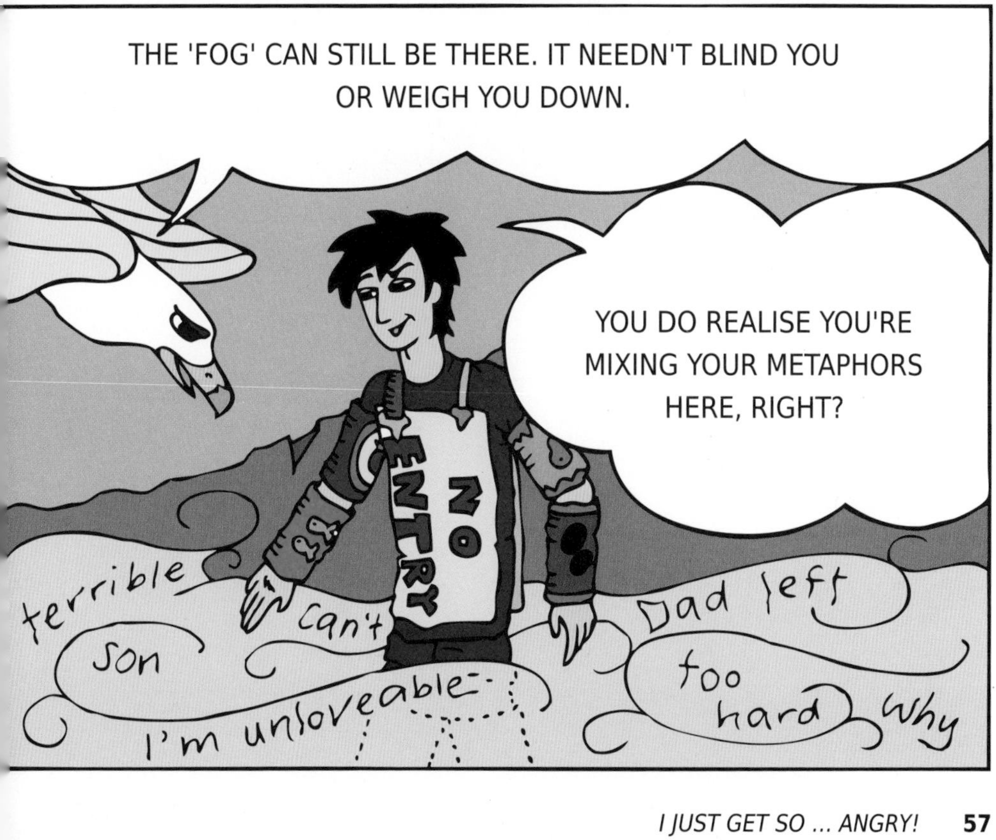
THE 'FOG' CAN STILL BE THERE. IT NEEDN'T BLIND YOU OR WEIGH YOU DOWN.
YOU DO REALISE YOU'RE MIXING YOUR METAPHORS HERE, RIGHT?
NO ENTRY
terrible son
can't
I'm unloveable
Dad left
too hard
why

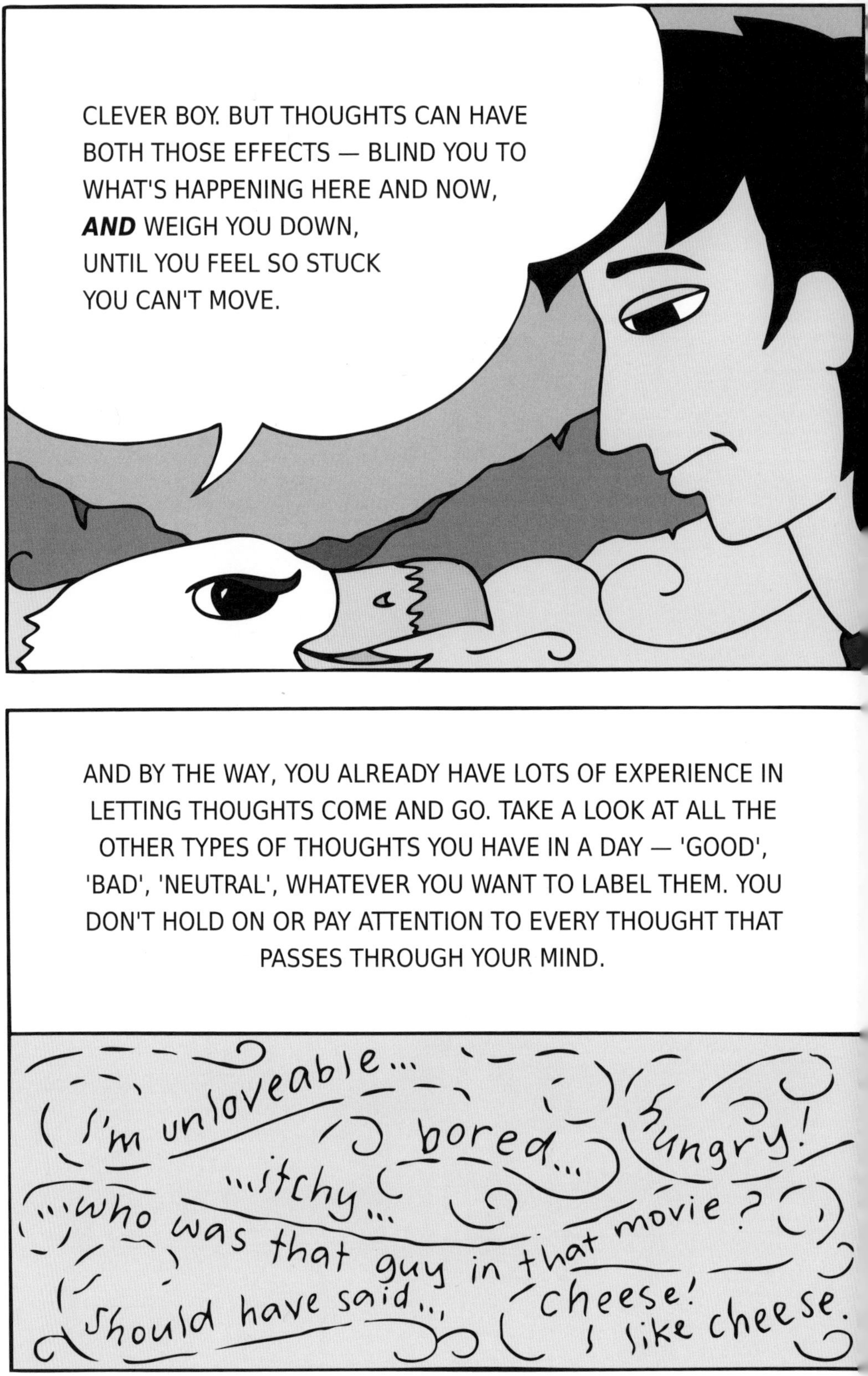
CLEVER BOY. BUT THOUGHTS CAN HAVE BOTH THOSE EFFECTS — BLIND YOU TO WHAT'S HAPPENING HERE AND NOW, ***AND*** WEIGH YOU DOWN, UNTIL YOU FEEL SO STUCK YOU CAN'T MOVE.
AND BY THE WAY, YOU ALREADY HAVE LOTS OF EXPERIENCE IN LETTING THOUGHTS COME AND GO. TAKE A LOOK AT ALL THE OTHER TYPES OF THOUGHTS YOU HAVE IN A DAY — 'GOOD', 'BAD', 'NEUTRAL', WHATEVER YOU WANT TO LABEL THEM. YOU DON'T HOLD ON OR PAY ATTENTION TO EVERY THOUGHT THAT PASSES THROUGH YOUR MIND.
I'm unloveable...
bored...
hungry!
...itchy...
...who was that guy in that movie?
should have said...
cheese! I like cheese.

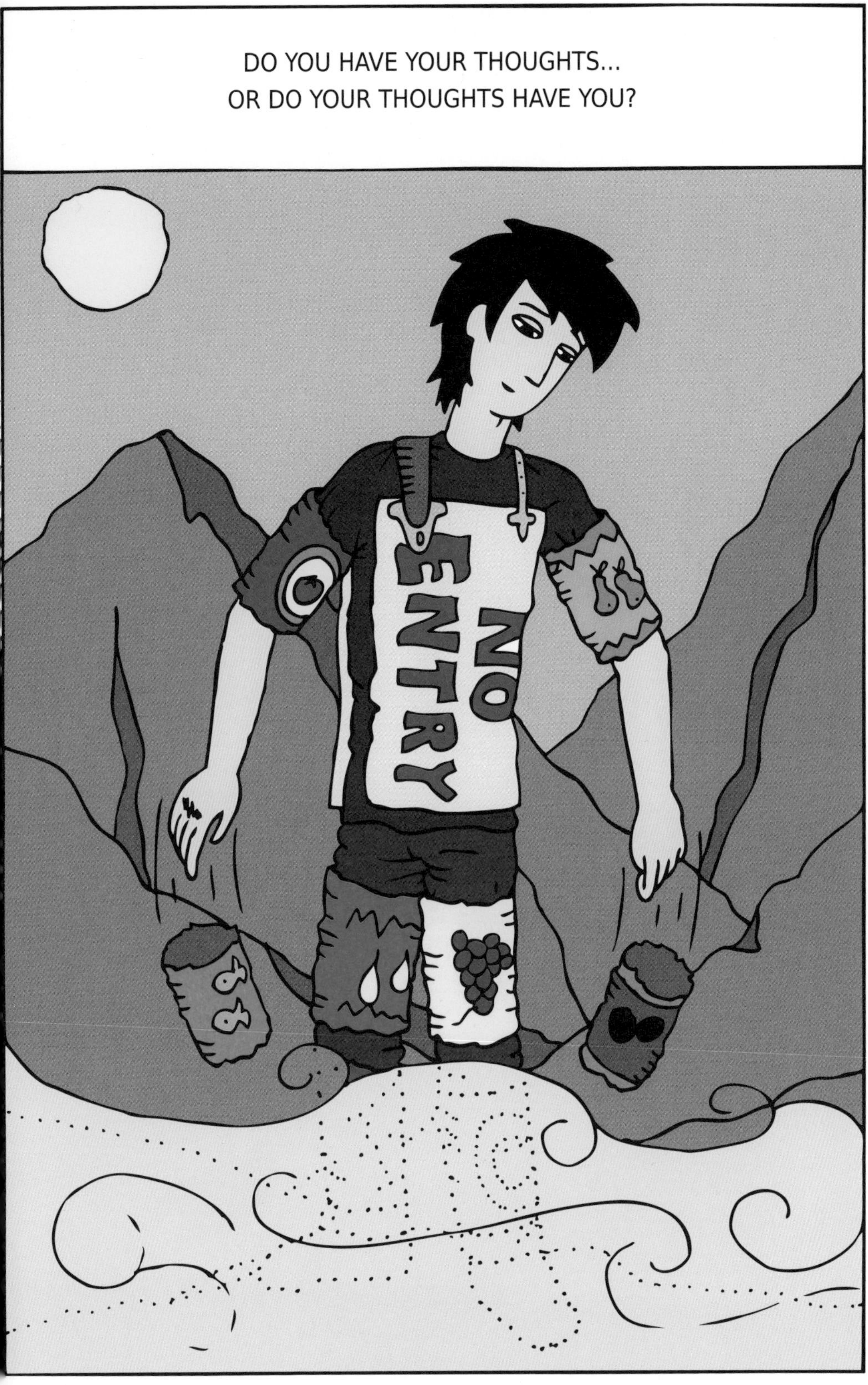
DO YOU HAVE YOUR THOUGHTS...
OR DO YOUR THOUGHTS HAVE YOU?
NO ENTRY

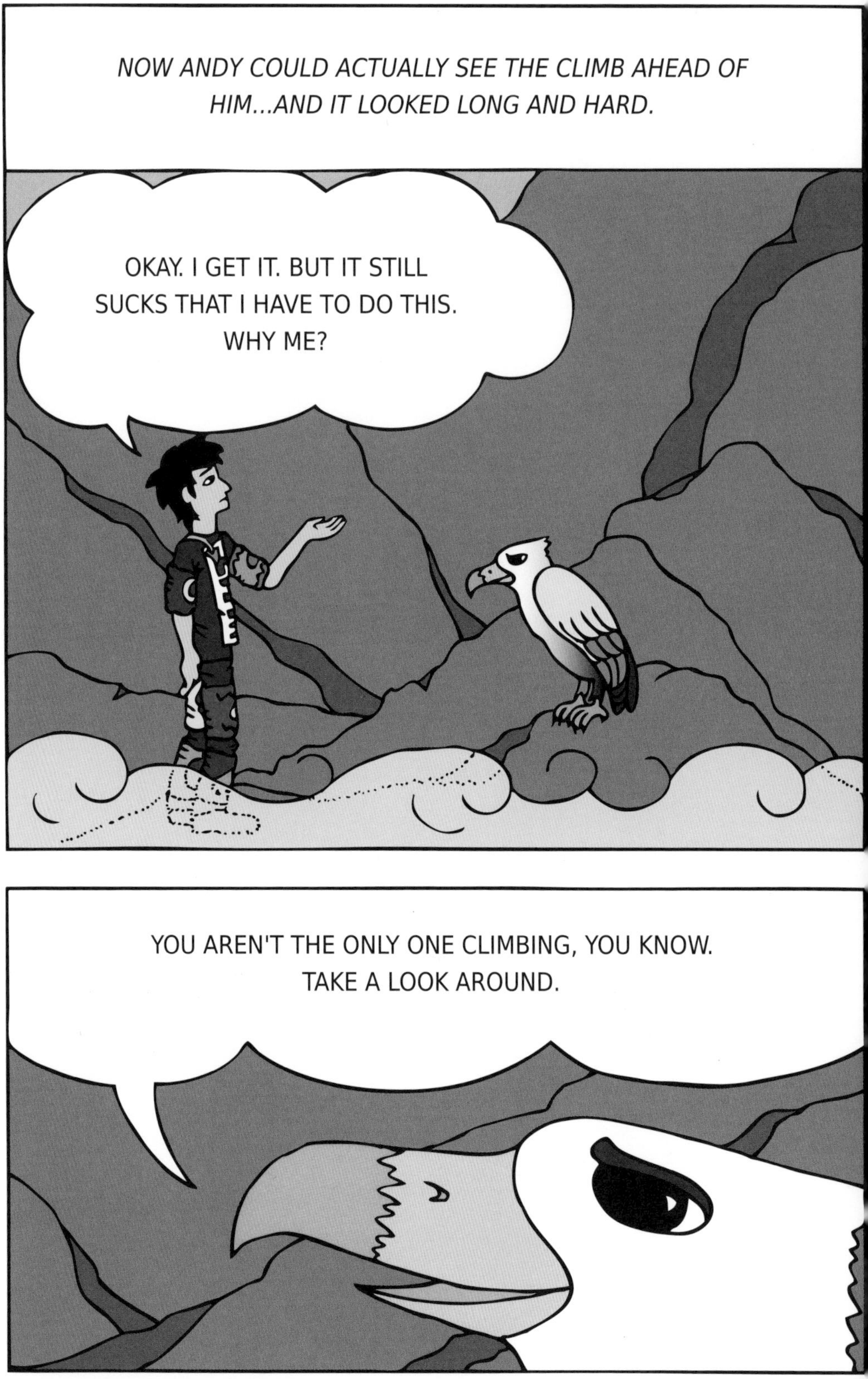
NOW ANDY COULD ACTUALLY SEE THE CLIMB AHEAD OF HIM...AND IT LOOKED LONG AND HARD.
OKAY. I GET IT. BUT IT STILL SUCKS THAT I HAVE TO DO THIS. WHY ME?
YOU AREN'T THE ONLY ONE CLIMBING, YOU KNOW. TAKE A LOOK AROUND.

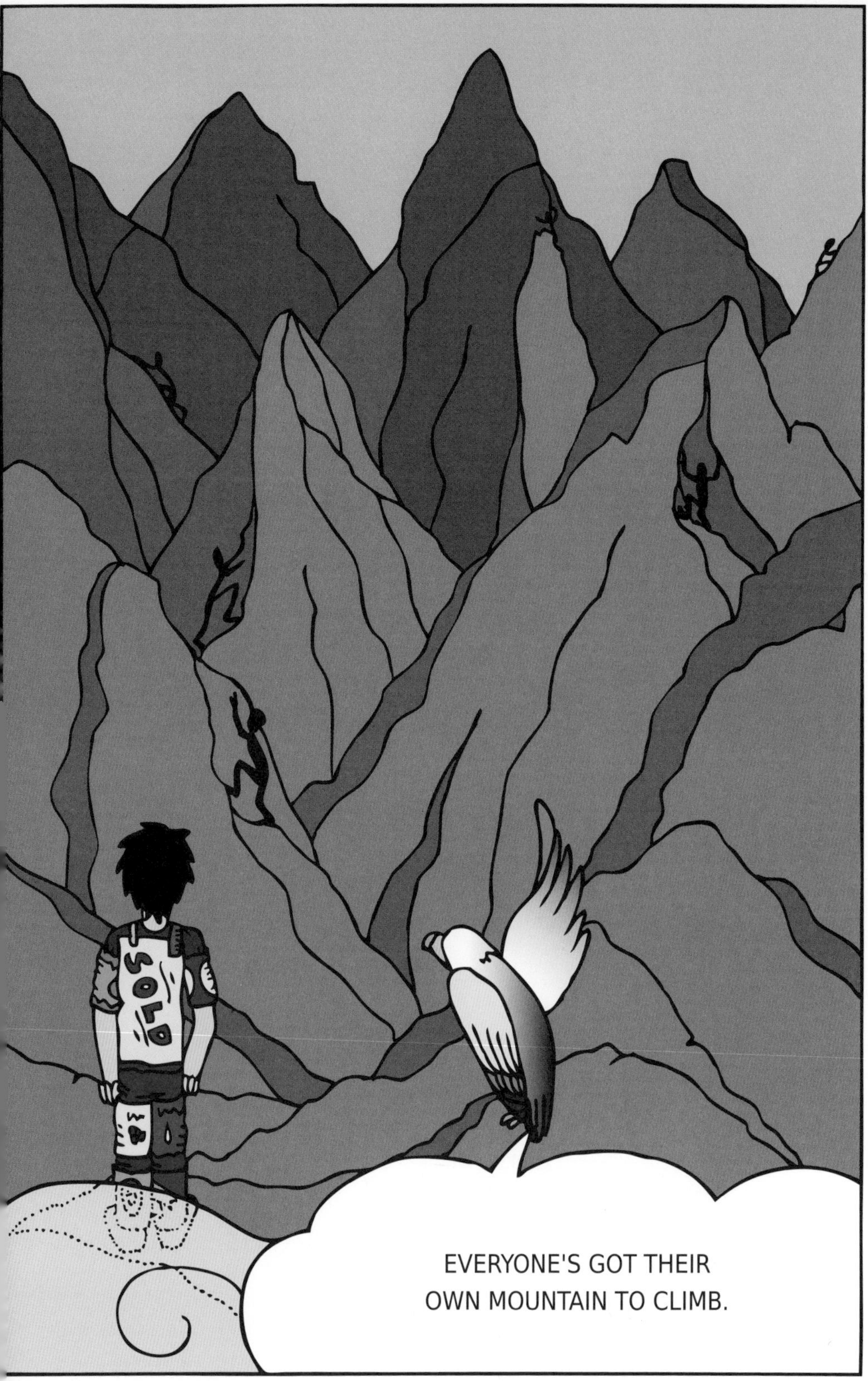
SOLD
EVERYONE'S GOT THEIR OWN MOUNTAIN TO CLIMB.

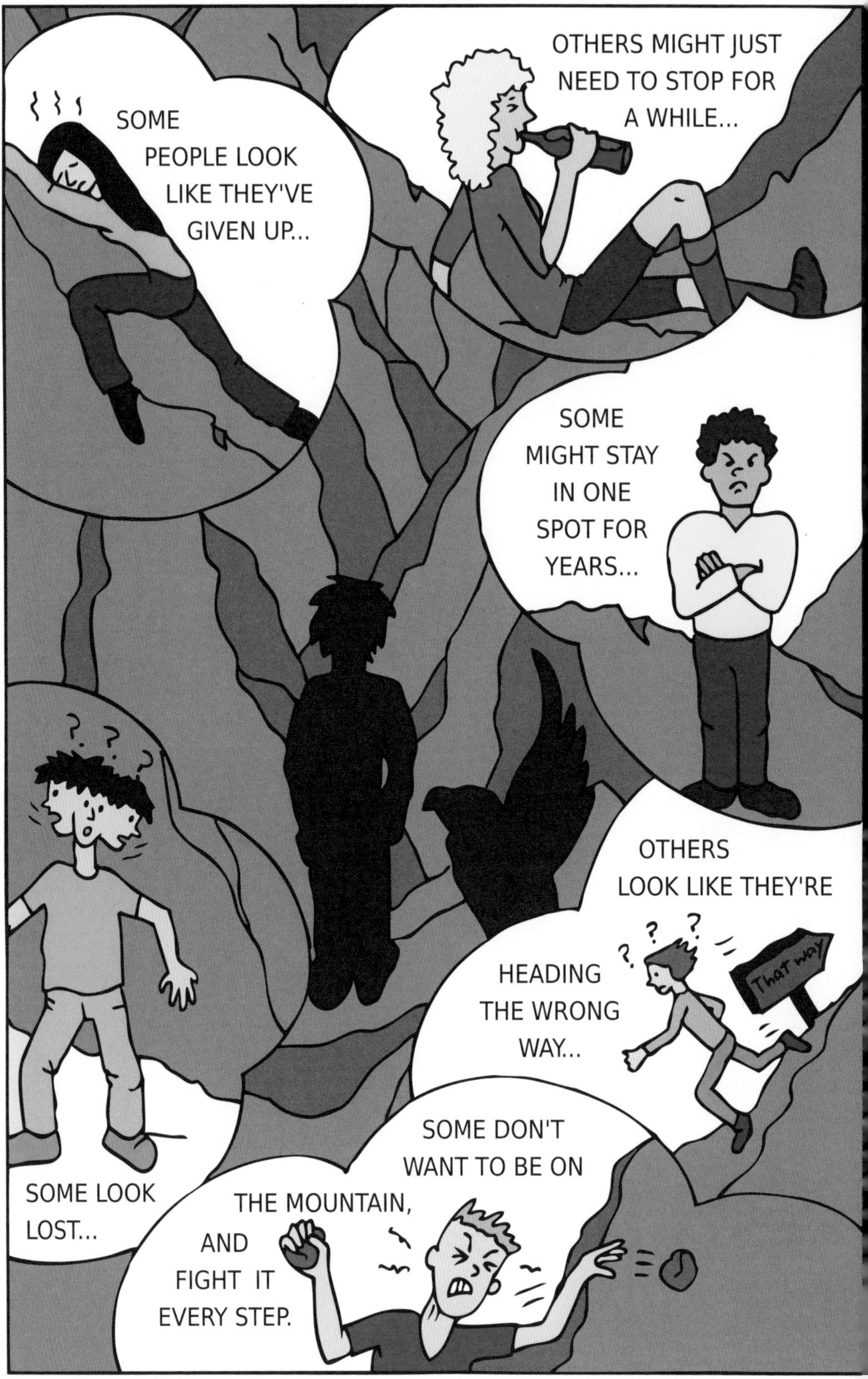
SOME PEOPLE LOOK LIKE THEY'VE GIVEN UP...
OTHERS MIGHT JUST NEED TO STOP FOR A WHILE...
SOME MIGHT STAY IN ONE SPOT FOR YEARS...
SOME LOOK LOST...
OTHERS LOOK LIKE THEY'RE HEADING THE WRONG WAY...
That way
SOME DON'T WANT TO BE ON THE MOUNTAIN,
AND FIGHT IT EVERY STEP.

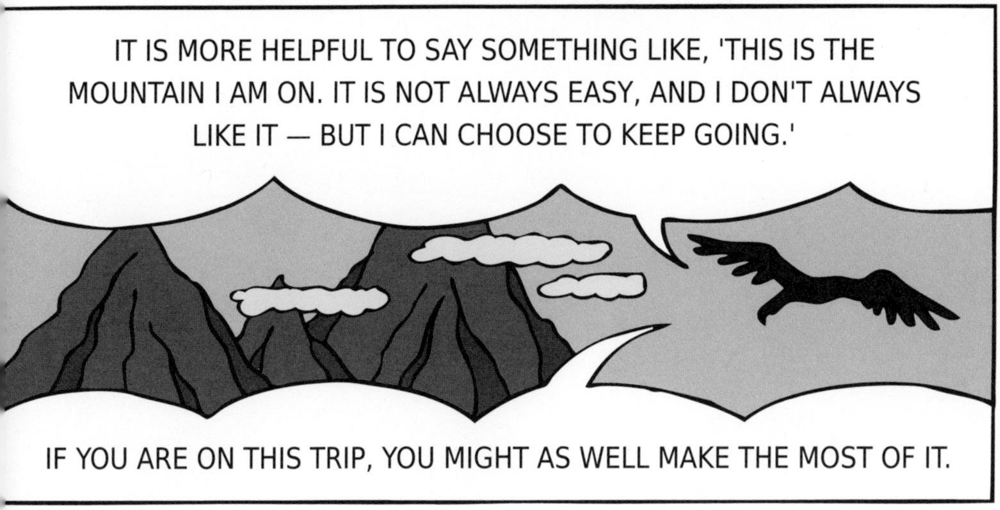
IT IS MORE HELPFUL TO SAY SOMETHING LIKE, 'THIS IS THE MOUNTAIN I AM ON. IT IS NOT ALWAYS EASY, AND I DON'T ALWAYS LIKE IT — BUT I CAN CHOOSE TO KEEP GOING.'
IF YOU ARE ON THIS TRIP, YOU MIGHT AS WELL MAKE THE MOST OF IT.

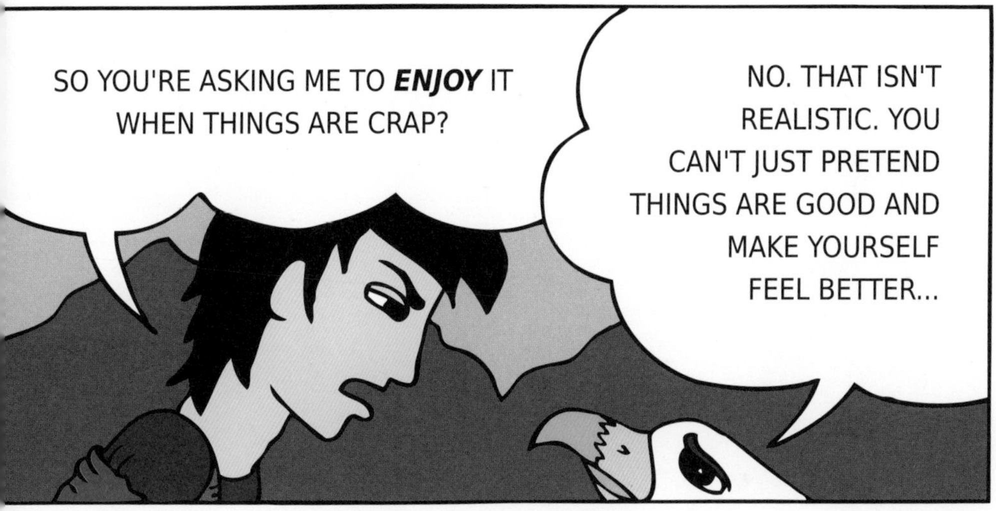
SO YOU'RE ASKING ME TO ***ENJOY*** IT WHEN THINGS ARE CRAP?
NO. THAT ISN'T REALISTIC. YOU CAN'T JUST PRETEND THINGS ARE GOOD AND MAKE YOURSELF FEEL BETTER...

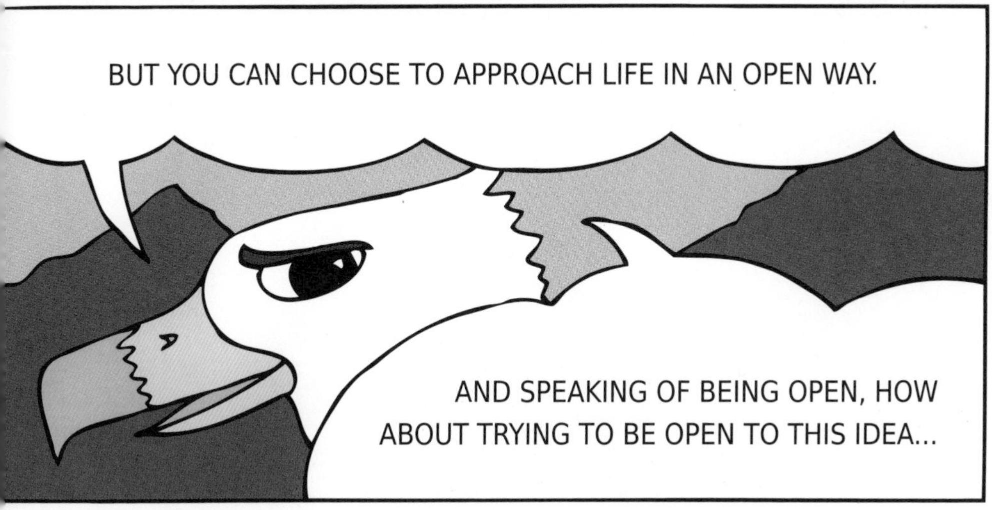
BUT YOU CAN CHOOSE TO APPROACH LIFE IN AN OPEN WAY.
AND SPEAKING OF BEING OPEN, HOW ABOUT TRYING TO BE OPEN TO THIS IDEA...

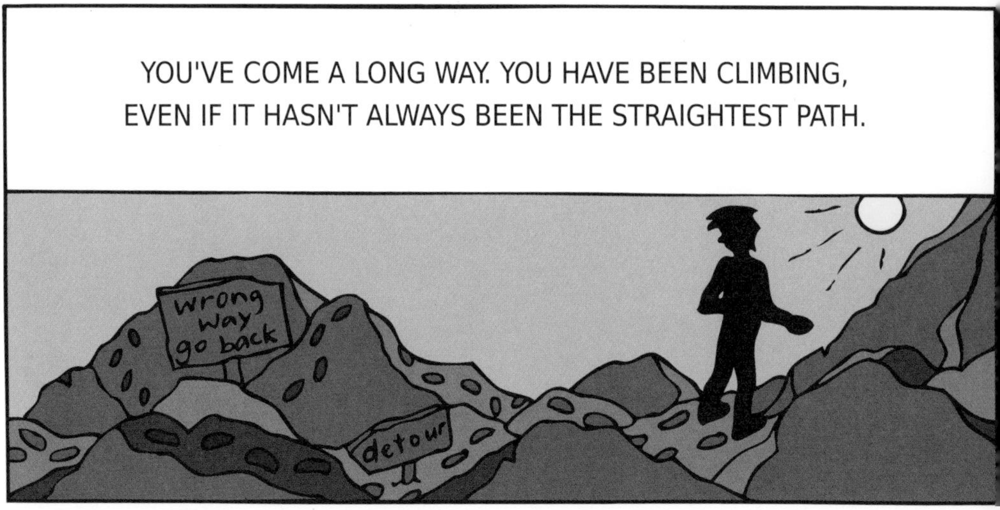
YOU'VE COME A LONG WAY. YOU HAVE BEEN CLIMBING, EVEN IF IT HASN'T ALWAYS BEEN THE STRAIGHTEST PATH.
wrong way go back
detour

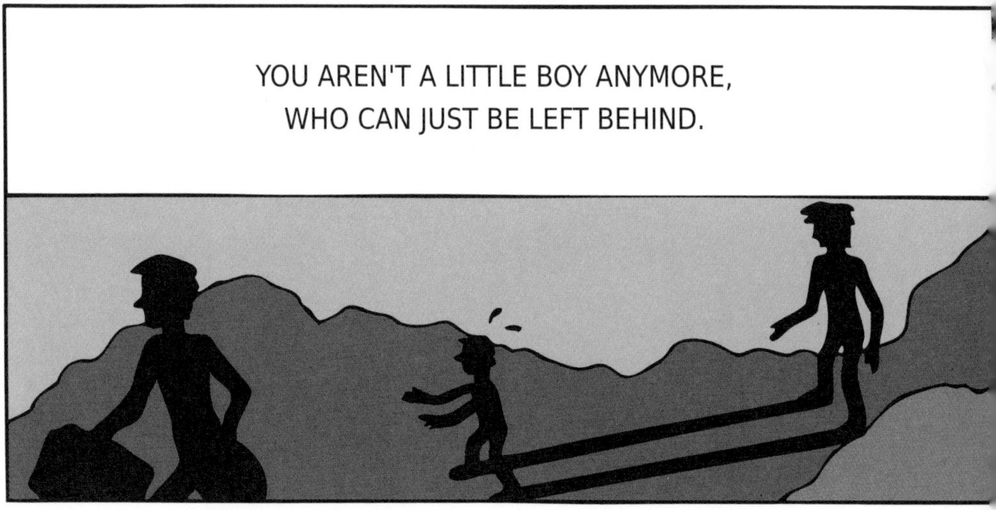
YOU AREN'T A LITTLE BOY ANYMORE, WHO CAN JUST BE LEFT BEHIND.

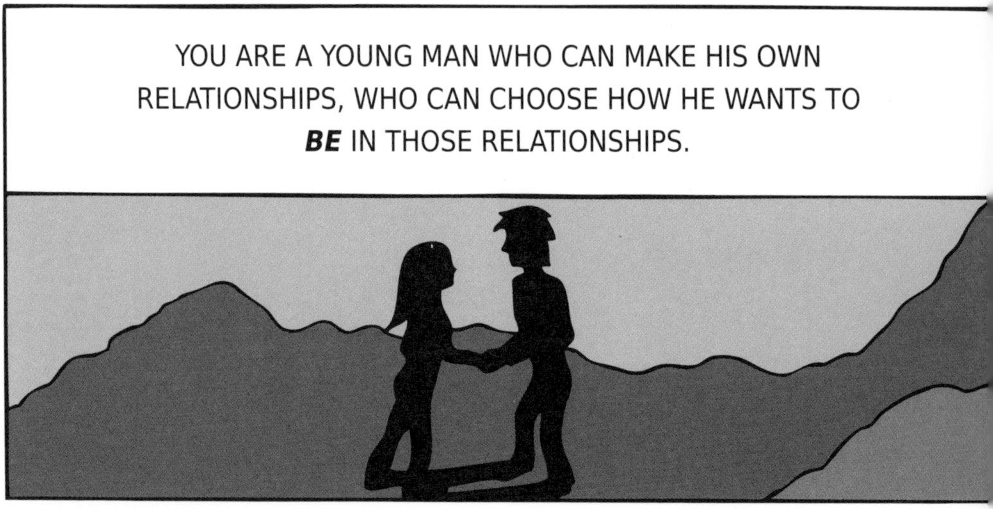
YOU ARE A YOUNG MAN WHO CAN MAKE HIS OWN RELATIONSHIPS, WHO CAN CHOOSE HOW HE WANTS TO ***BE*** IN THOSE RELATIONSHIPS.

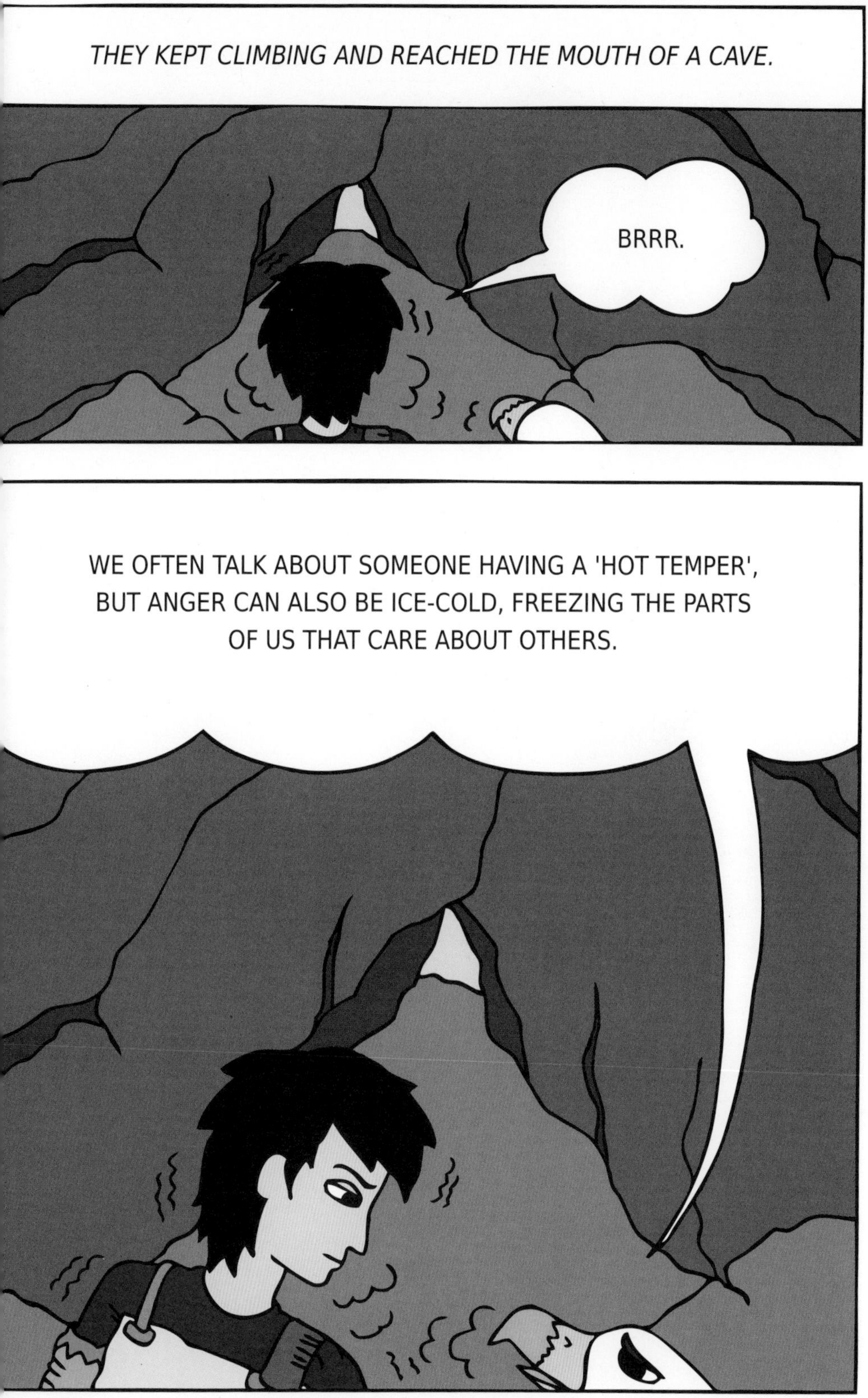
THEY KEPT CLIMBING AND REACHED THE MOUTH OF A CAVE.
BRRR.
WE OFTEN TALK ABOUT SOMEONE HAVING A 'HOT TEMPER', BUT ANGER CAN ALSO BE ICE-COLD, FREEZING THE PARTS OF US THAT CARE ABOUT OTHERS.

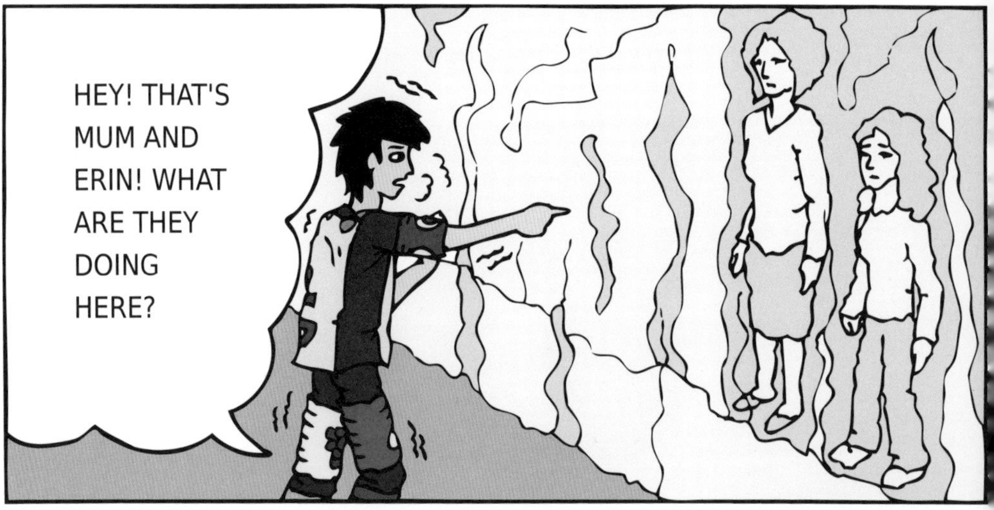
HEY! THAT'S MUM AND ERIN! WHAT ARE THEY DOING HERE?

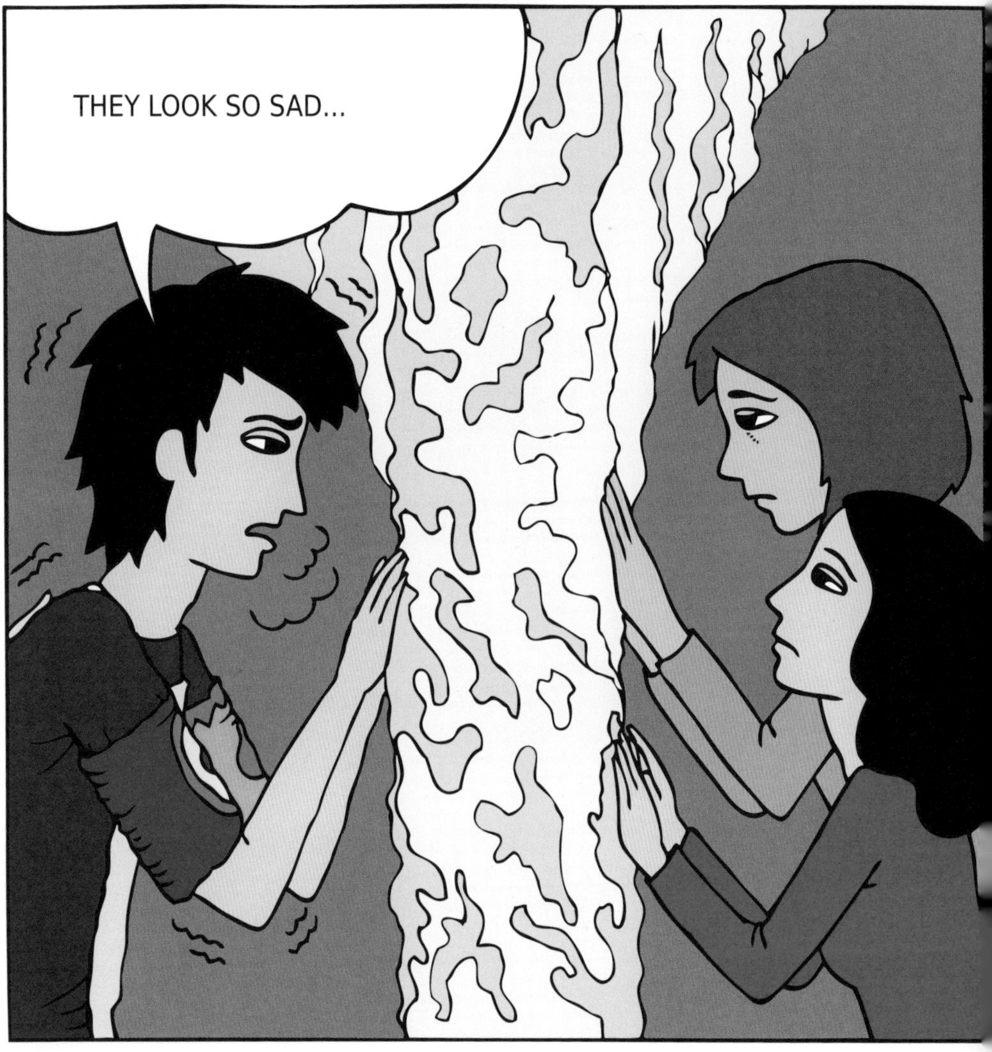
THEY LOOK SO SAD...

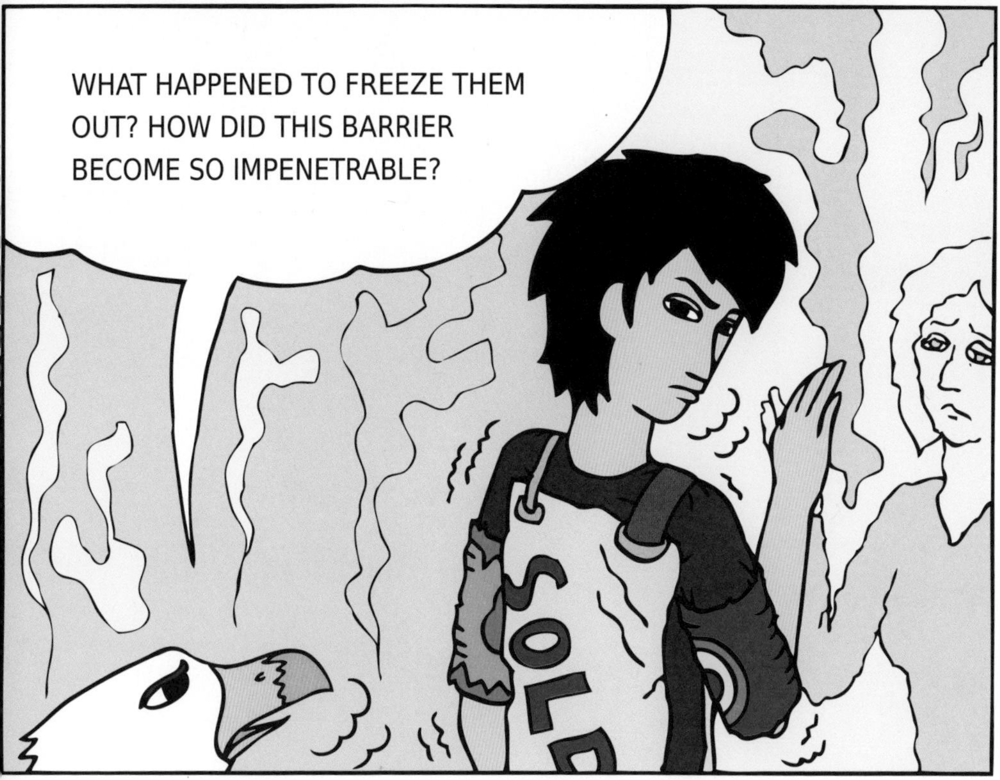
WHAT HAPPENED TO FREEZE THEM OUT? HOW DID THIS BARRIER BECOME SO IMPENETRABLE?
SOLD

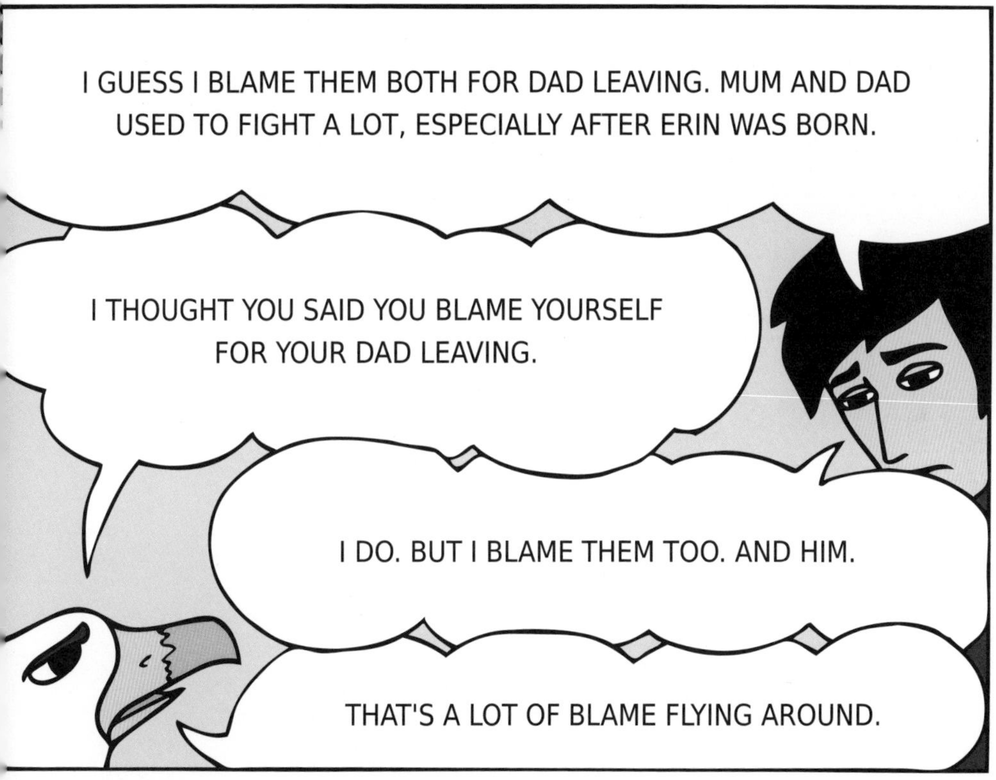
I GUESS I BLAME THEM BOTH FOR DAD LEAVING. MUM AND DAD USED TO FIGHT A LOT, ESPECIALLY AFTER ERIN WAS BORN.
I THOUGHT YOU SAID YOU BLAME YOURSELF FOR YOUR DAD LEAVING.
I DO. BUT I BLAME THEM TOO. AND HIM.
THAT'S A LOT OF BLAME FLYING AROUND.

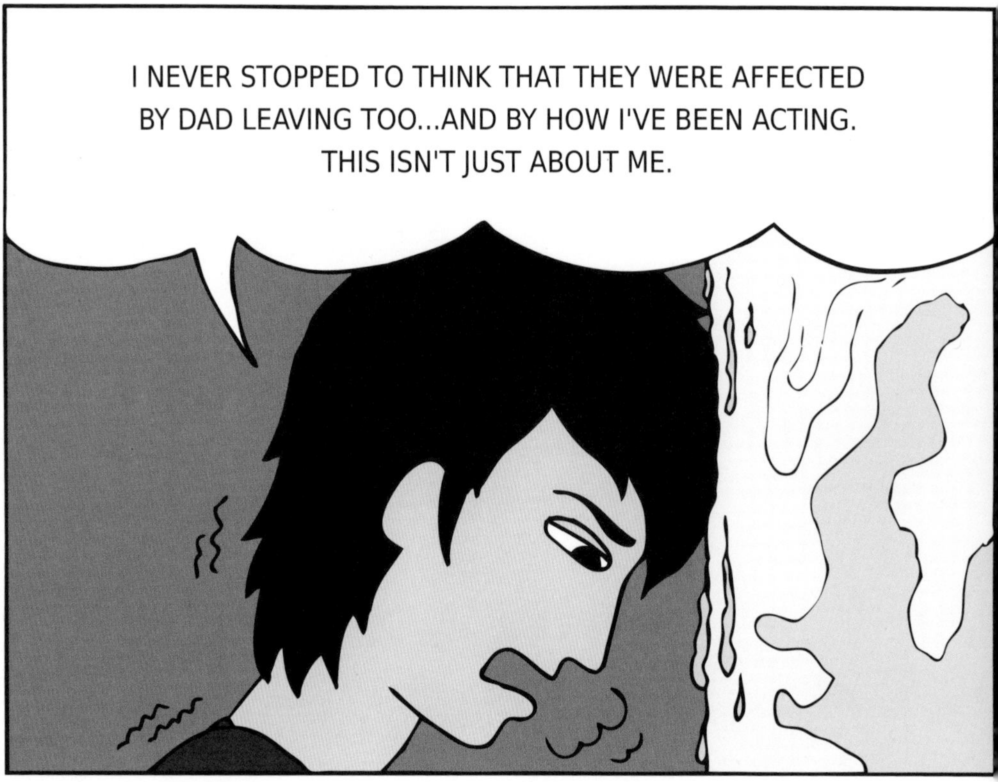
I NEVER STOPPED TO THINK THAT THEY WERE AFFECTED BY DAD LEAVING TOO...AND BY HOW I'VE BEEN ACTING. THIS ISN'T JUST ABOUT ME.

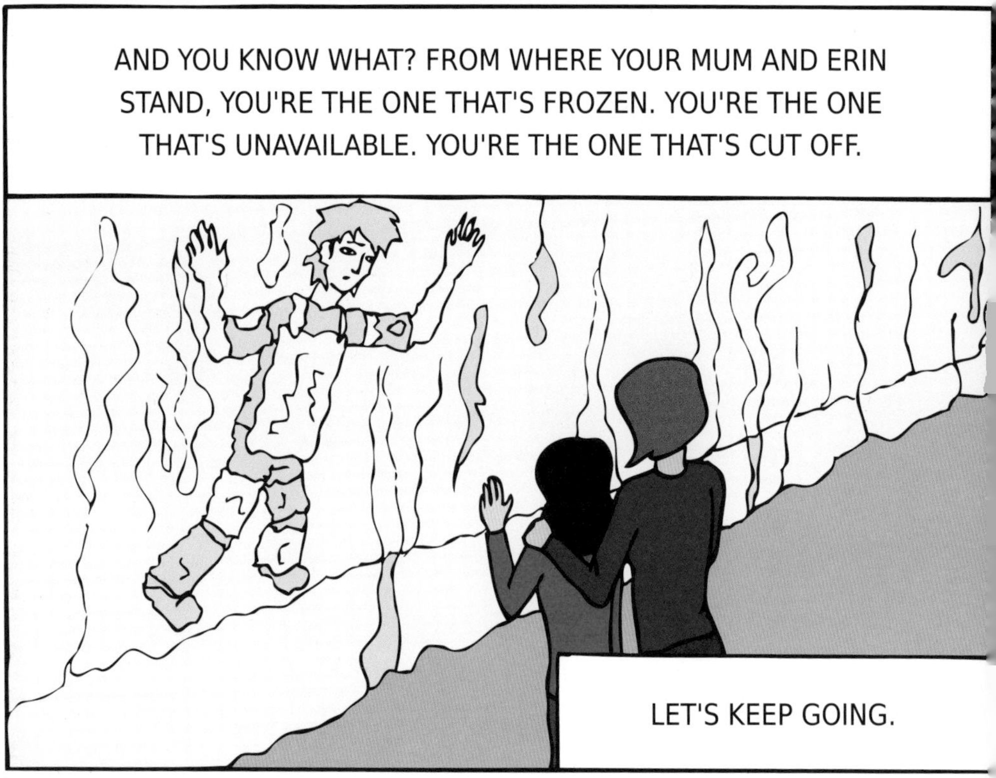
AND YOU KNOW WHAT? FROM WHERE YOUR MUM AND ERIN STAND, YOU'RE THE ONE THAT'S FROZEN. YOU'RE THE ONE THAT'S UNAVAILABLE. YOU'RE THE ONE THAT'S CUT OFF.
LET'S KEEP GOING.

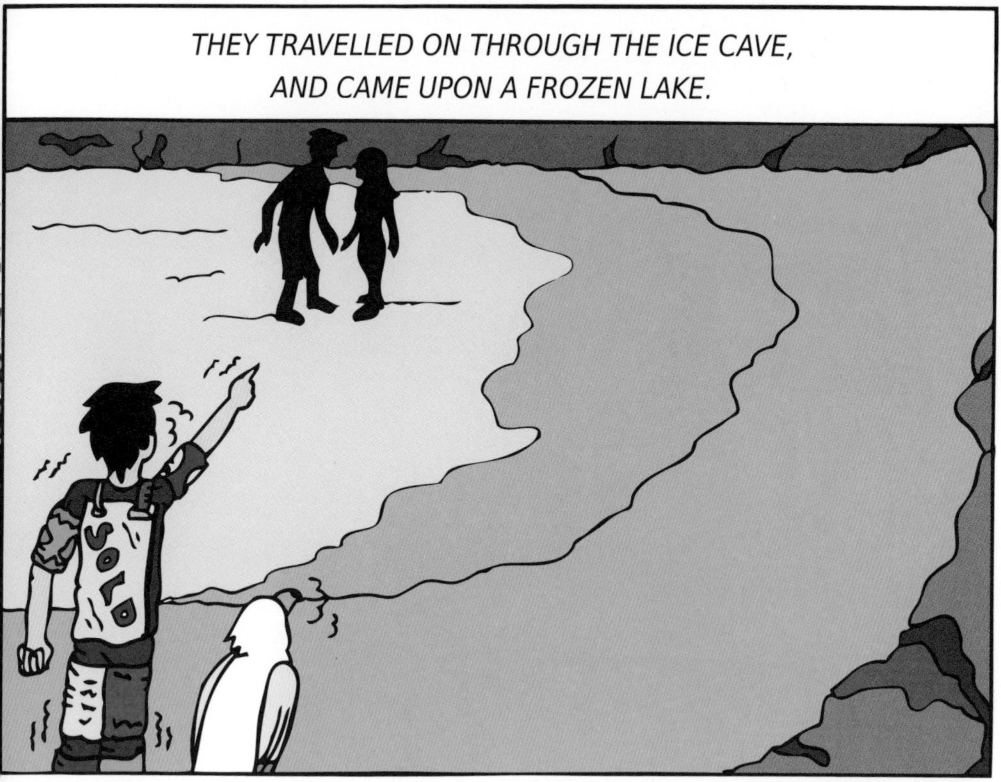
THEY TRAVELLED ON THROUGH THE ICE CAVE, AND CAME UPON A FROZEN LAKE.
SOLD

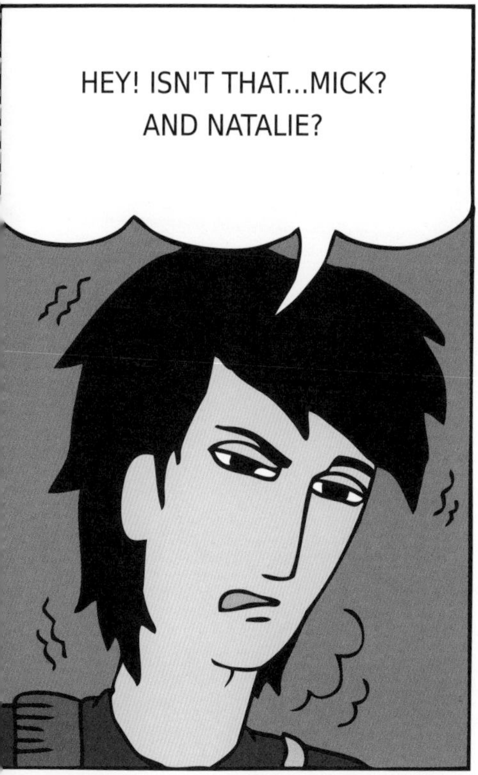
HEY! ISN'T THAT...MICK? AND NATALIE?

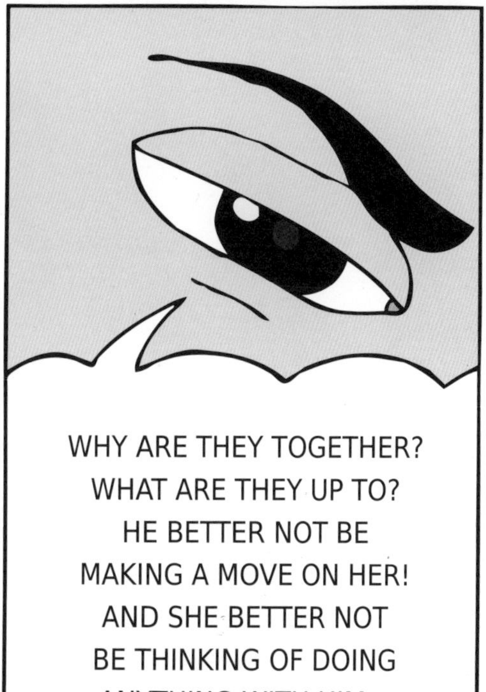
WHY ARE THEY TOGETHER? WHAT ARE THEY UP TO? HE BETTER NOT BE MAKING A MOVE ON HER! AND SHE BETTER NOT BE THINKING OF DOING ANYTHING WITH HIM...

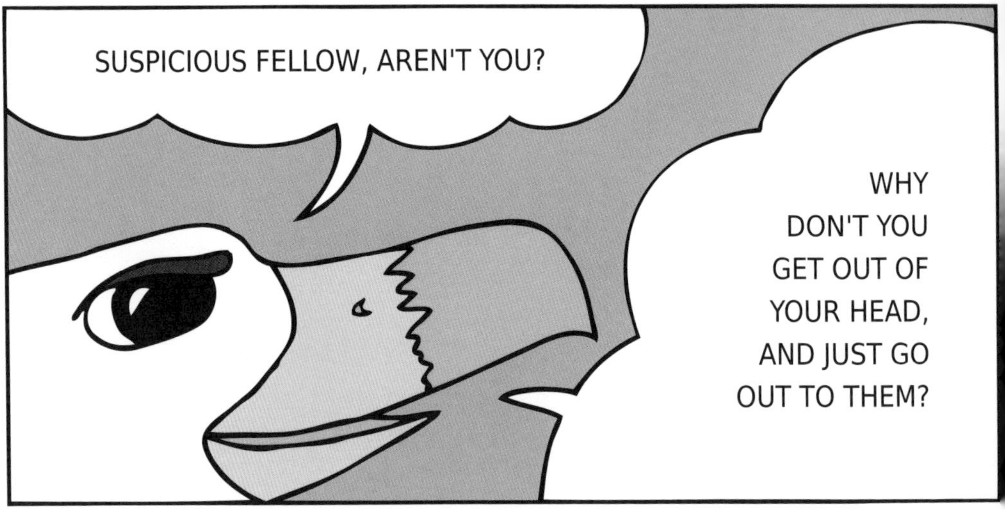
SUSPICIOUS FELLOW, AREN'T YOU?
WHY DON'T YOU GET OUT OF YOUR HEAD, AND JUST GO OUT TO THEM?

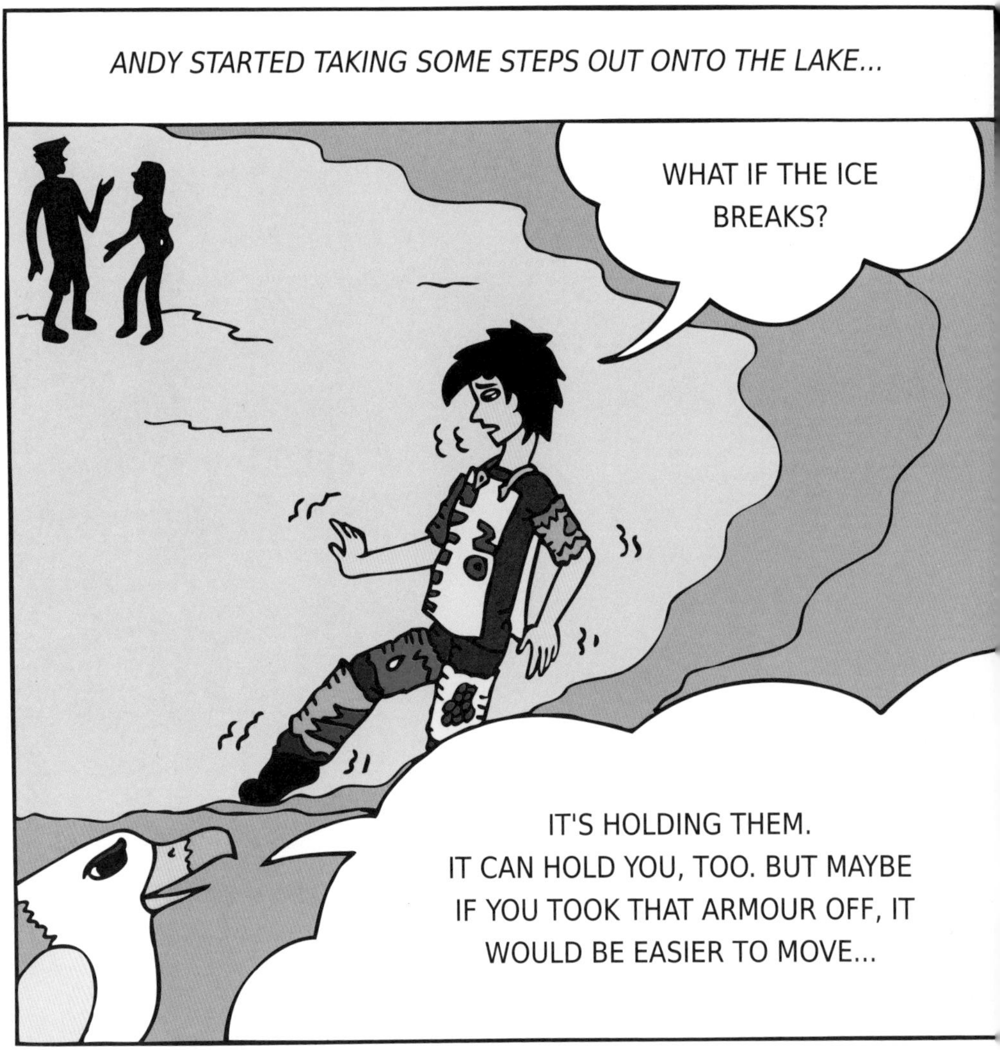
ANDY STARTED TAKING SOME STEPS OUT ONTO THE LAKE...
WHAT IF THE ICE BREAKS?
IT'S HOLDING THEM. IT CAN HOLD YOU, TOO. BUT MAYBE IF YOU TOOK THAT ARMOUR OFF, IT WOULD BE EASIER TO MOVE...

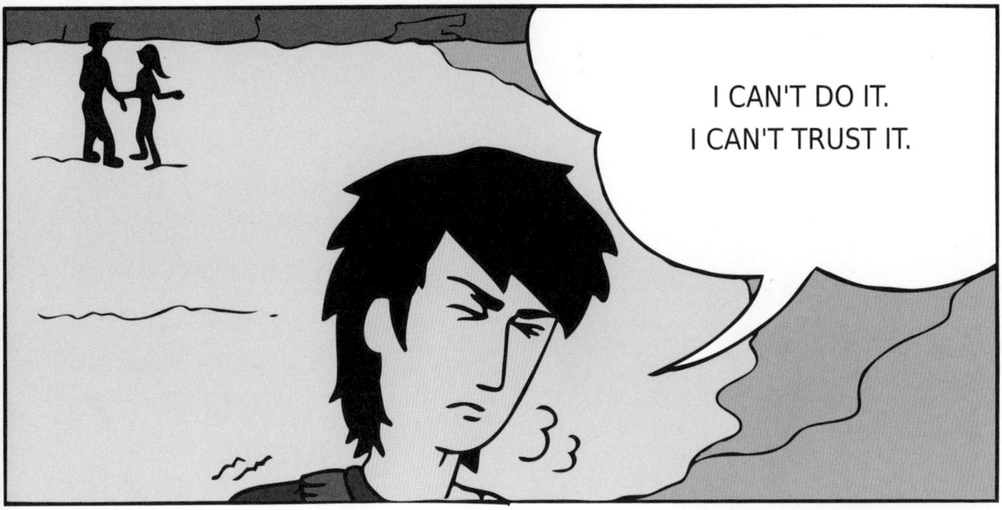
I CAN'T DO IT.
I CAN'T TRUST IT.

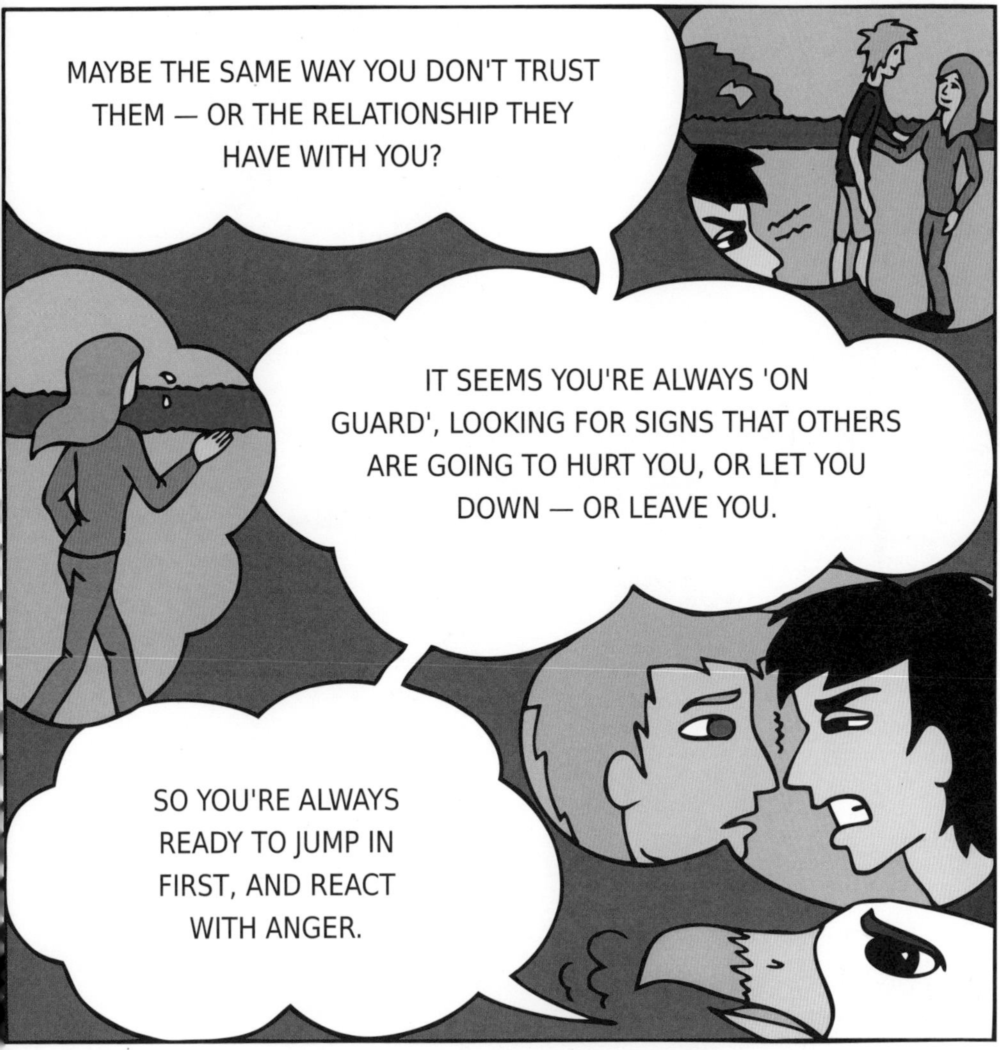
MAYBE THE SAME WAY YOU DON'T TRUST THEM — OR THE RELATIONSHIP THEY HAVE WITH YOU?
IT SEEMS YOU'RE ALWAYS 'ON GUARD', LOOKING FOR SIGNS THAT OTHERS ARE GOING TO HURT YOU, OR LET YOU DOWN — OR LEAVE YOU.
SO YOU'RE ALWAYS READY TO JUMP IN FIRST, AND REACT WITH ANGER.

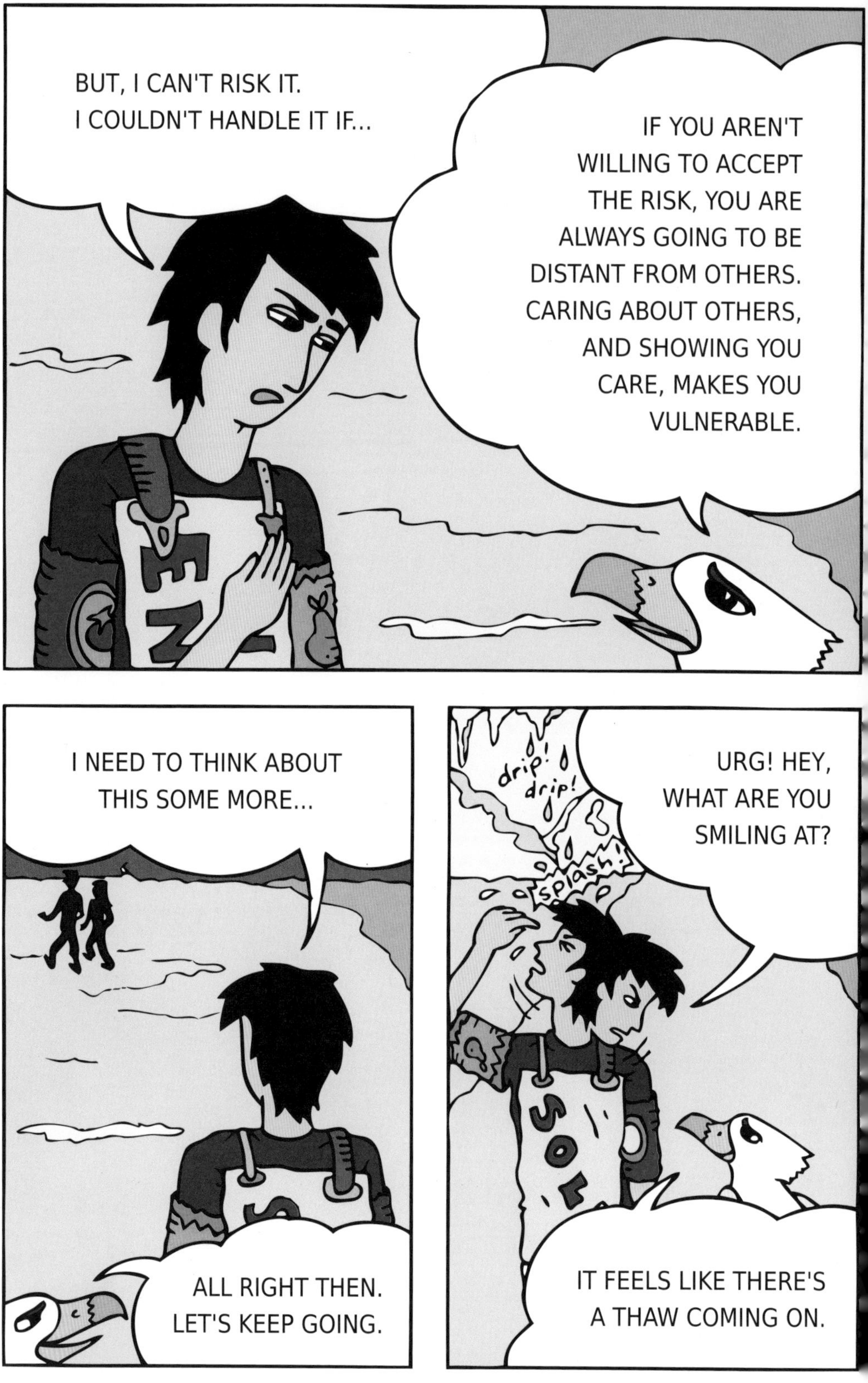
BUT, I CAN'T RISK IT.
I COULDN'T HANDLE IT IF...
IF YOU AREN'T WILLING TO ACCEPT THE RISK, YOU ARE ALWAYS GOING TO BE DISTANT FROM OTHERS. CARING ABOUT OTHERS, AND SHOWING YOU CARE, MAKES YOU VULNERABLE.
I NEED TO THINK ABOUT THIS SOME MORE...
ALL RIGHT THEN. LET'S KEEP GOING.
drip! drip!
splash!
URG! HEY, WHAT ARE YOU SMILING AT?
IT FEELS LIKE THERE'S A THAW COMING ON.

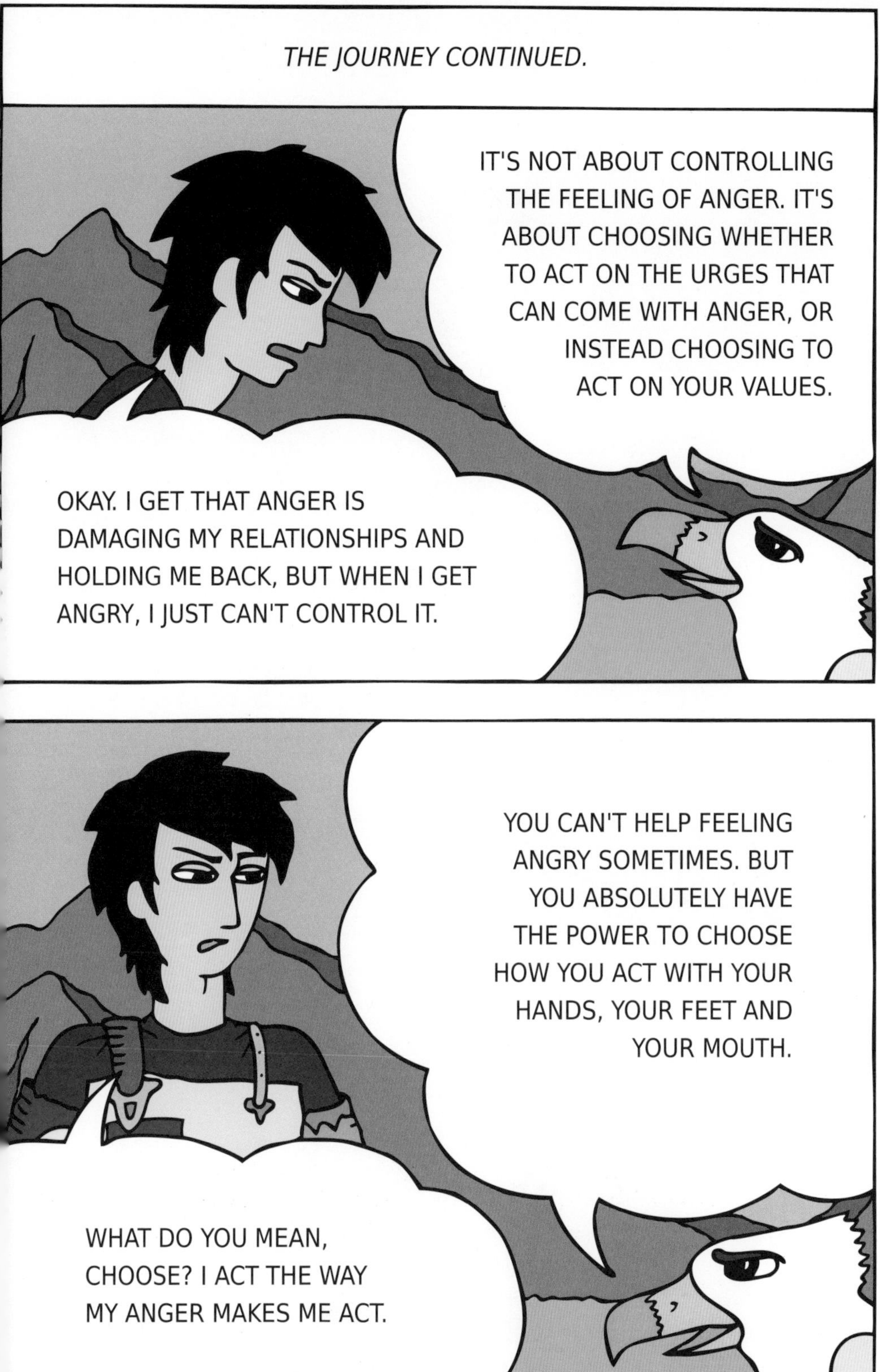
THE JOURNEY CONTINUED.
IT'S NOT ABOUT CONTROLLING THE FEELING OF ANGER. IT'S ABOUT CHOOSING WHETHER TO ACT ON THE URGES THAT CAN COME WITH ANGER, OR INSTEAD CHOOSING TO ACT ON YOUR VALUES.
OKAY. I GET THAT ANGER IS DAMAGING MY RELATIONSHIPS AND HOLDING ME BACK, BUT WHEN I GET ANGRY, I JUST CAN'T CONTROL IT.
YOU CAN'T HELP FEELING ANGRY SOMETIMES. BUT YOU ABSOLUTELY HAVE THE POWER TO CHOOSE HOW YOU ACT WITH YOUR HANDS, YOUR FEET AND YOUR MOUTH.
WHAT DO YOU MEAN, CHOOSE? I ACT THE WAY MY ANGER MAKES ME ACT.

FOR EXAMPLE, YOU CAN PUSH PEOPLE AWAY
OR BE OPEN TO WHAT THEY SAY.

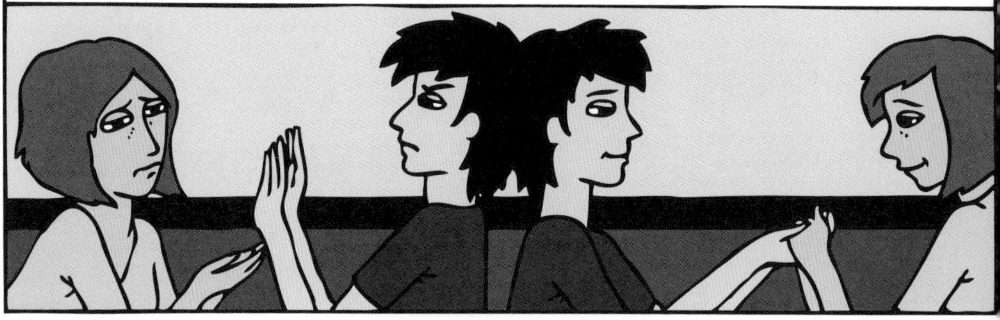

YOU CAN WALK INTO AN ARGUMENT
OR CHOOSE TO WALK AWAY.

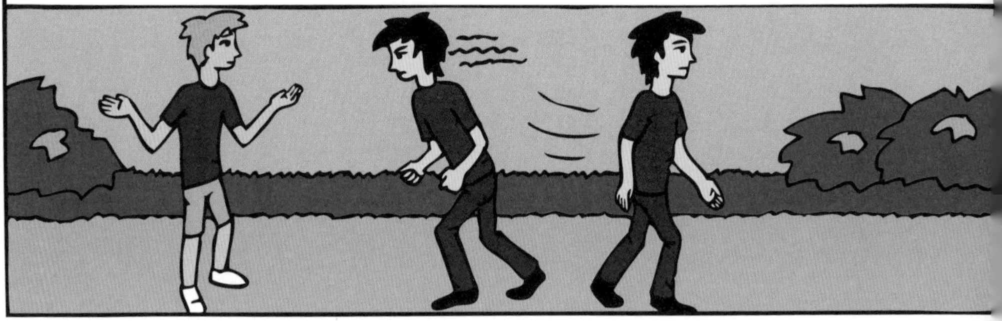

YOU CAN LET ANGER DO THE TALKING, TRY TO SORT THINGS
OUT — OR EVEN JUST HOLD YOUR TONGUE AND SAY NOTHING.

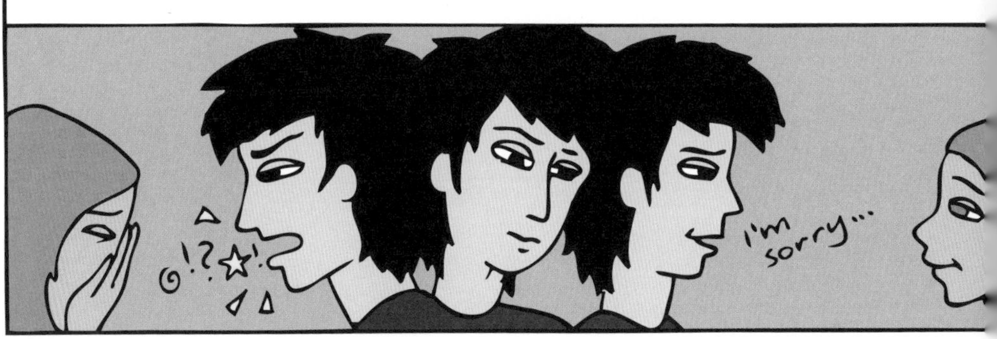
I'm sorry...

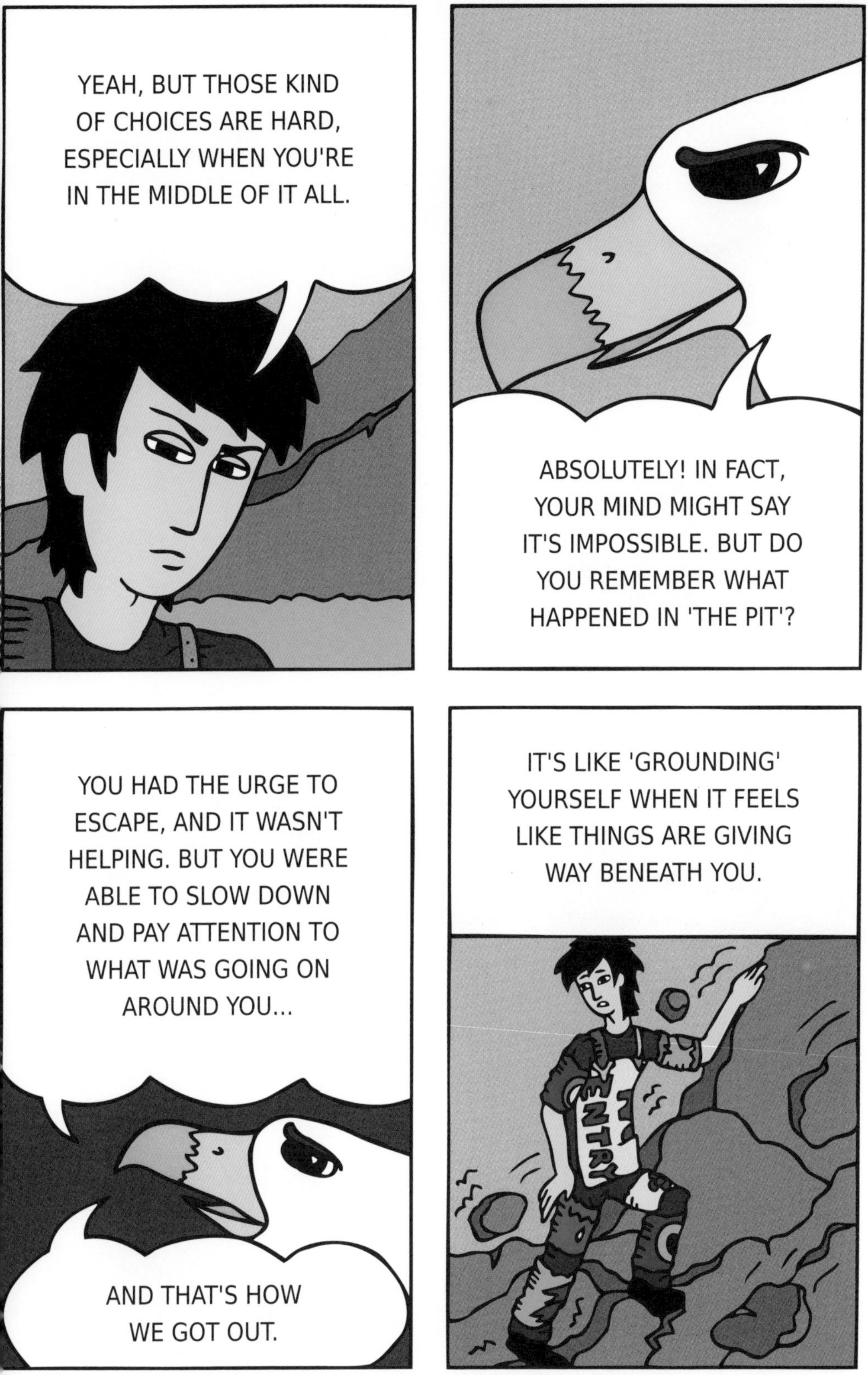
YEAH, BUT THOSE KIND OF CHOICES ARE HARD, ESPECIALLY WHEN YOU'RE IN THE MIDDLE OF IT ALL.
ABSOLUTELY! IN FACT, YOUR MIND MIGHT SAY IT'S IMPOSSIBLE. BUT DO YOU REMEMBER WHAT HAPPENED IN 'THE PIT'?
YOU HAD THE URGE TO ESCAPE, AND IT WASN'T HELPING. BUT YOU WERE ABLE TO SLOW DOWN AND PAY ATTENTION TO WHAT WAS GOING ON AROUND YOU...
AND THAT'S HOW WE GOT OUT.
IT'S LIKE 'GROUNDING' YOURSELF WHEN IT FEELS LIKE THINGS ARE GIVING WAY BENEATH YOU.

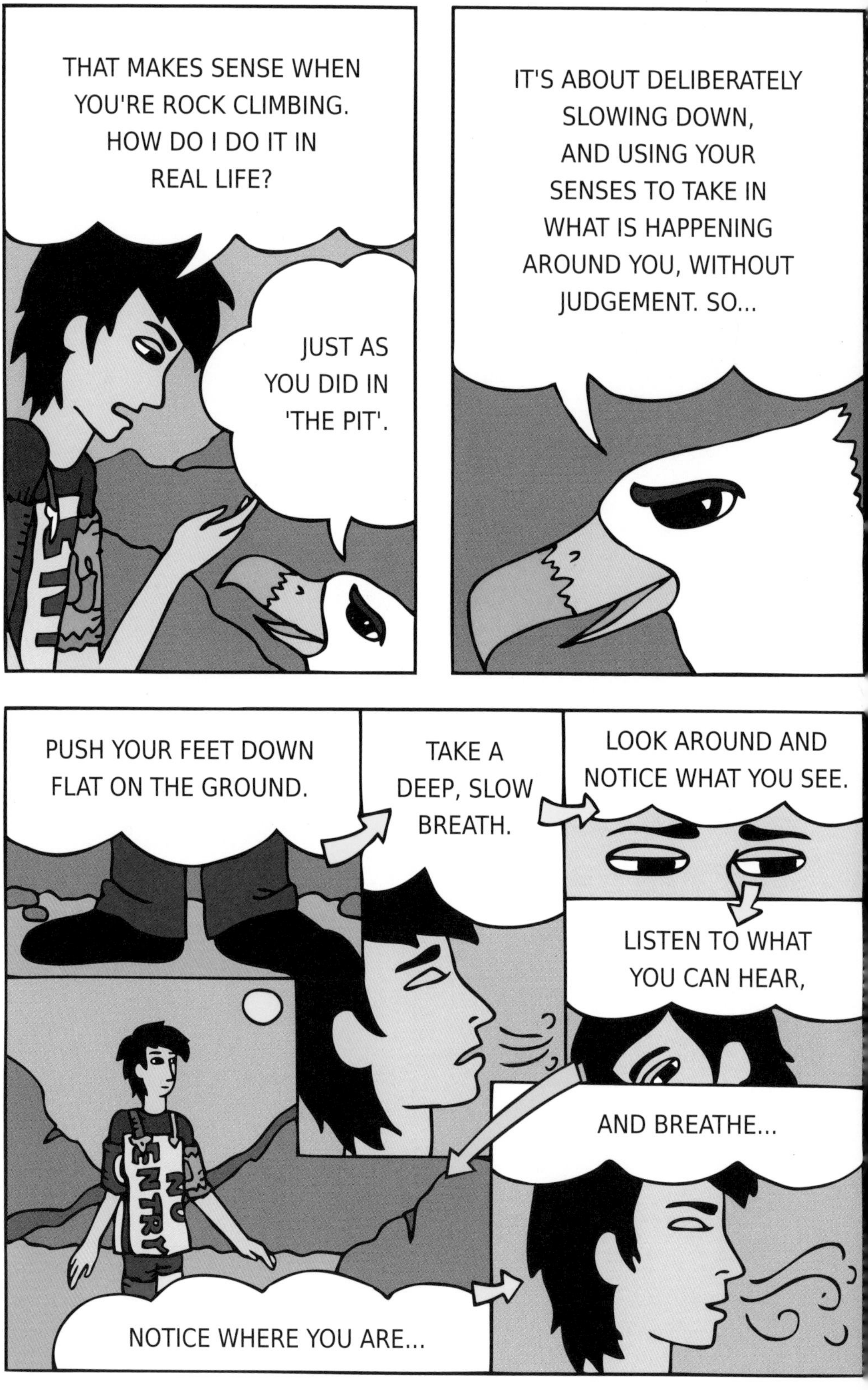
THAT MAKES SENSE WHEN YOU'RE ROCK CLIMBING. HOW DO I DO IT IN REAL LIFE?
JUST AS YOU DID IN 'THE PIT'.
IT'S ABOUT DELIBERATELY SLOWING DOWN, AND USING YOUR SENSES TO TAKE IN WHAT IS HAPPENING AROUND YOU, WITHOUT JUDGEMENT. SO...
PUSH YOUR FEET DOWN FLAT ON THE GROUND.
TAKE A DEEP, SLOW BREATH.
LOOK AROUND AND NOTICE WHAT YOU SEE.
LISTEN TO WHAT YOU CAN HEAR,
AND BREATHE...
NOTICE WHERE YOU ARE...

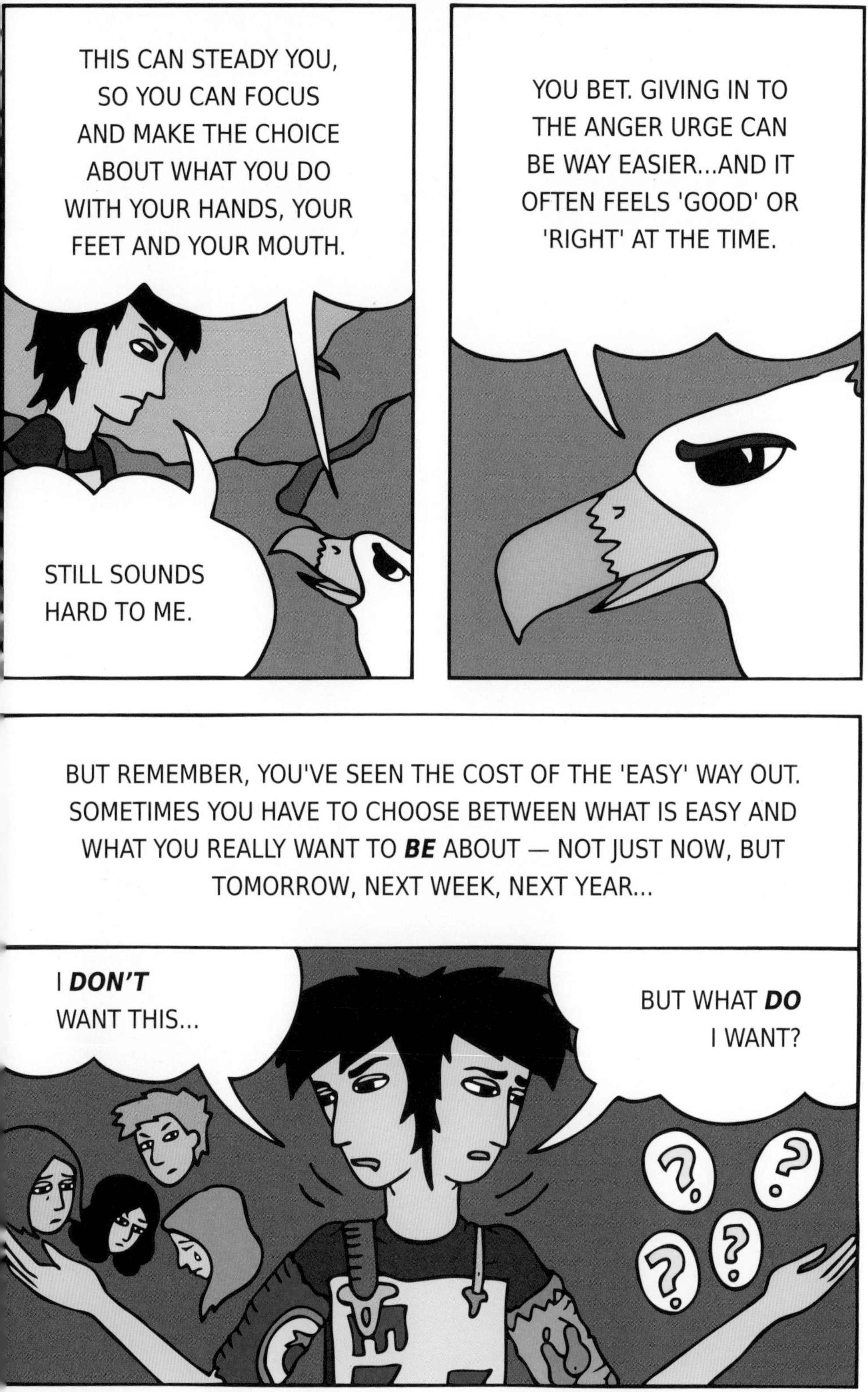
THIS CAN STEADY YOU, SO YOU CAN FOCUS AND MAKE THE CHOICE ABOUT WHAT YOU DO WITH YOUR HANDS, YOUR FEET AND YOUR MOUTH.
STILL SOUNDS HARD TO ME.
YOU BET. GIVING IN TO THE ANGER URGE CAN BE WAY EASIER...AND IT OFTEN FEELS 'GOOD' OR 'RIGHT' AT THE TIME.
BUT REMEMBER, YOU'VE SEEN THE COST OF THE 'EASY' WAY OUT. SOMETIMES YOU HAVE TO CHOOSE BETWEEN WHAT IS EASY AND WHAT YOU REALLY WANT TO ***BE*** ABOUT — NOT JUST NOW, BUT TOMORROW, NEXT WEEK, NEXT YEAR...
I ***DON'T*** WANT THIS...
BUT WHAT ***DO*** I WANT?

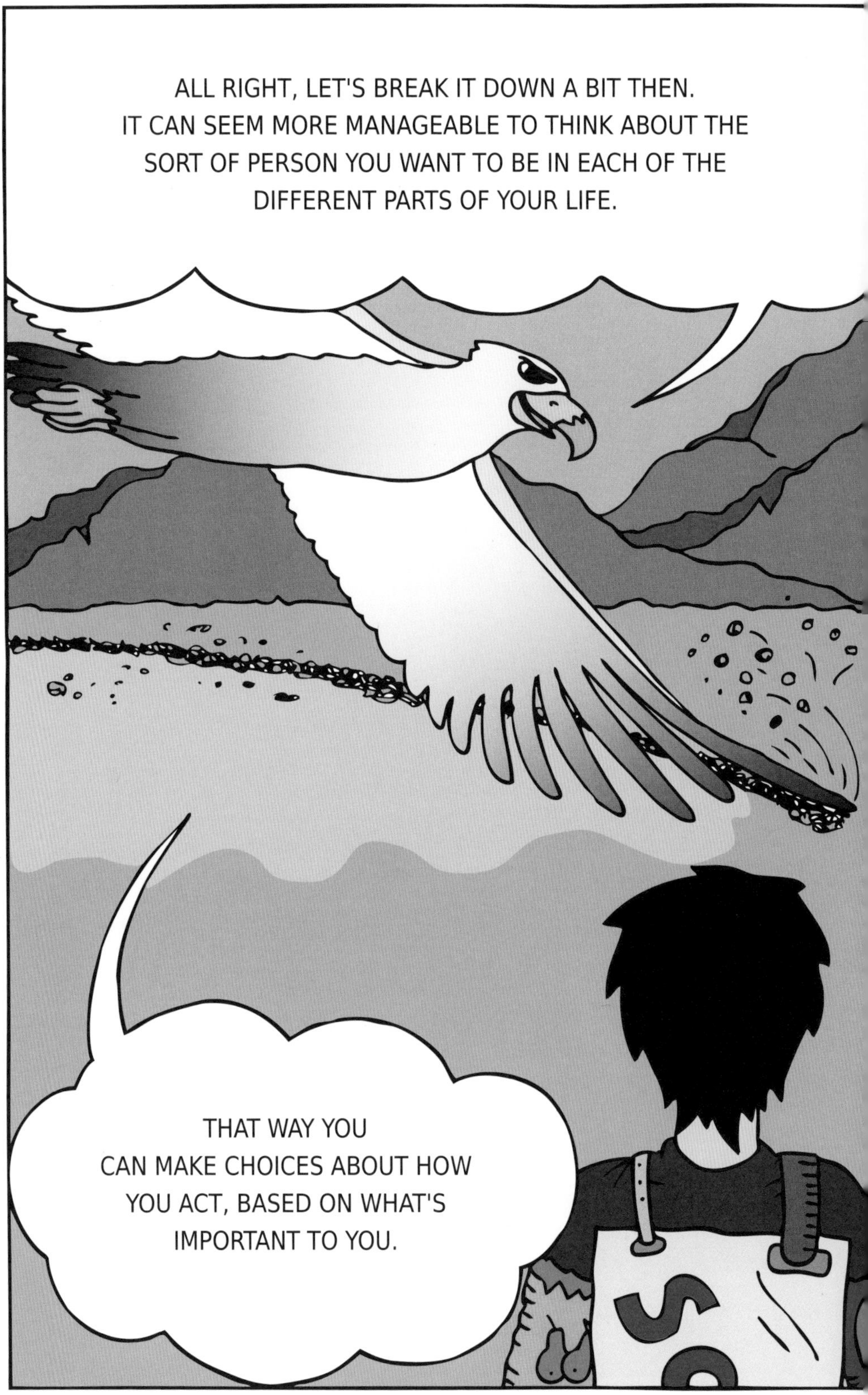
ALL RIGHT, LET'S BREAK IT DOWN A BIT THEN. IT CAN SEEM MORE MANAGEABLE TO THINK ABOUT THE SORT OF PERSON YOU WANT TO BE IN EACH OF THE DIFFERENT PARTS OF YOUR LIFE.
THAT WAY YOU CAN MAKE CHOICES ABOUT HOW YOU ACT, BASED ON WHAT'S IMPORTANT TO YOU.

SO, IF THESE ARE ALL PART OF WHAT MAKES UP YOUR LIFE, HOW DO YOU WANT TO BE AS A FRIEND? FAMILY MEMBER? STUDENT? PERSON?

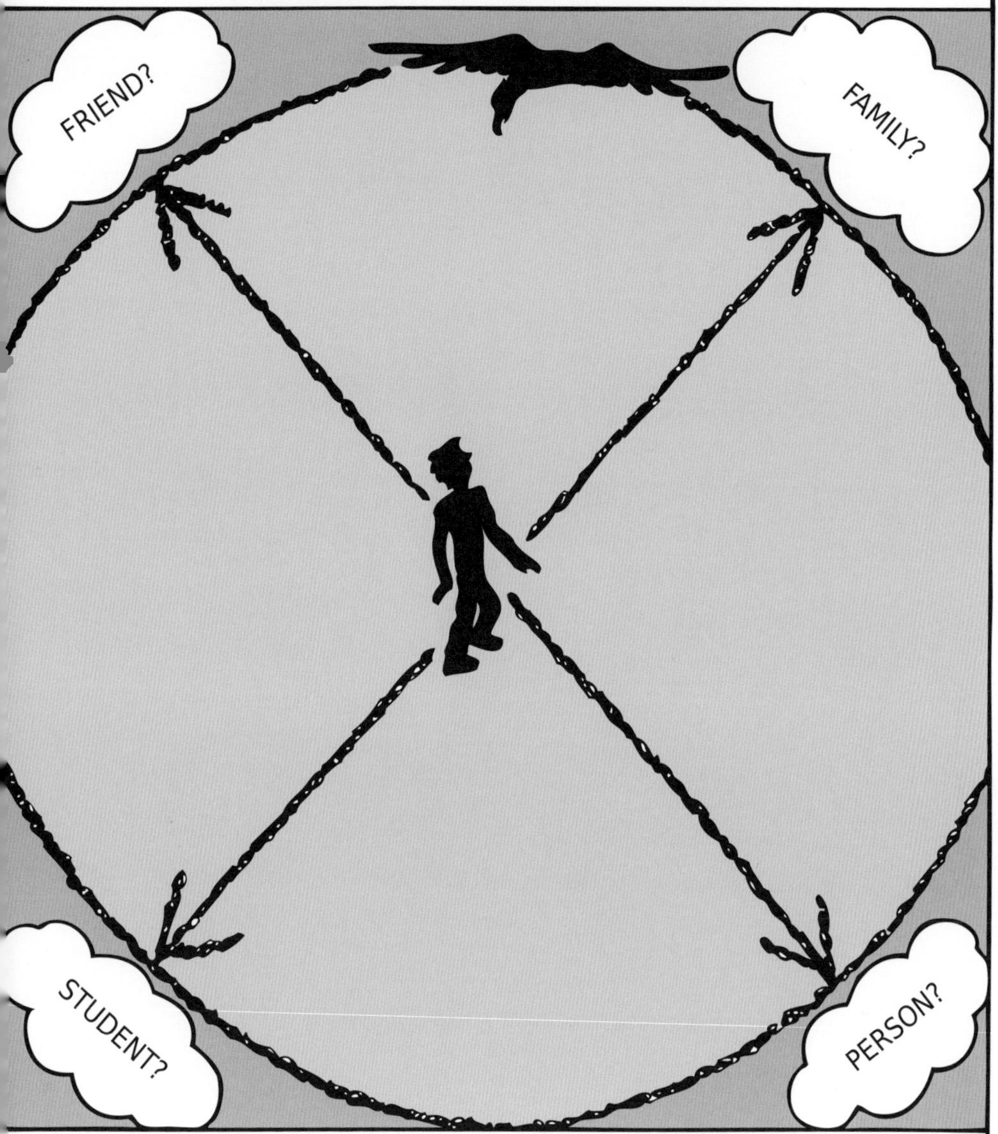
FRIEND?
FAMILY?
STUDENT?
PERSON?

IF THE OUTSIDE OF THE CIRCLE IS YOU FULLY BEING HOW YOU WANT TO BE IN EACH AREA, SHOW ME HOW FAR ALONG YOU FEEL YOU ARE AT THE MOMENT.

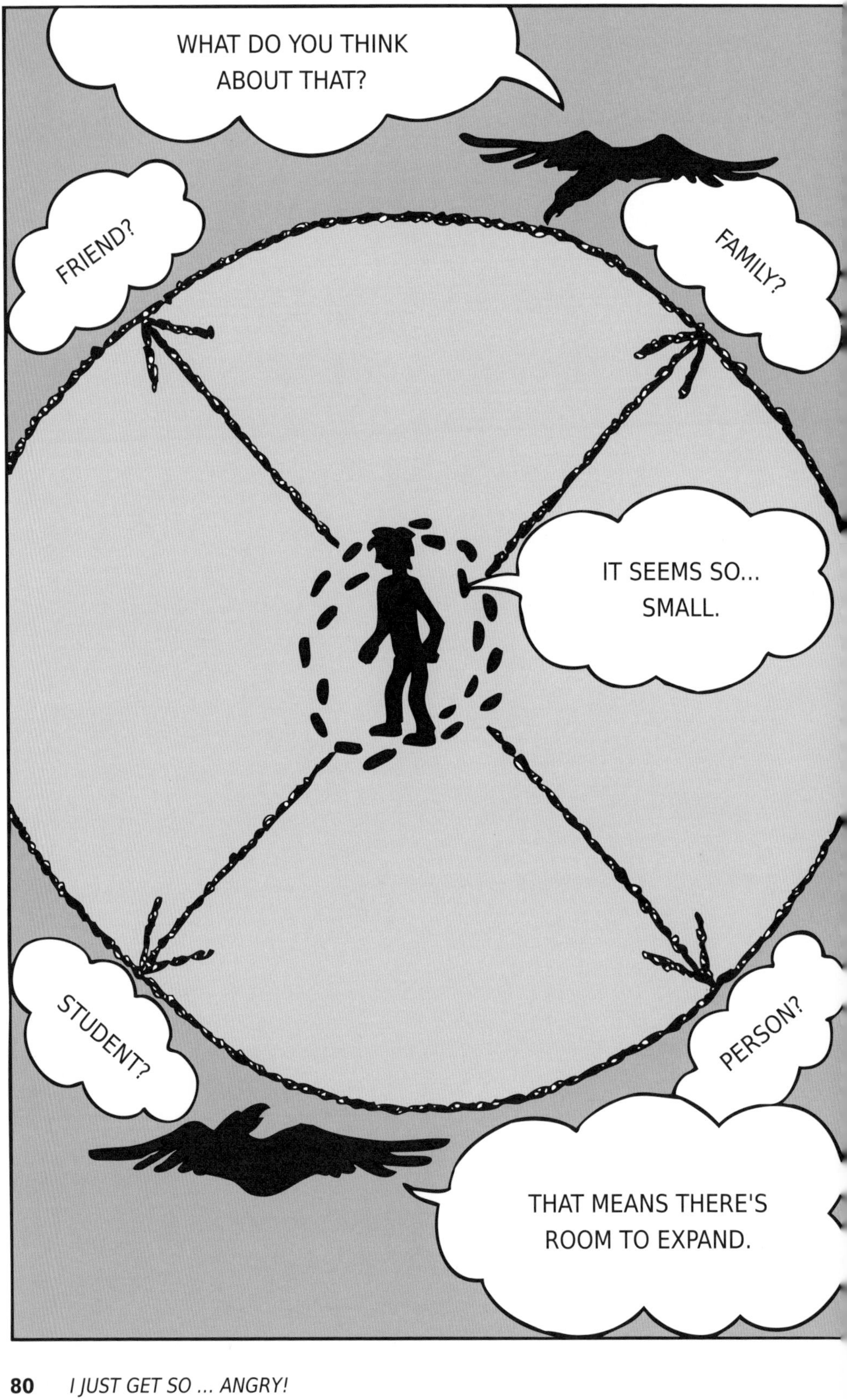
WHAT DO YOU THINK ABOUT THAT?
FRIEND?
FAMILY?
IT SEEMS SO... SMALL.
STUDENT?
PERSON?
THAT MEANS THERE'S ROOM TO EXPAND.

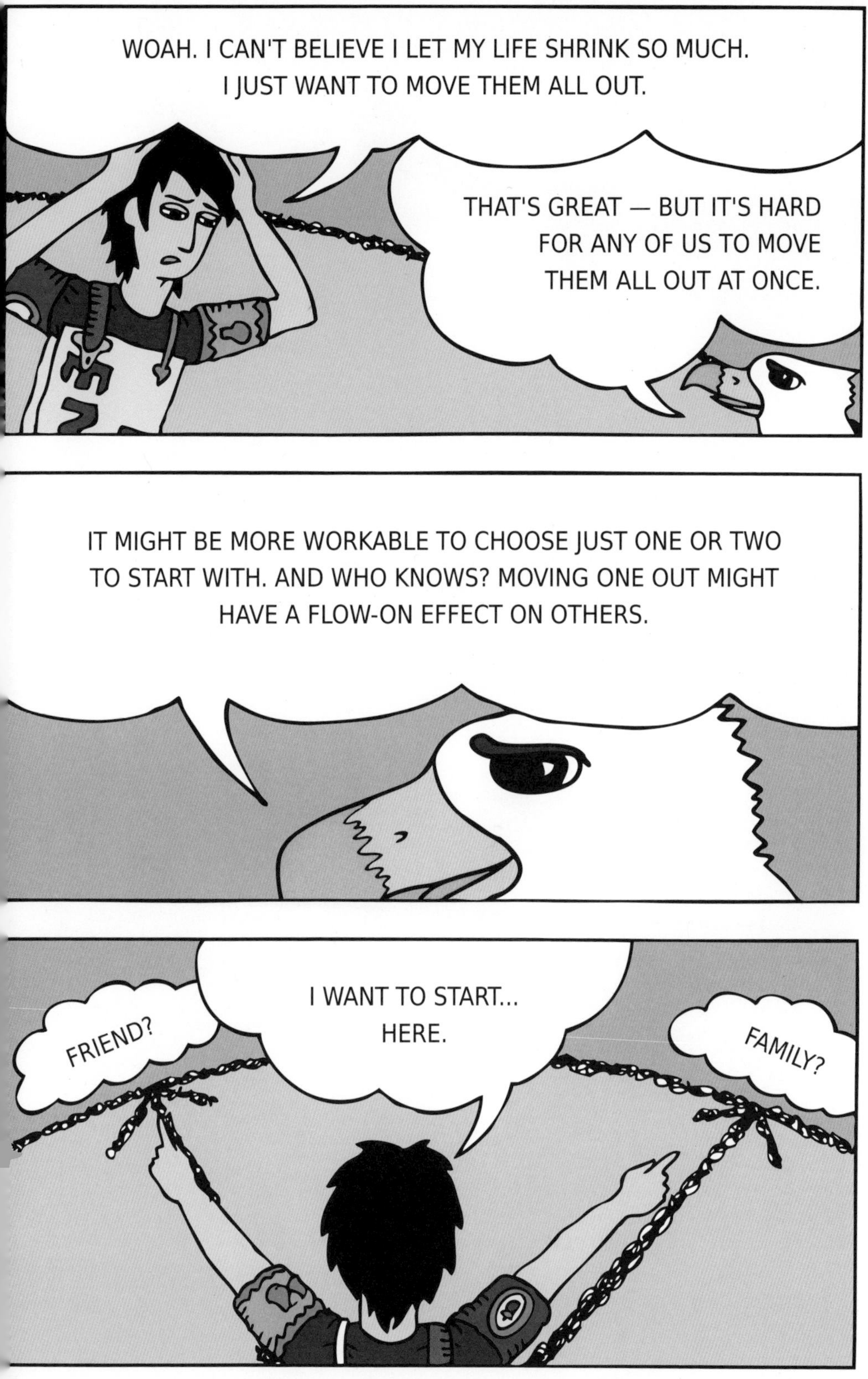
WOAH. I CAN'T BELIEVE I LET MY LIFE SHRINK SO MUCH. I JUST WANT TO MOVE THEM ALL OUT.
THAT'S GREAT — BUT IT'S HARD FOR ANY OF US TO MOVE THEM ALL OUT AT ONCE.
IT MIGHT BE MORE WORKABLE TO CHOOSE JUST ONE OR TWO TO START WITH. AND WHO KNOWS? MOVING ONE OUT MIGHT HAVE A FLOW-ON EFFECT ON OTHERS.
FRIEND?
I WANT TO START... HERE.
FAMILY?

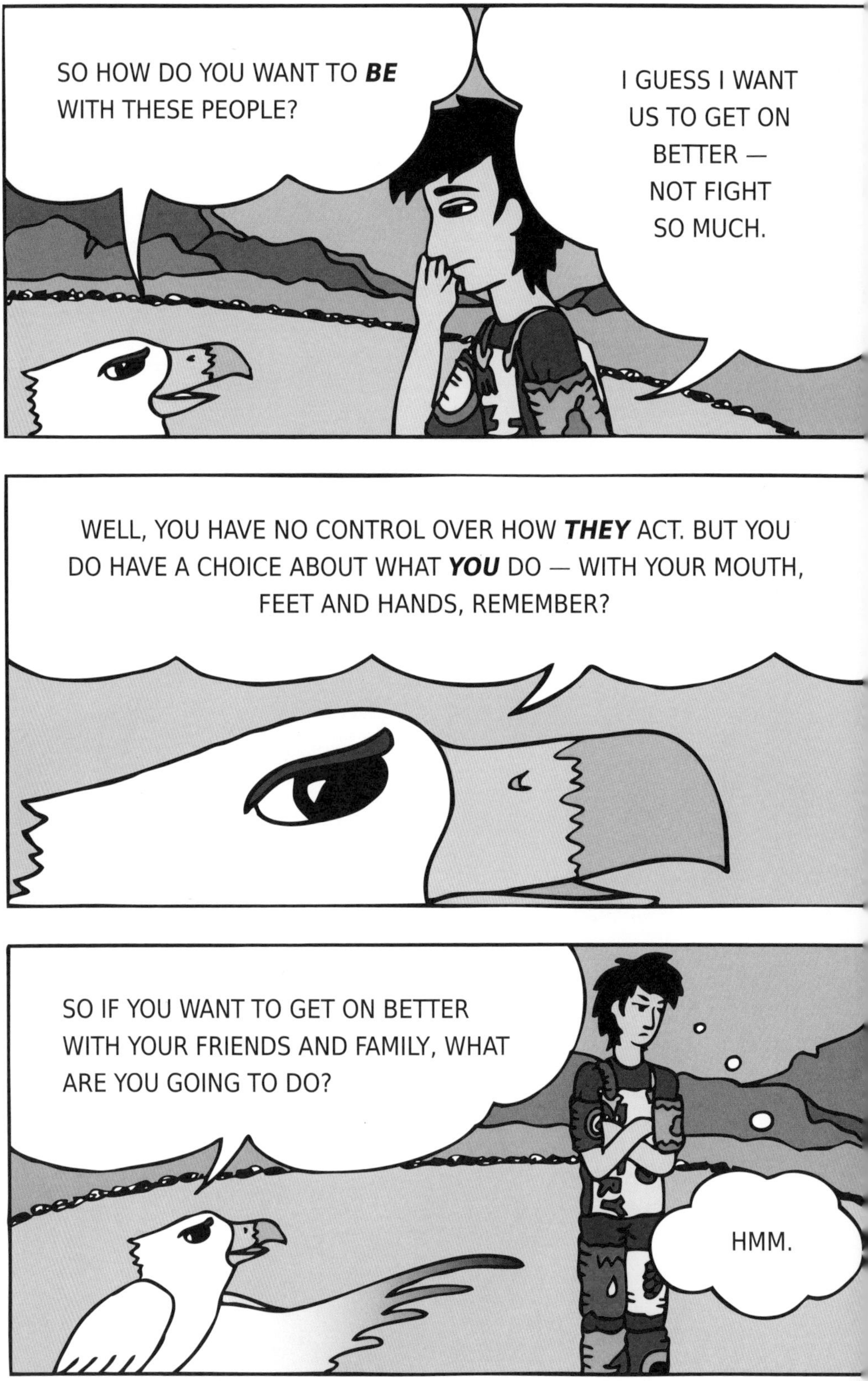
SO HOW DO YOU WANT TO **BE** WITH THESE PEOPLE?
I GUESS I WANT US TO GET ON BETTER — NOT FIGHT SO MUCH.
WELL, YOU HAVE NO CONTROL OVER HOW **THEY** ACT. BUT YOU DO HAVE A CHOICE ABOUT WHAT **YOU** DO — WITH YOUR MOUTH, FEET AND HANDS, REMEMBER?
SO IF YOU WANT TO GET ON BETTER WITH YOUR FRIENDS AND FAMILY, WHAT ARE YOU GOING TO DO?
HMM.

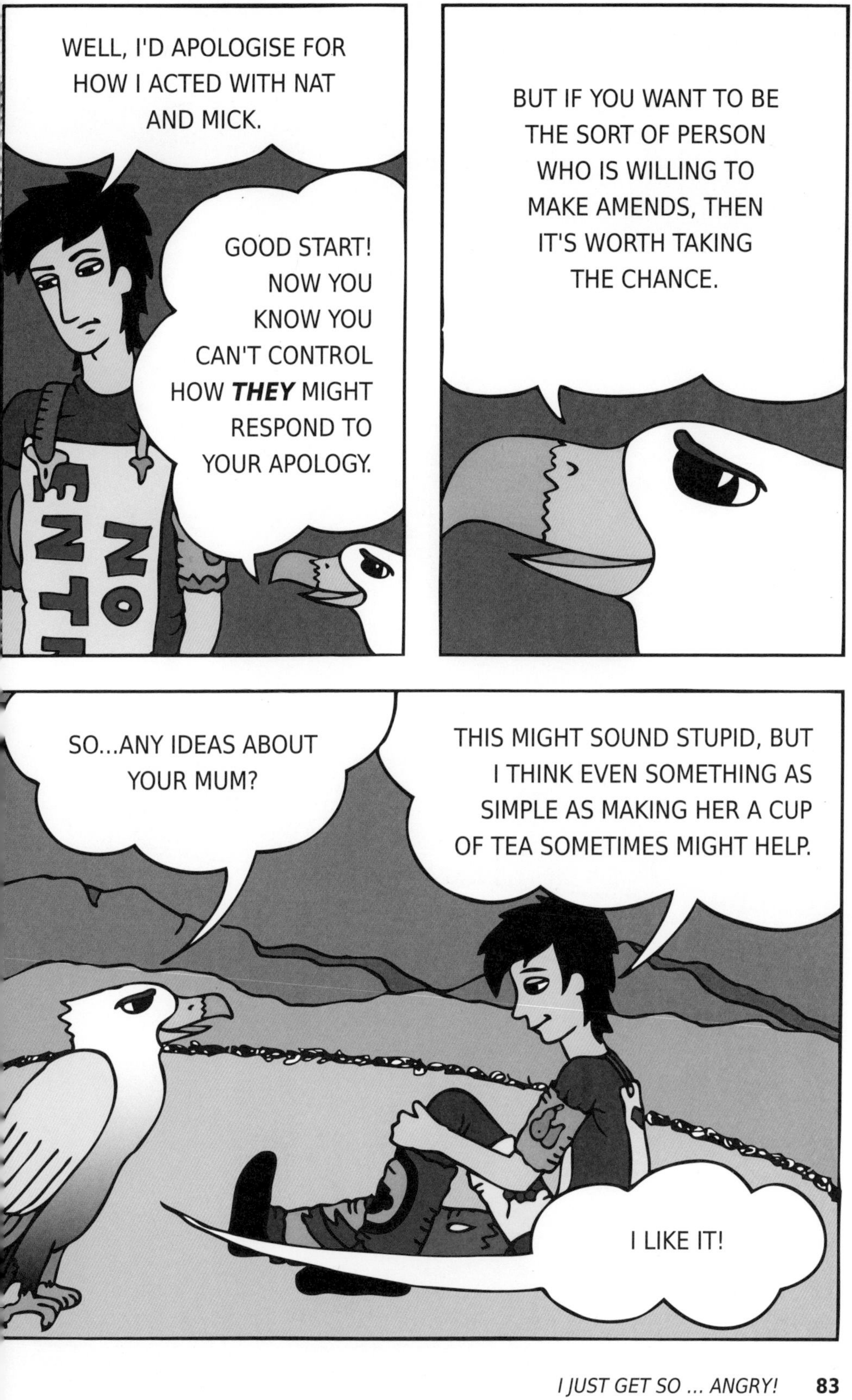
WELL, I'D APOLOGISE FOR HOW I ACTED WITH NAT AND MICK.
GOOD START! NOW YOU KNOW YOU CAN'T CONTROL HOW ***THEY*** MIGHT RESPOND TO YOUR APOLOGY.
BUT IF YOU WANT TO BE THE SORT OF PERSON WHO IS WILLING TO MAKE AMENDS, THEN IT'S WORTH TAKING THE CHANCE.
SO...ANY IDEAS ABOUT YOUR MUM?
THIS MIGHT SOUND STUPID, BUT I THINK EVEN SOMETHING AS SIMPLE AS MAKING HER A CUP OF TEA SOMETIMES MIGHT HELP.
I LIKE IT!

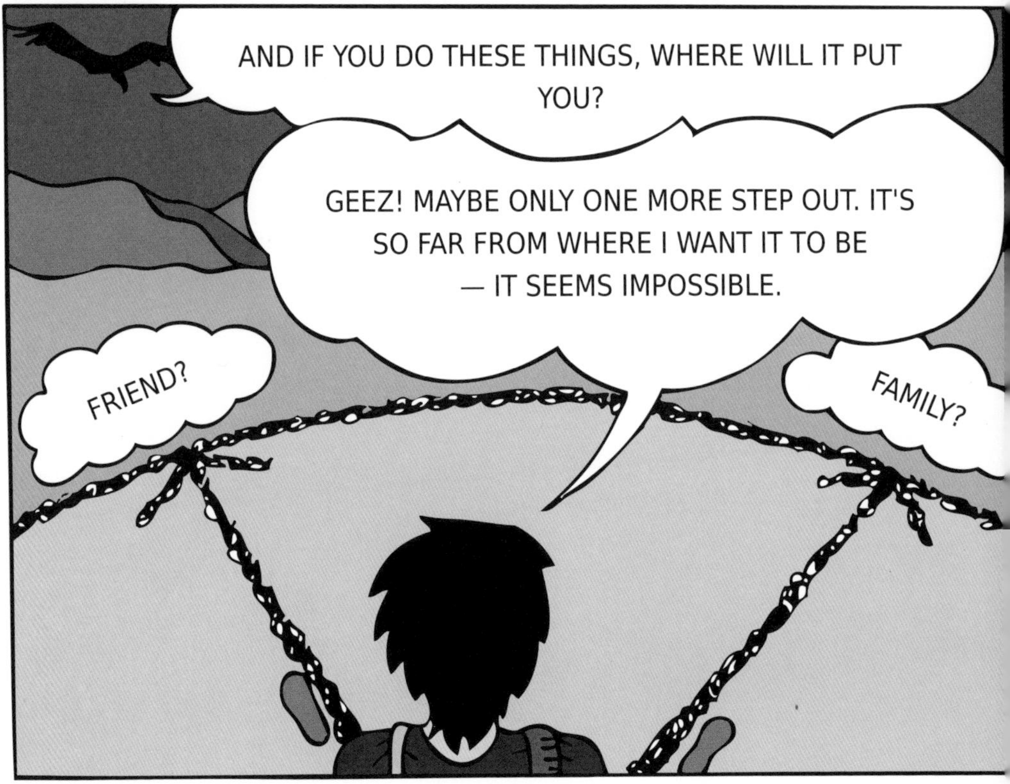
AND IF YOU DO THESE THINGS, WHERE WILL IT PUT YOU?
GEEZ! MAYBE ONLY ONE MORE STEP OUT. IT'S SO FAR FROM WHERE I WANT IT TO BE — IT SEEMS IMPOSSIBLE.
FRIEND?
FAMILY?

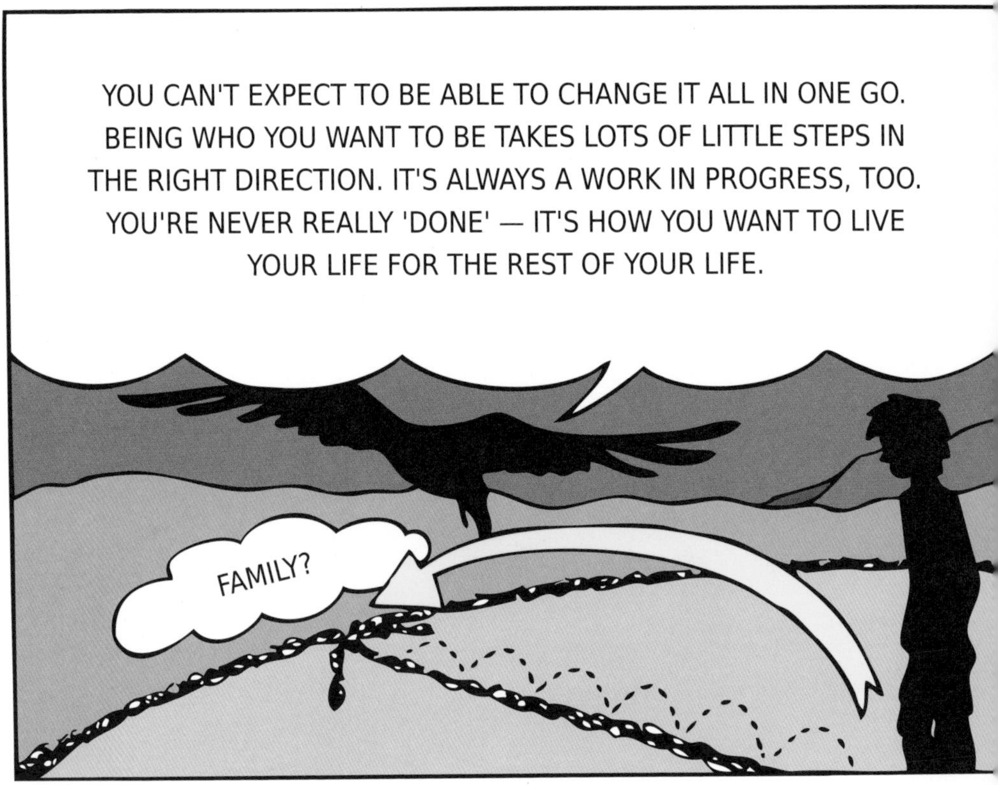
YOU CAN'T EXPECT TO BE ABLE TO CHANGE IT ALL IN ONE GO. BEING WHO YOU WANT TO BE TAKES LOTS OF LITTLE STEPS IN THE RIGHT DIRECTION. IT'S ALWAYS A WORK IN PROGRESS, TOO. YOU'RE NEVER REALLY 'DONE' — IT'S HOW YOU WANT TO LIVE YOUR LIFE FOR THE REST OF YOUR LIFE.
FAMILY?

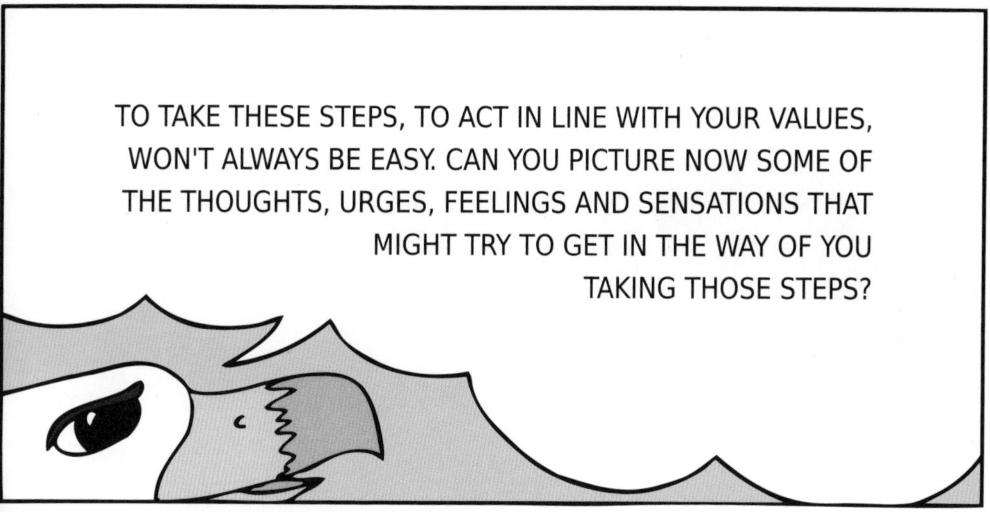
TO TAKE THESE STEPS, TO ACT IN LINE WITH YOUR VALUES, WON'T ALWAYS BE EASY. CAN YOU PICTURE NOW SOME OF THE THOUGHTS, URGES, FEELINGS AND SENSATIONS THAT MIGHT TRY TO GET IN THE WAY OF YOU TAKING THOSE STEPS?

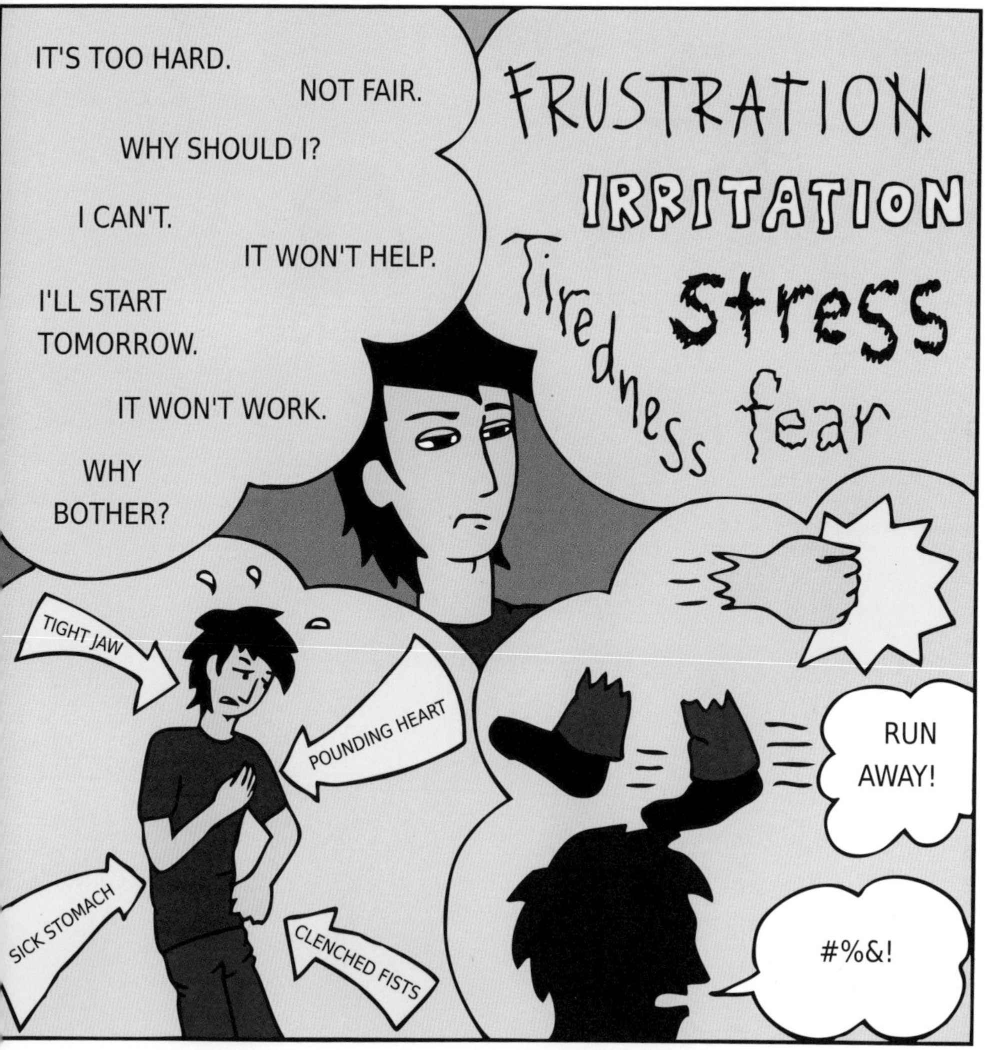
IT'S TOO HARD.
NOT FAIR.
WHY SHOULD I?
I CAN'T.
IT WON'T HELP.
I'LL START TOMORROW.
IT WON'T WORK.
WHY BOTHER?
FRUSTRATION
IRRITATION
Tiredness
Stress
fear
TIGHT JAW
POUNDING HEART
SICK STOMACH
CLENCHED FISTS
RUN AWAY!
#%&!

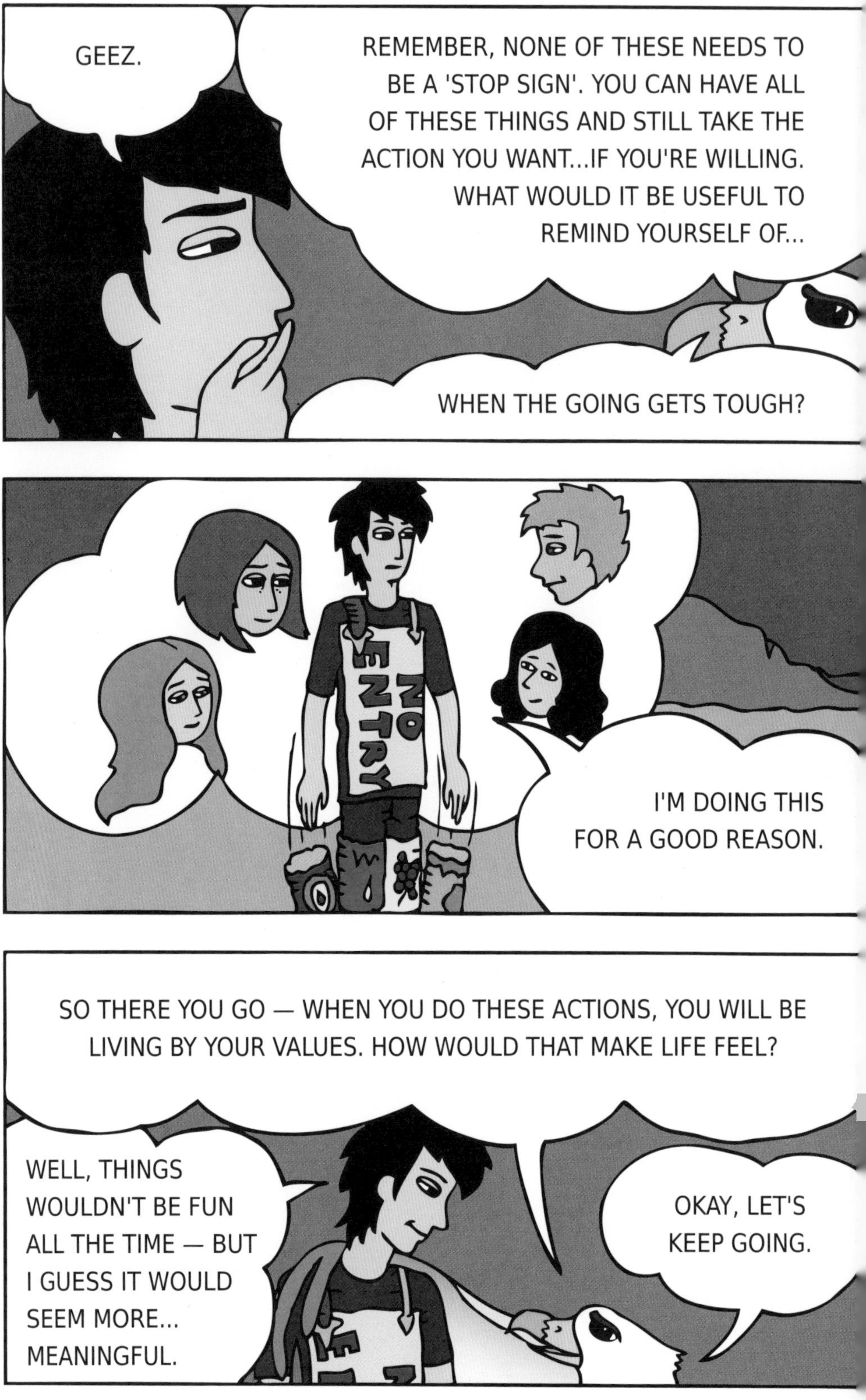
GEEZ.
REMEMBER, NONE OF THESE NEEDS TO BE A 'STOP SIGN'. YOU CAN HAVE ALL OF THESE THINGS AND STILL TAKE THE ACTION YOU WANT...IF YOU'RE WILLING. WHAT WOULD IT BE USEFUL TO REMIND YOURSELF OF...
WHEN THE GOING GETS TOUGH?
NO ENTRY
I'M DOING THIS FOR A GOOD REASON.
SO THERE YOU GO — WHEN YOU DO THESE ACTIONS, YOU WILL BE LIVING BY YOUR VALUES. HOW WOULD THAT MAKE LIFE FEEL?
WELL, THINGS WOULDN'T BE FUN ALL THE TIME — BUT I GUESS IT WOULD SEEM MORE... MEANINGFUL.
OKAY, LET'S KEEP GOING.

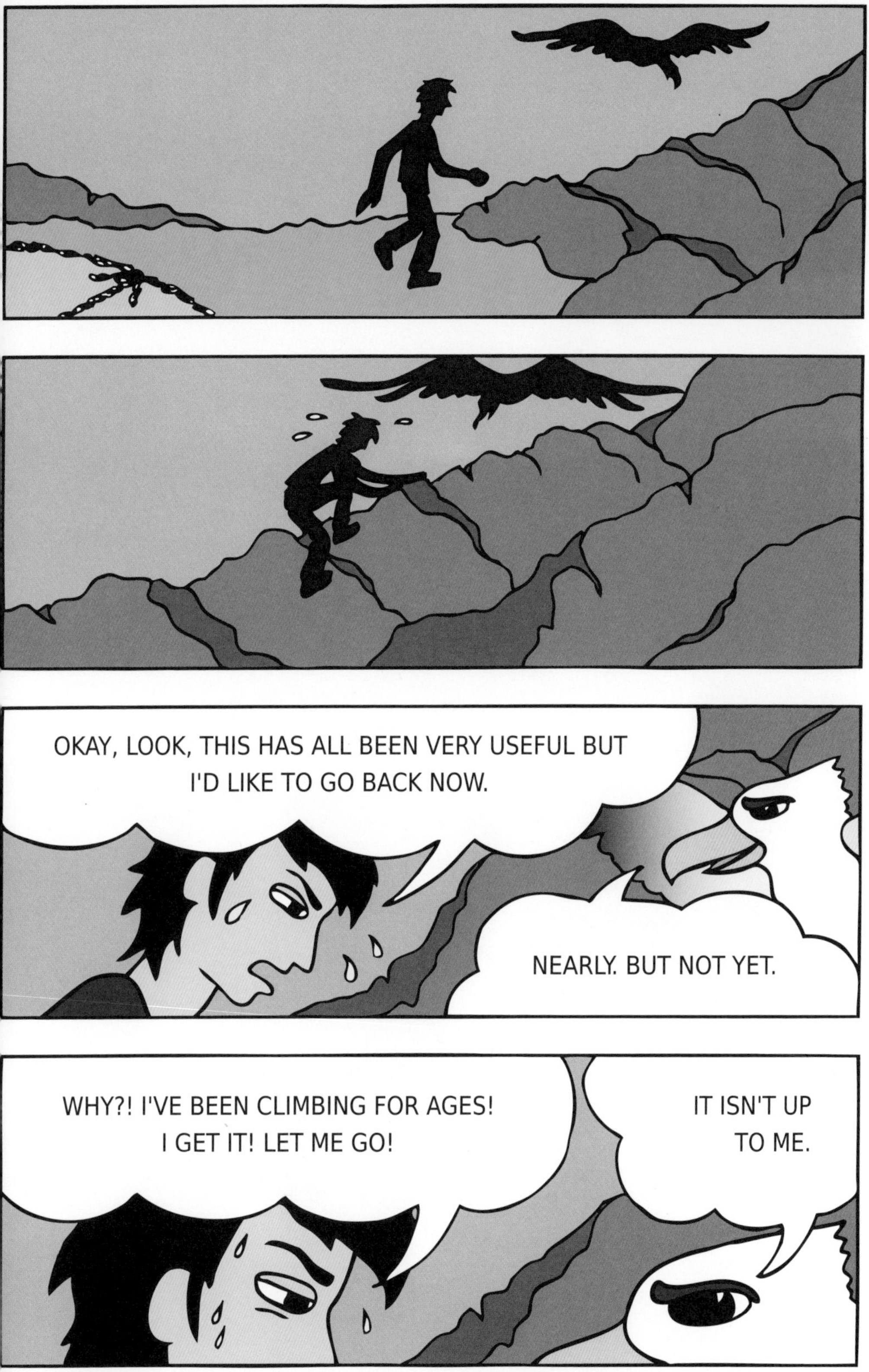
OKAY, LOOK, THIS HAS ALL BEEN VERY USEFUL BUT I'D LIKE TO GO BACK NOW.
NEARLY. BUT NOT YET.
WHY?! I'VE BEEN CLIMBING FOR AGES! I GET IT! LET ME GO!
IT ISN'T UP TO ME.

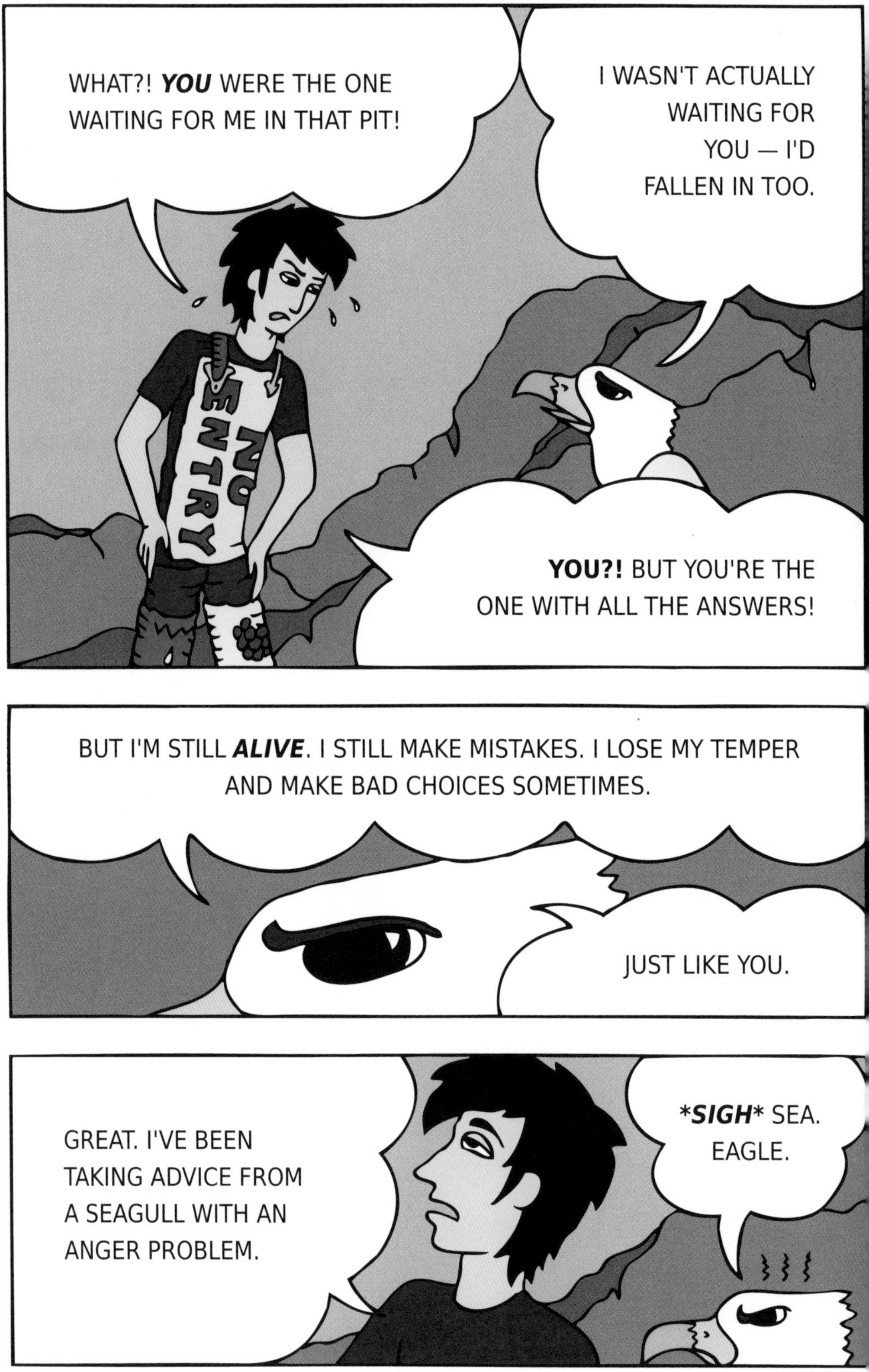
WHAT?! ***YOU*** WERE THE ONE WAITING FOR ME IN THAT PIT!
I WASN'T ACTUALLY WAITING FOR YOU — I'D FALLEN IN TOO.
NO ENTRY
YOU?! BUT YOU'RE THE ONE WITH ALL THE ANSWERS!
BUT I'M STILL ***ALIVE***. I STILL MAKE MISTAKES. I LOSE MY TEMPER AND MAKE BAD CHOICES SOMETIMES.
JUST LIKE YOU.
GREAT. I'VE BEEN TAKING ADVICE FROM A SEAGULL WITH AN ANGER PROBLEM.
****SIGH**** SEA. EAGLE.

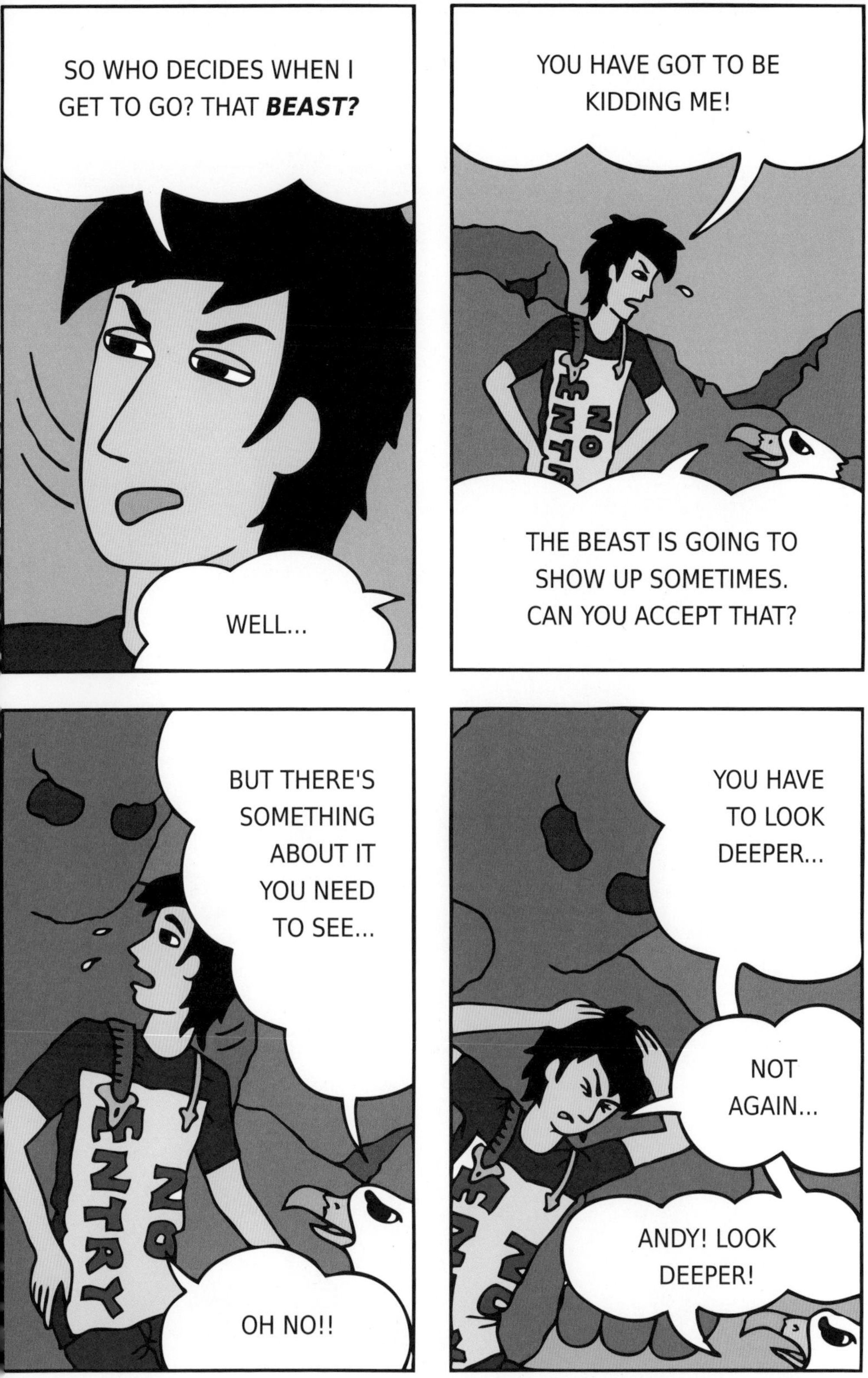
SO WHO DECIDES WHEN I GET TO GO? THAT ***BEAST?***
WELL...
YOU HAVE GOT TO BE KIDDING ME!
NO ENTRY
THE BEAST IS GOING TO SHOW UP SOMETIMES. CAN YOU ACCEPT THAT?
BUT THERE'S SOMETHING ABOUT IT YOU NEED TO SEE...
NO ENTRY
OH NO!!
YOU HAVE TO LOOK DEEPER...
NOT AGAIN...
ANDY! LOOK DEEPER!

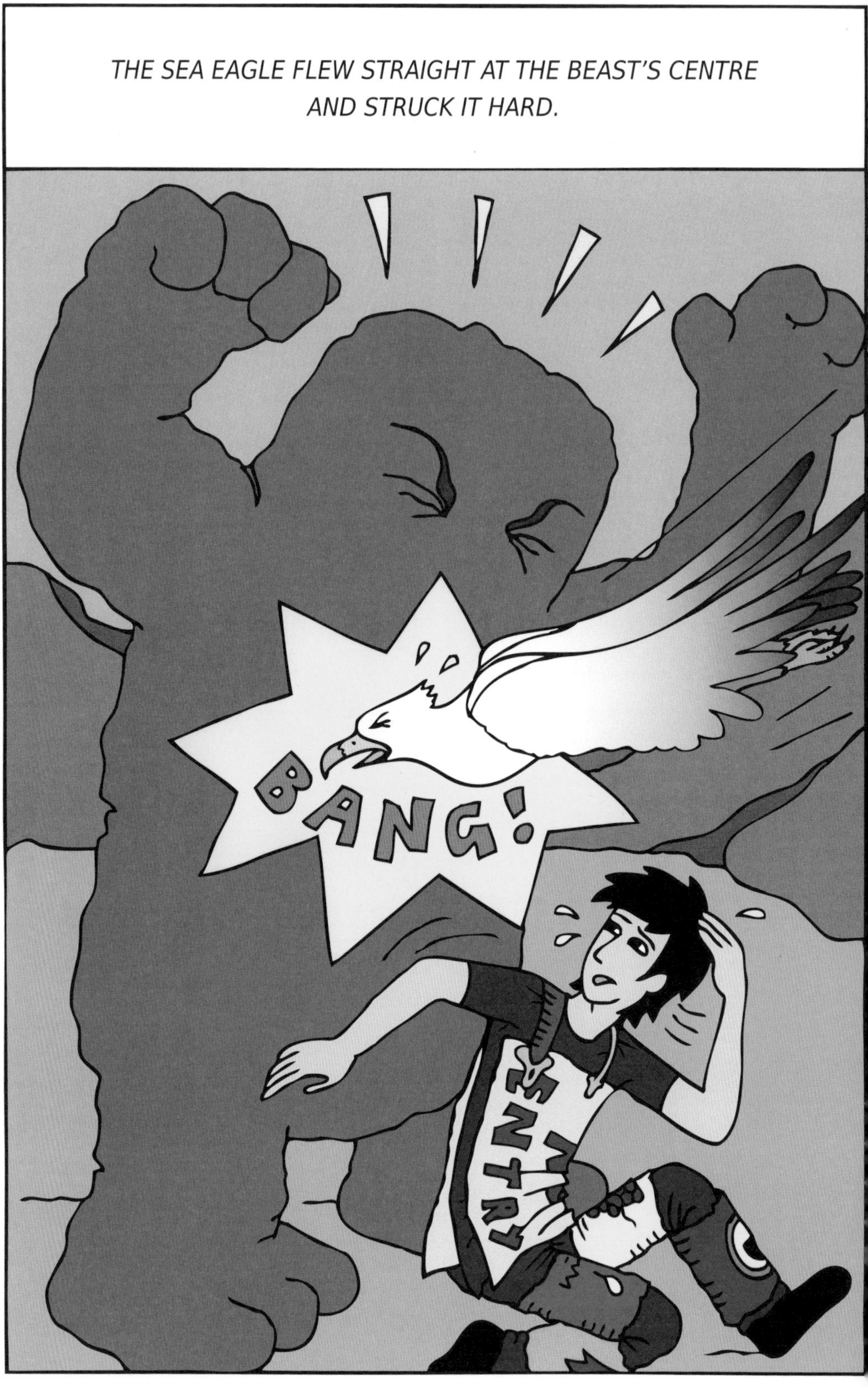
THE SEA EAGLE FLEW STRAIGHT AT THE BEAST'S CENTRE AND STRUCK IT HARD.
BANG!

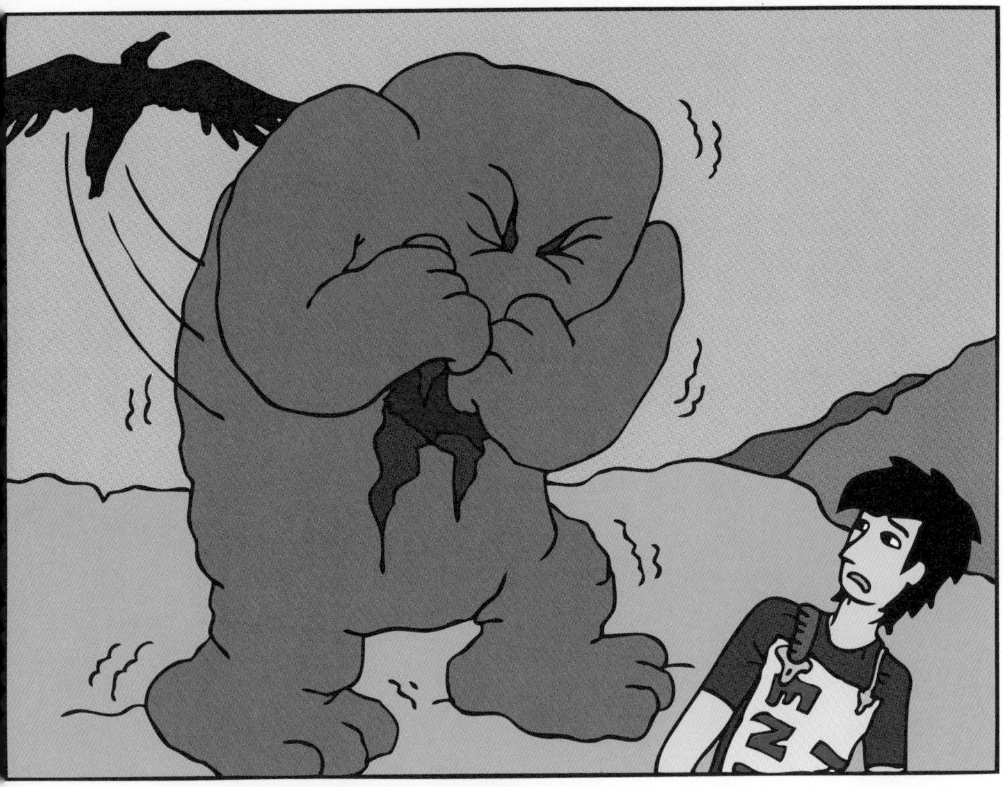

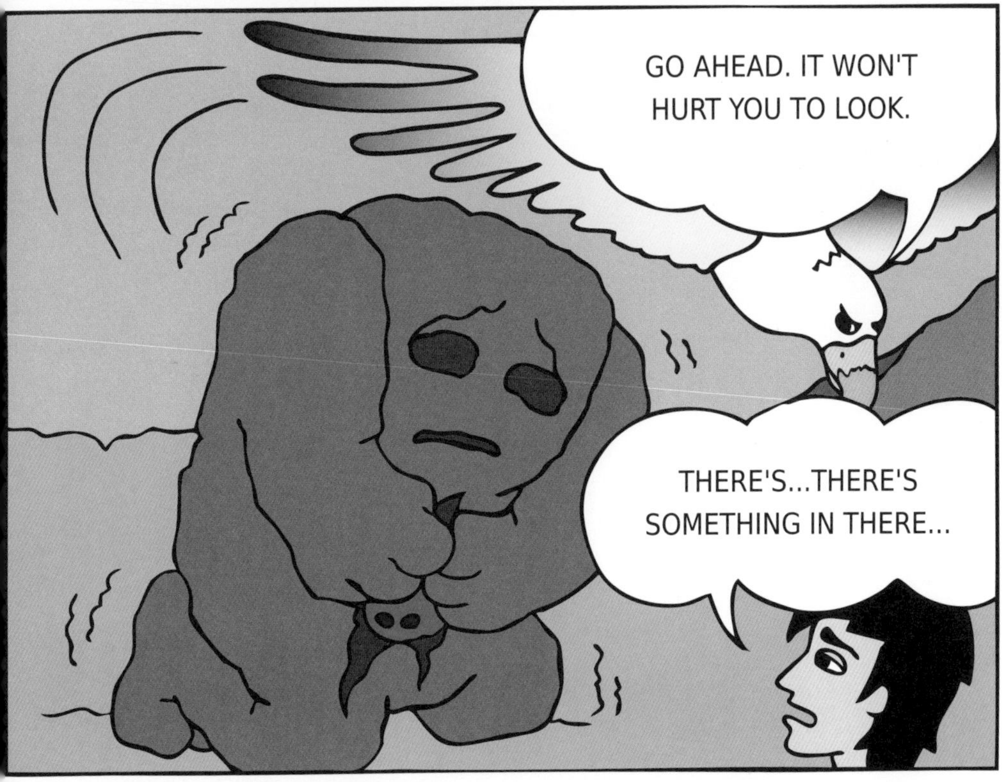
GO AHEAD. IT WON'T HURT YOU TO LOOK.
THERE'S...THERE'S SOMETHING IN THERE...

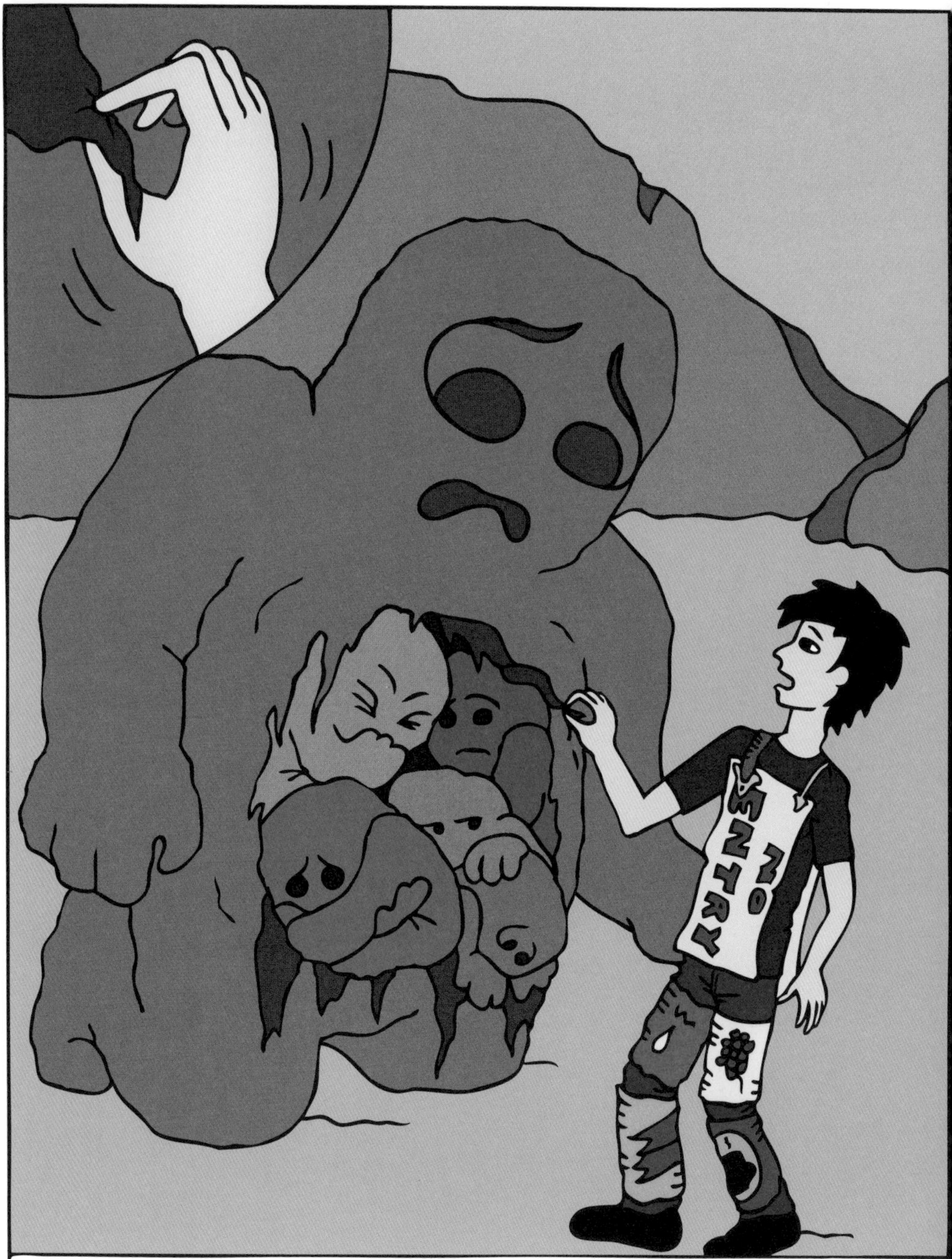
NO ENTRY

BENEATH THE BEAST'S SKIN, TIGHTLY PACKED, LAY A HEAVY MASS OF LONG-HIDDEN EMOTIONS — GRIEF...FEAR... LONELINESS...SADNESS...DESPAIR.

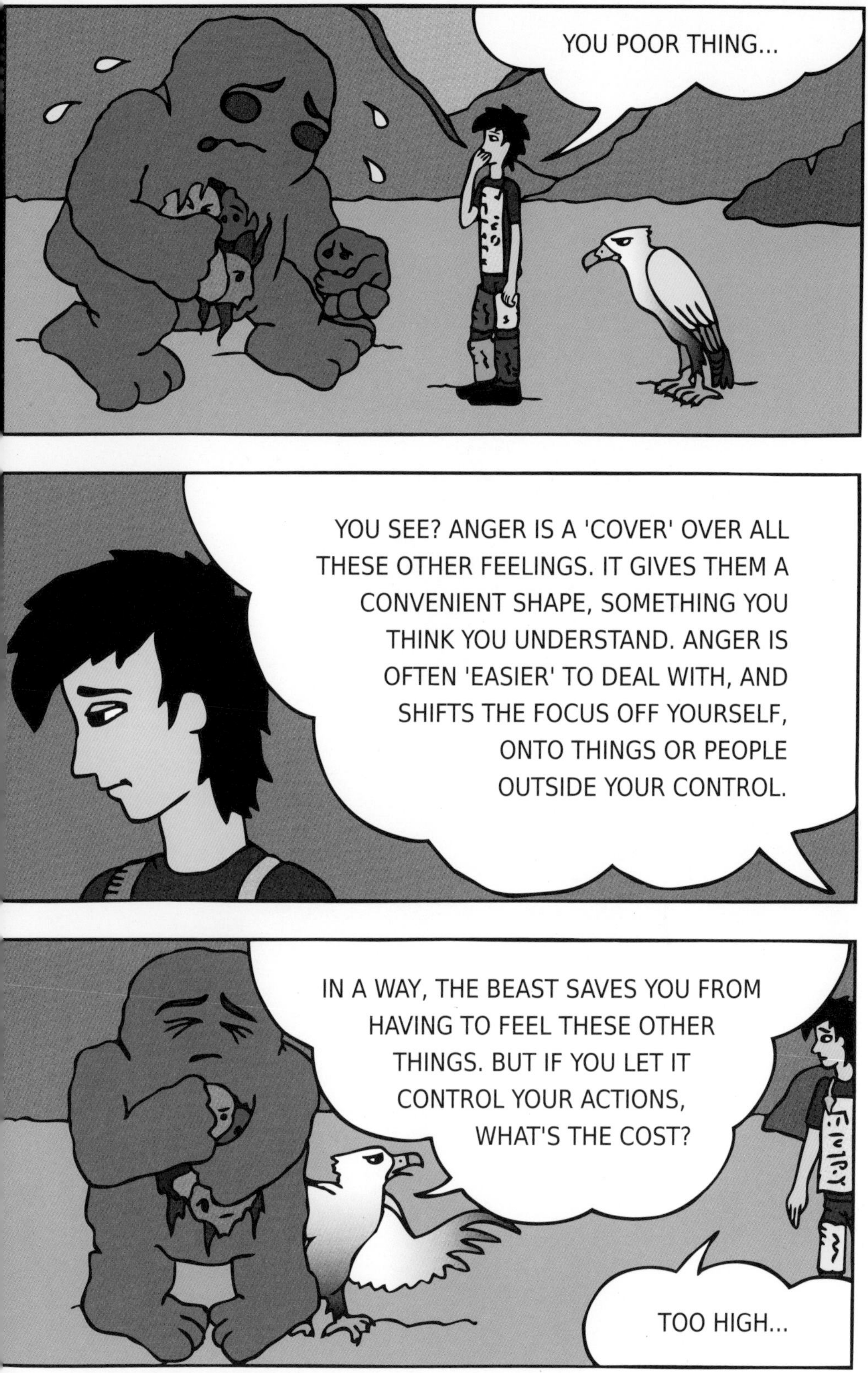
YOU POOR THING...
YOU SEE? ANGER IS A 'COVER' OVER ALL THESE OTHER FEELINGS. IT GIVES THEM A CONVENIENT SHAPE, SOMETHING YOU THINK YOU UNDERSTAND. ANGER IS OFTEN 'EASIER' TO DEAL WITH, AND SHIFTS THE FOCUS OFF YOURSELF, ONTO THINGS OR PEOPLE OUTSIDE YOUR CONTROL.
IN A WAY, THE BEAST SAVES YOU FROM HAVING TO FEEL THESE OTHER THINGS. BUT IF YOU LET IT CONTROL YOUR ACTIONS, WHAT'S THE COST?
TOO HIGH...

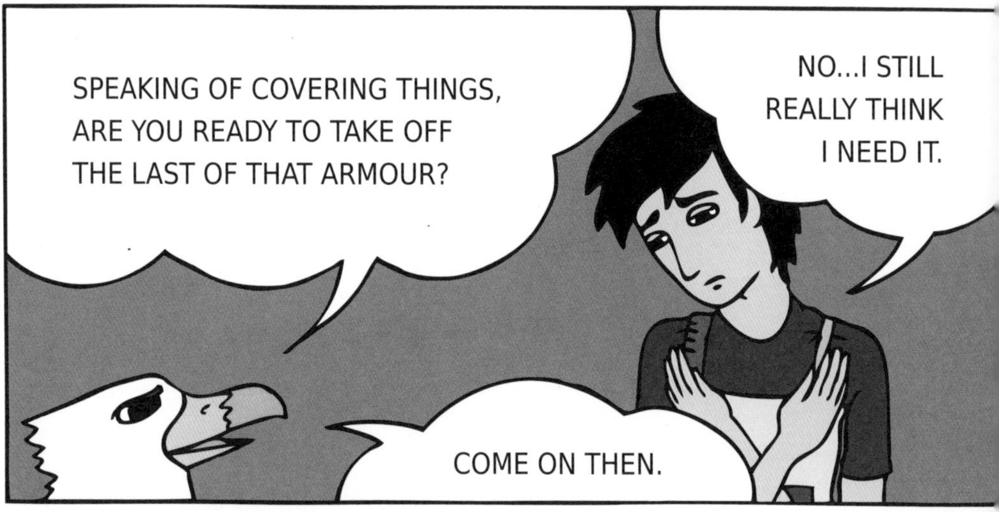
SPEAKING OF COVERING THINGS, ARE YOU READY TO TAKE OFF THE LAST OF THAT ARMOUR?
NO...I STILL REALLY THINK I NEED IT.
COME ON THEN.

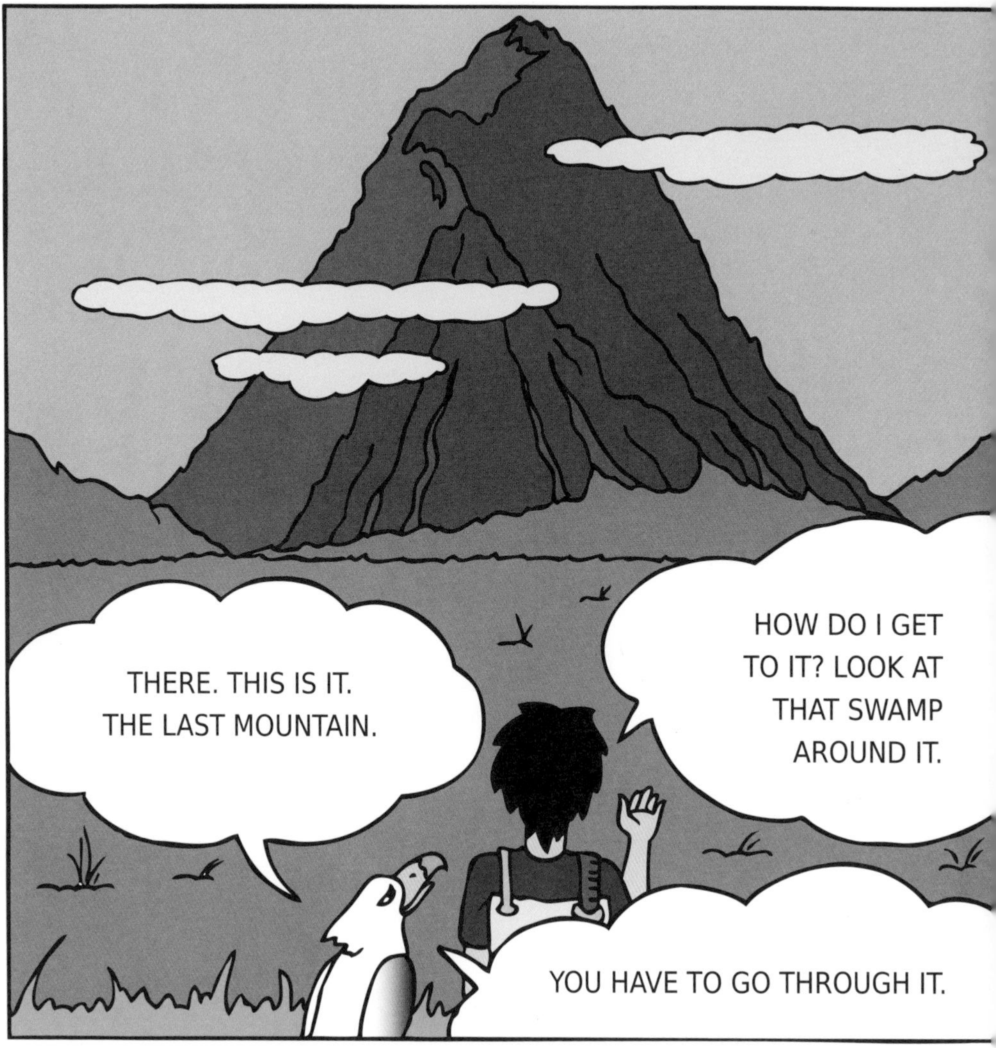
THERE. THIS IS IT. THE LAST MOUNTAIN.
HOW DO I GET TO IT? LOOK AT THAT SWAMP AROUND IT.
YOU HAVE TO GO THROUGH IT.

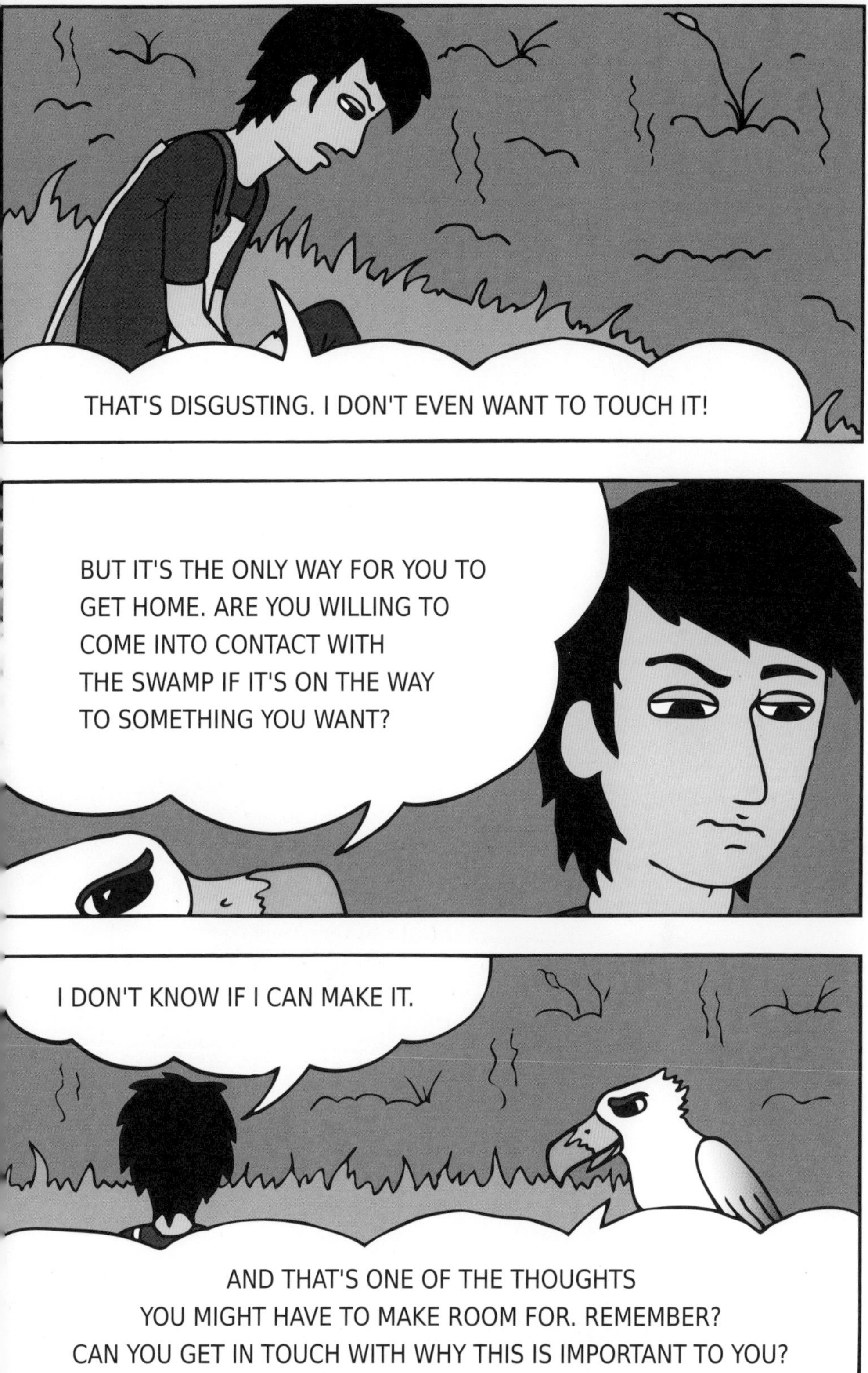
THAT'S DISGUSTING. I DON'T EVEN WANT TO TOUCH IT!
BUT IT'S THE ONLY WAY FOR YOU TO GET HOME. ARE YOU WILLING TO COME INTO CONTACT WITH THE SWAMP IF IT'S ON THE WAY TO SOMETHING YOU WANT?
I DON'T KNOW IF I CAN MAKE IT.
AND THAT'S ONE OF THE THOUGHTS YOU MIGHT HAVE TO MAKE ROOM FOR. REMEMBER? CAN YOU GET IN TOUCH WITH WHY THIS IS IMPORTANT TO YOU?

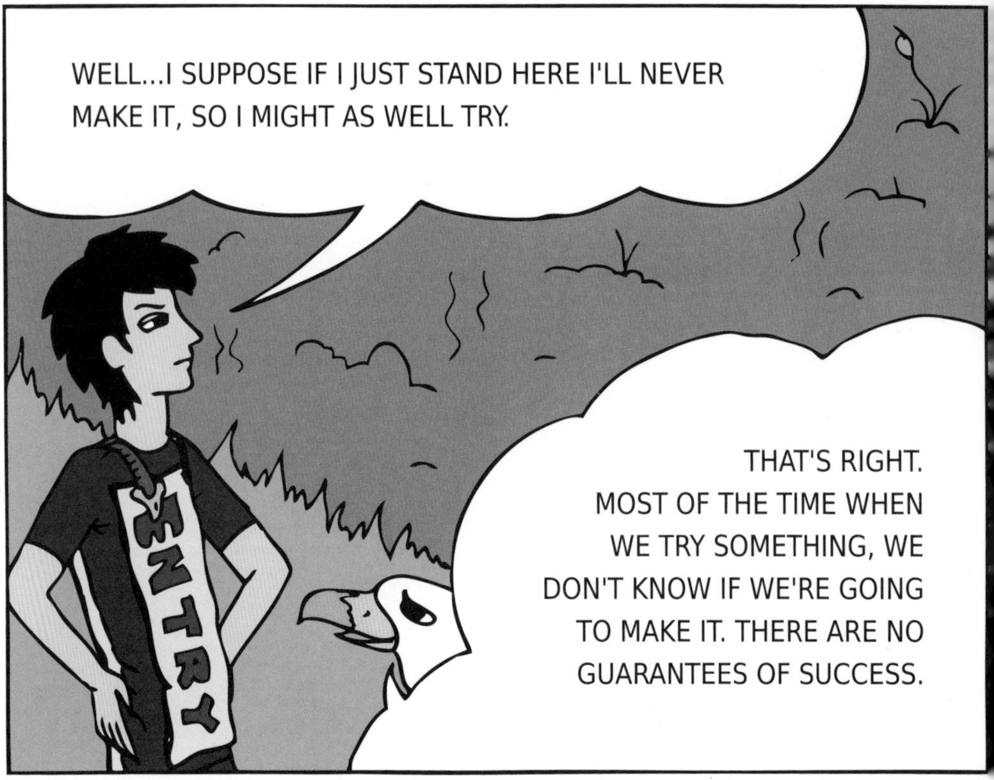
WELL...I SUPPOSE IF I JUST STAND HERE I'LL NEVER MAKE IT, SO I MIGHT AS WELL TRY.
THAT'S RIGHT. MOST OF THE TIME WHEN WE TRY SOMETHING, WE DON'T KNOW IF WE'RE GOING TO MAKE IT. THERE ARE NO GUARANTEES OF SUCCESS.

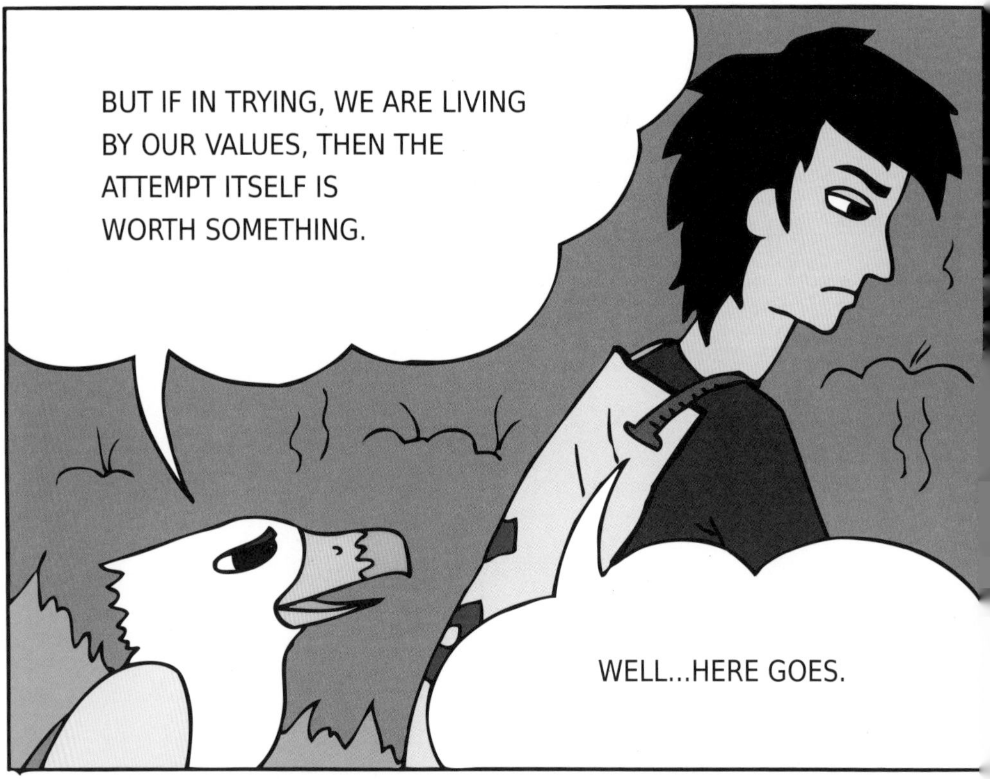
BUT IF IN TRYING, WE ARE LIVING BY OUR VALUES, THEN THE ATTEMPT ITSELF IS WORTH SOMETHING.
WELL...HERE GOES.

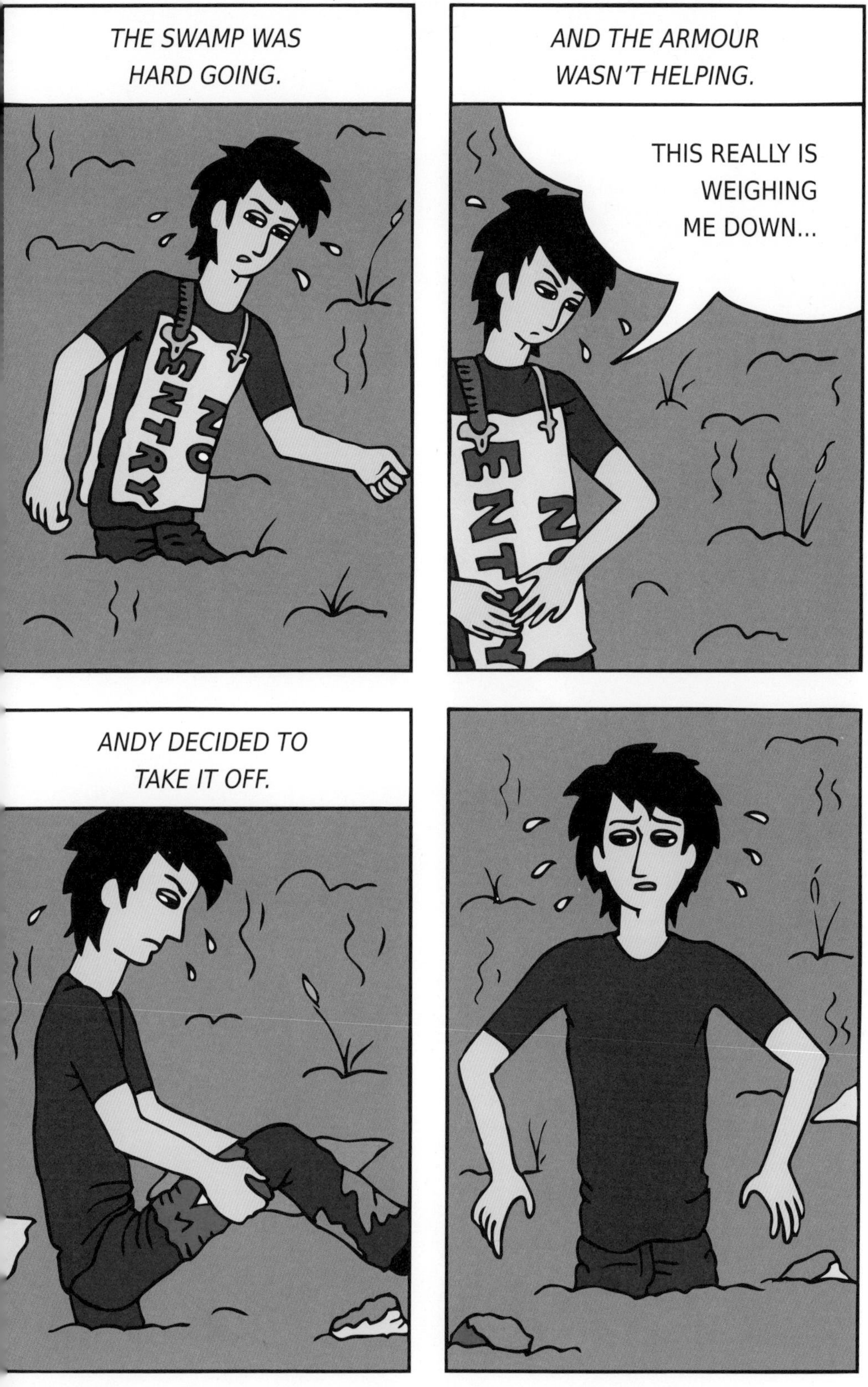
THE SWAMP WAS HARD GOING.
NO ENTRY
AND THE ARMOUR WASN'T HELPING.
THIS REALLY IS WEIGHING ME DOWN...
ANDY DECIDED TO TAKE IT OFF.

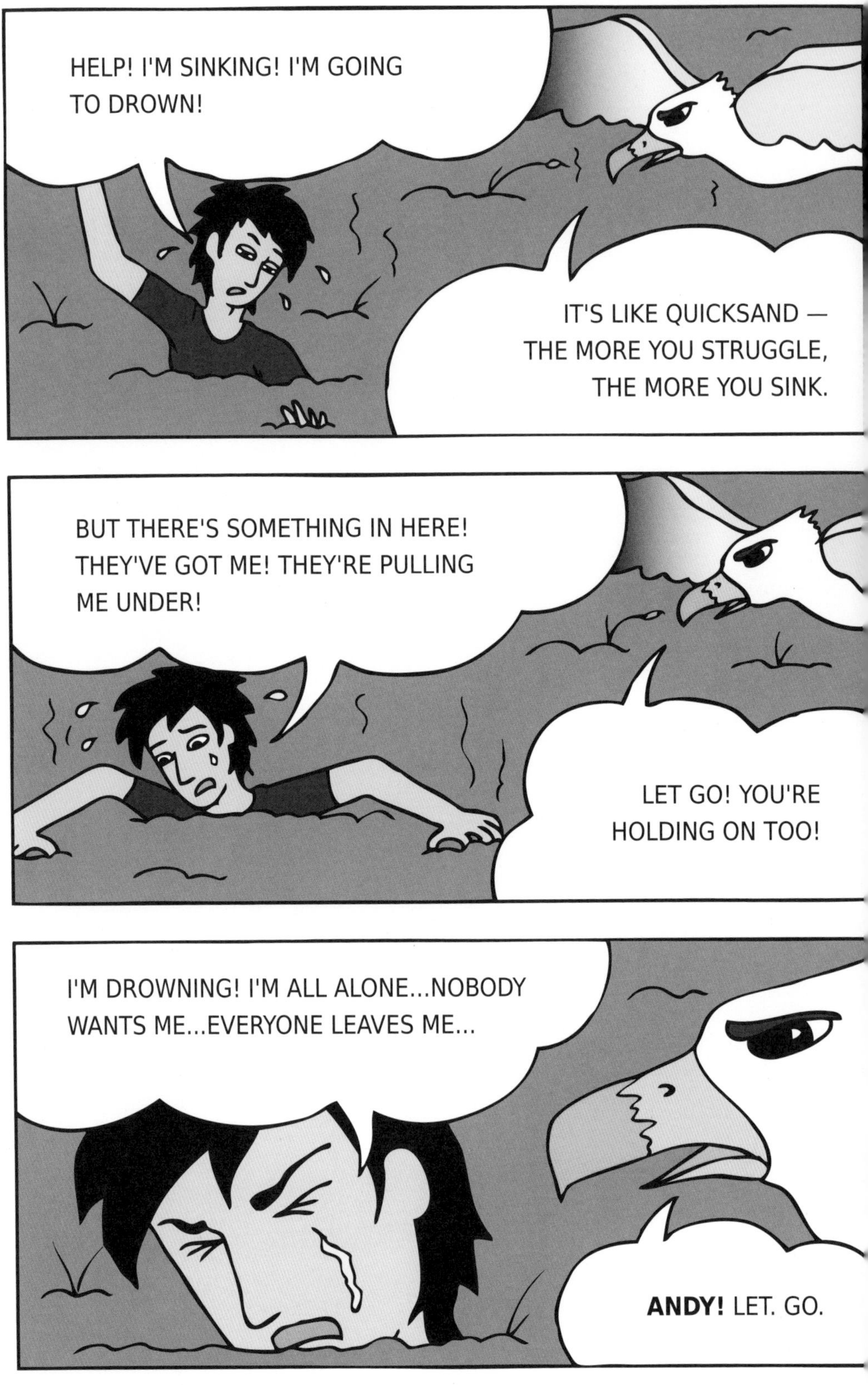
HELP! I'M SINKING! I'M GOING TO DROWN!
IT'S LIKE QUICKSAND — THE MORE YOU STRUGGLE, THE MORE YOU SINK.
BUT THERE'S SOMETHING IN HERE! THEY'VE GOT ME! THEY'RE PULLING ME UNDER!
LET GO! YOU'RE HOLDING ON TOO!
I'M DROWNING! I'M ALL ALONE...NOBODY WANTS ME...EVERYONE LEAVES ME...
ANDY! LET. GO.

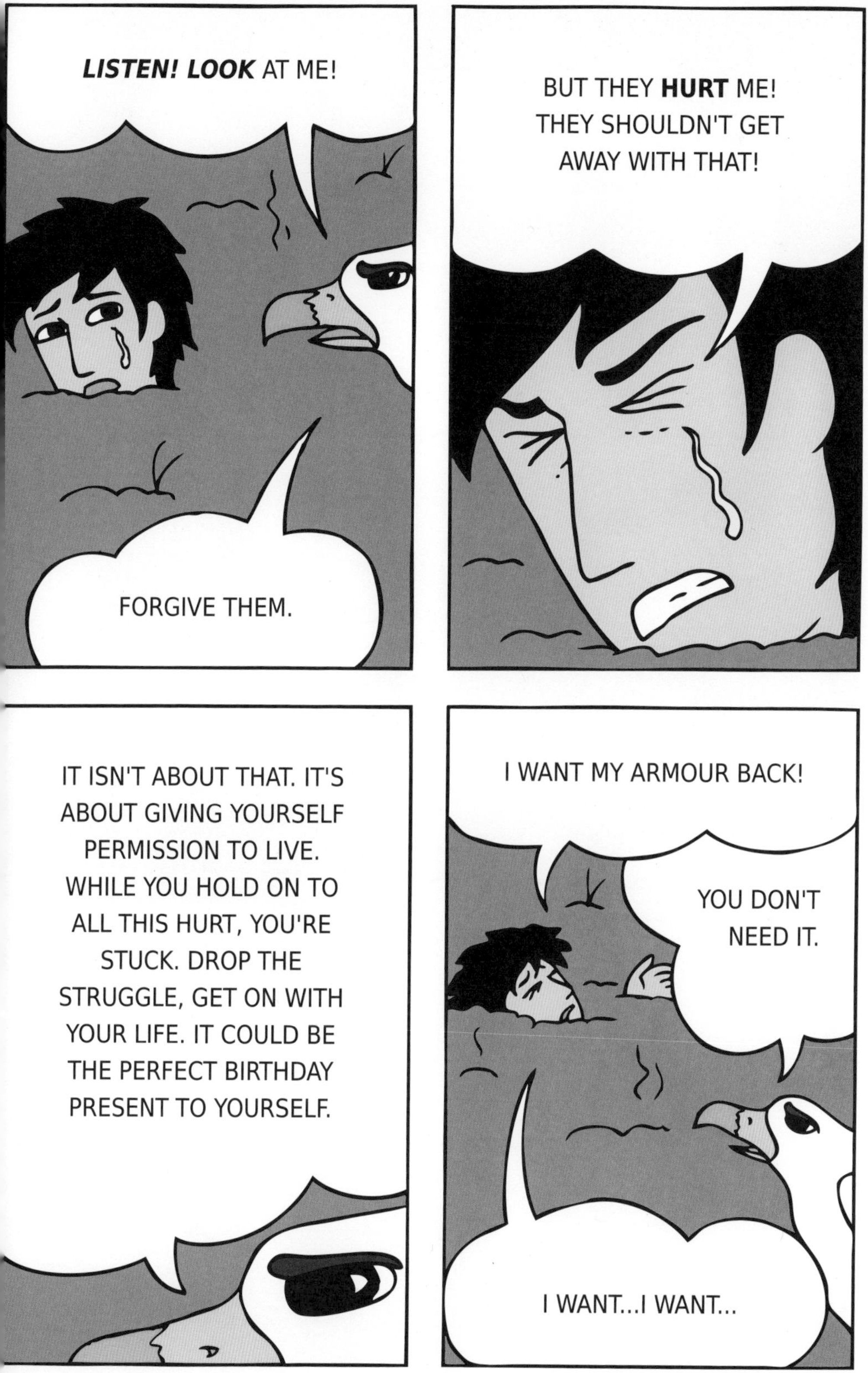
LISTEN! LOOK AT ME!
FORGIVE THEM.
BUT THEY **HURT** ME! THEY SHOULDN'T GET AWAY WITH THAT!
IT ISN'T ABOUT THAT. IT'S ABOUT GIVING YOURSELF PERMISSION TO LIVE. WHILE YOU HOLD ON TO ALL THIS HURT, YOU'RE STUCK. DROP THE STRUGGLE, GET ON WITH YOUR LIFE. IT COULD BE THE PERFECT BIRTHDAY PRESENT TO YOURSELF.
I WANT MY ARMOUR BACK!
YOU DON'T NEED IT.
I WANT...I WANT...

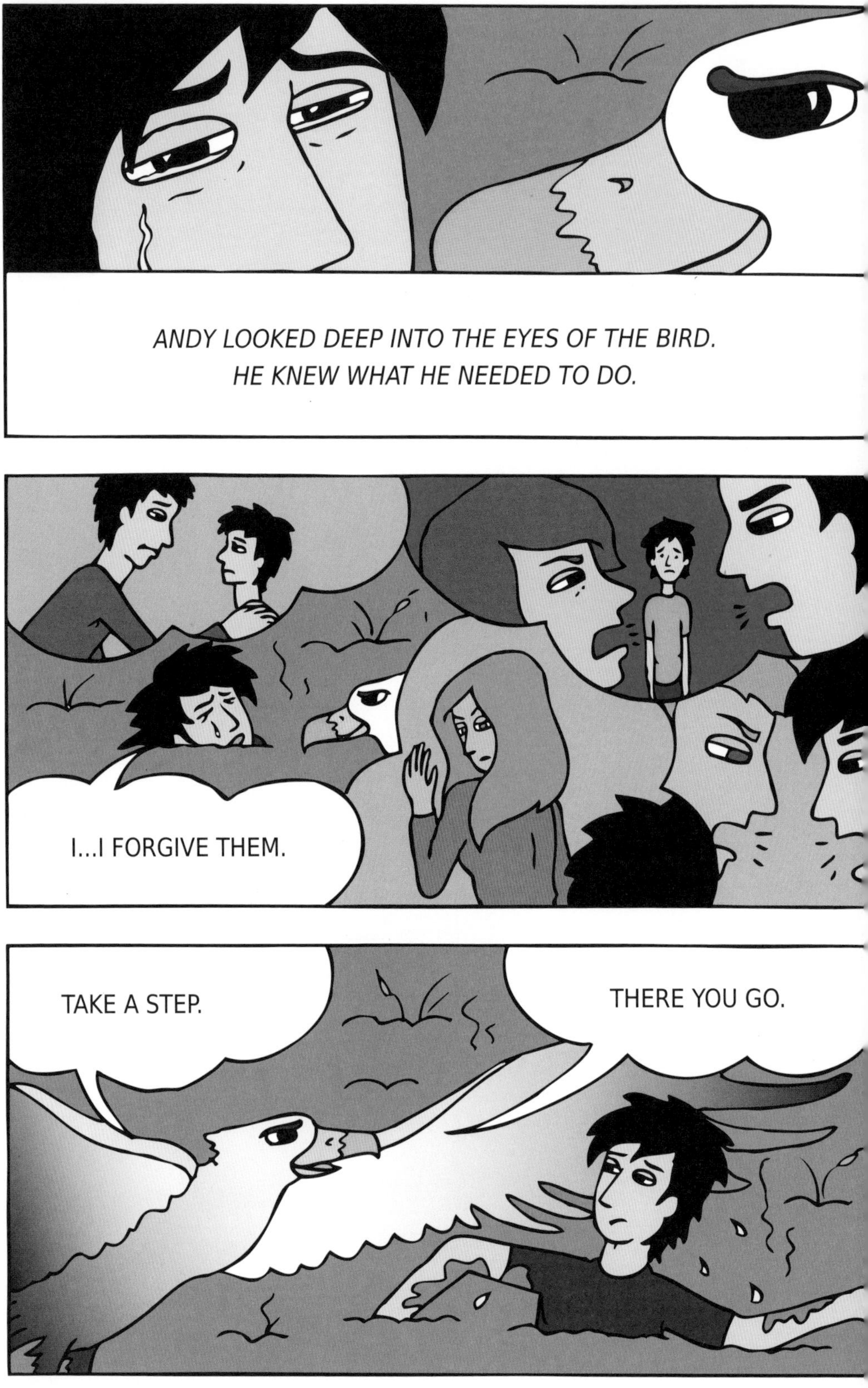
ANDY LOOKED DEEP INTO THE EYES OF THE BIRD.
HE KNEW WHAT HE NEEDED TO DO.
I...I FORGIVE THEM.
TAKE A STEP.
THERE YOU GO.

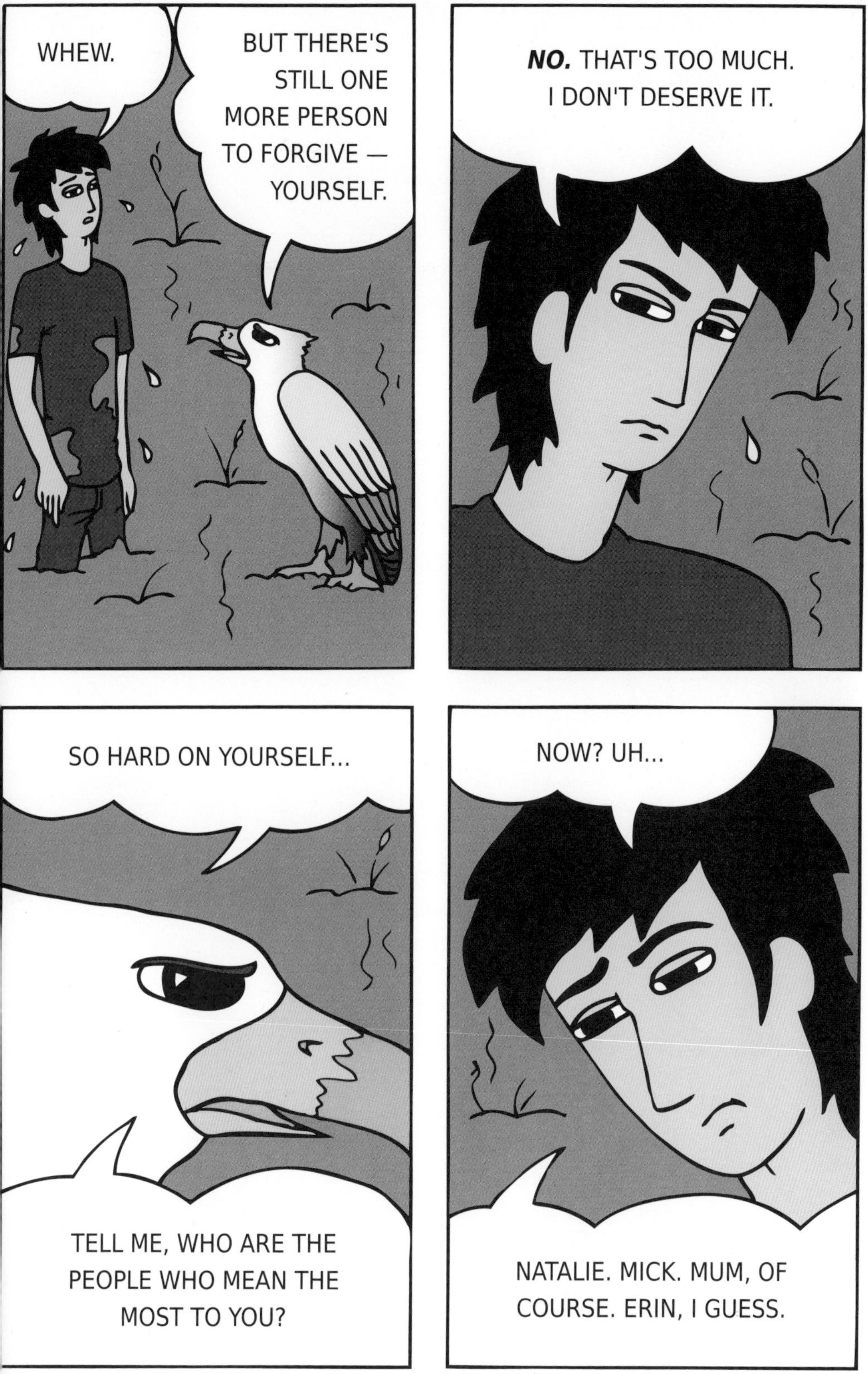
WHEW.
BUT THERE'S STILL ONE MORE PERSON TO FORGIVE — YOURSELF.
NO. THAT'S TOO MUCH. I DON'T DESERVE IT.
SO HARD ON YOURSELF...
TELL ME, WHO ARE THE PEOPLE WHO MEAN THE MOST TO YOU?
NOW? UH...
NATALIE. MICK. MUM, OF COURSE. ERIN, I GUESS.

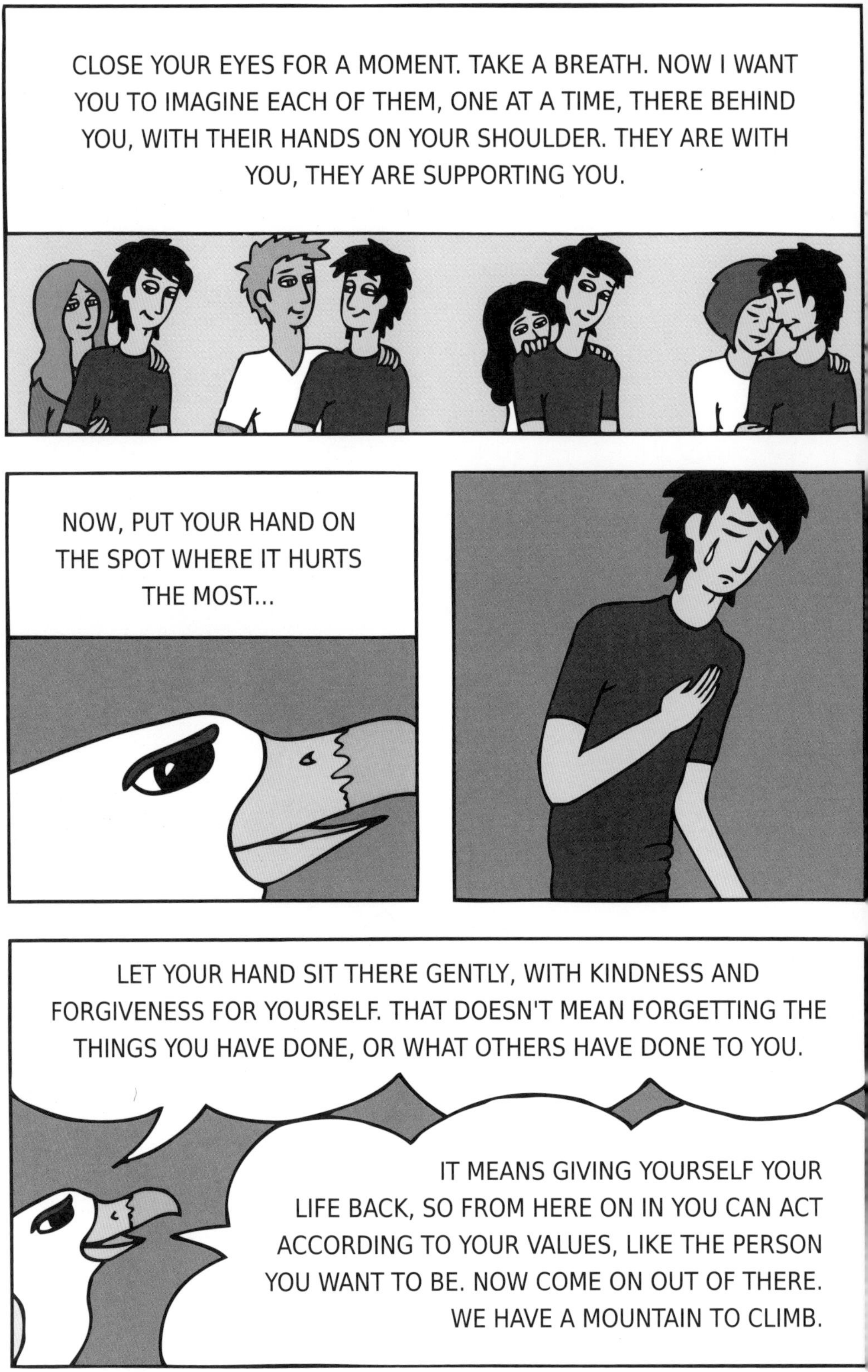
CLOSE YOUR EYES FOR A MOMENT. TAKE A BREATH. NOW I WANT YOU TO IMAGINE EACH OF THEM, ONE AT A TIME, THERE BEHIND YOU, WITH THEIR HANDS ON YOUR SHOULDER. THEY ARE WITH YOU, THEY ARE SUPPORTING YOU.
NOW, PUT YOUR HAND ON THE SPOT WHERE IT HURTS THE MOST...
LET YOUR HAND SIT THERE GENTLY, WITH KINDNESS AND FORGIVENESS FOR YOURSELF. THAT DOESN'T MEAN FORGETTING THE THINGS YOU HAVE DONE, OR WHAT OTHERS HAVE DONE TO YOU.
IT MEANS GIVING YOURSELF YOUR LIFE BACK, SO FROM HERE ON IN YOU CAN ACT ACCORDING TO YOUR VALUES, LIKE THE PERSON YOU WANT TO BE. NOW COME ON OUT OF THERE. WE HAVE A MOUNTAIN TO CLIMB.

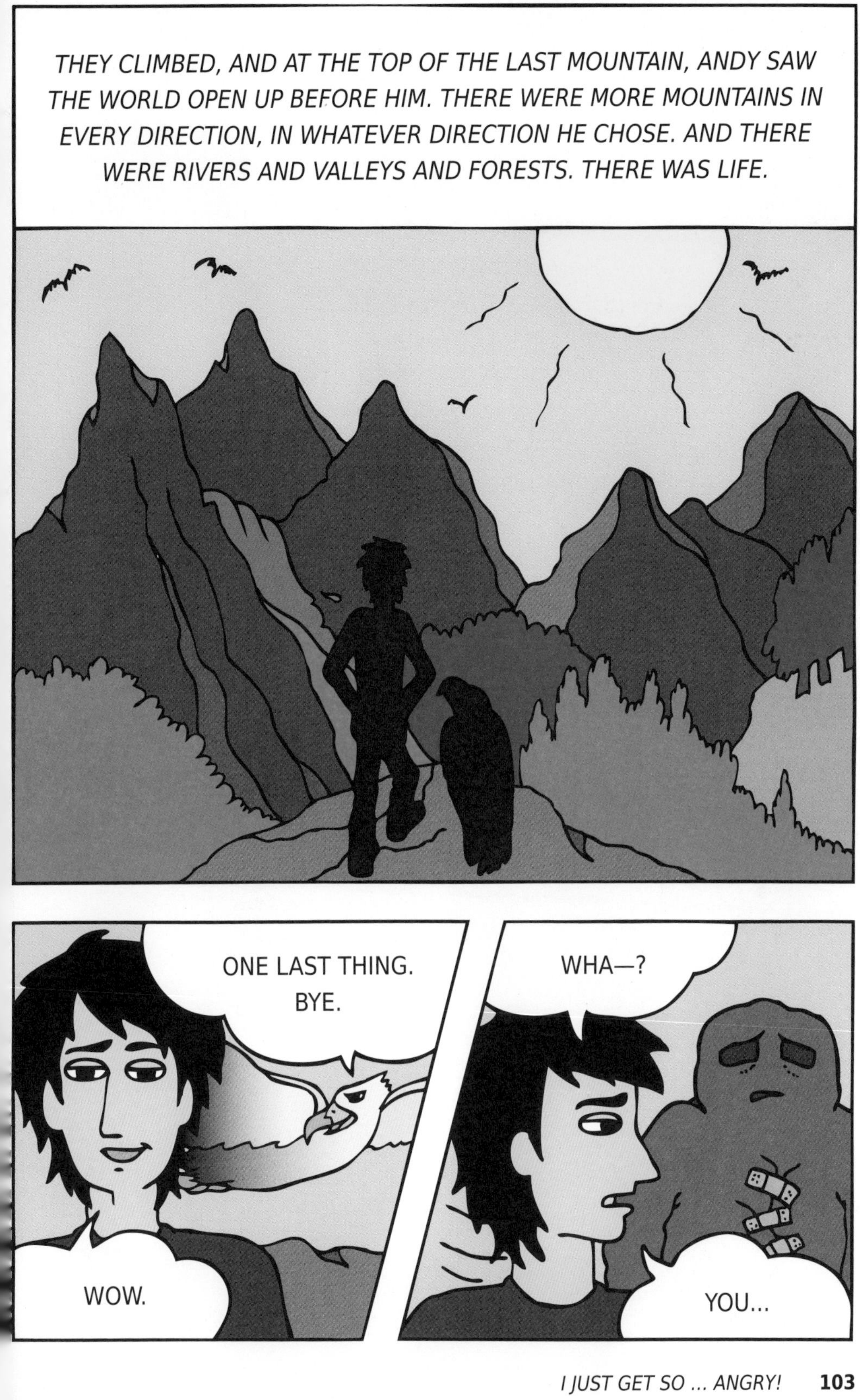
THEY CLIMBED, AND AT THE TOP OF THE LAST MOUNTAIN, ANDY SAW THE WORLD OPEN UP BEFORE HIM. THERE WERE MORE MOUNTAINS IN EVERY DIRECTION, IN WHATEVER DIRECTION HE CHOSE. AND THERE WERE RIVERS AND VALLEYS AND FORESTS. THERE WAS LIFE.
ONE LAST THING. BYE.
WOW.
WHA—?
YOU...

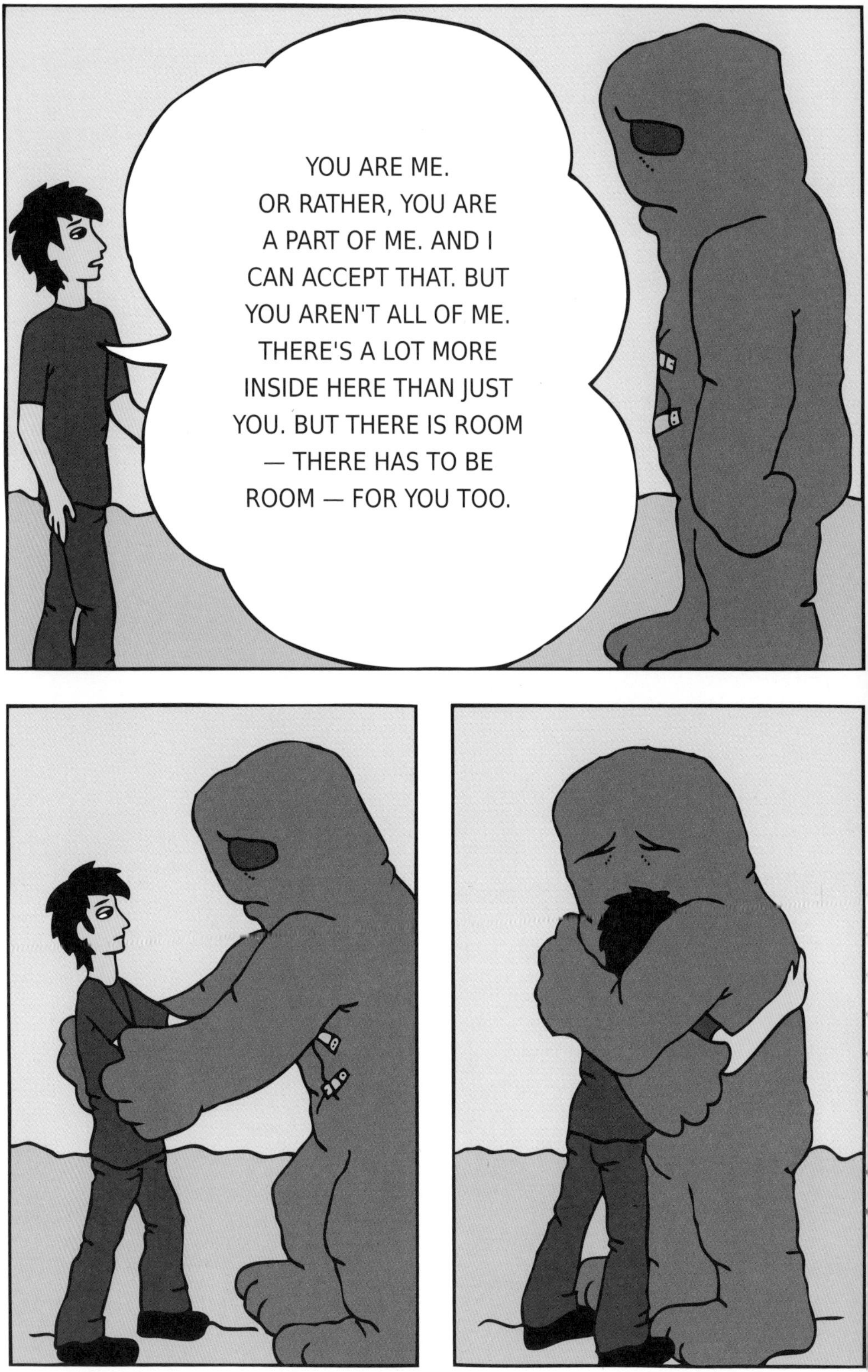
YOU ARE ME.
OR RATHER, YOU ARE
A PART OF ME. AND I
CAN ACCEPT THAT. BUT
YOU AREN'T ALL OF ME.
THERE'S A LOT MORE
INSIDE HERE THAN JUST
YOU. BUT THERE IS ROOM
— THERE HAS TO BE
ROOM — FOR YOU TOO.

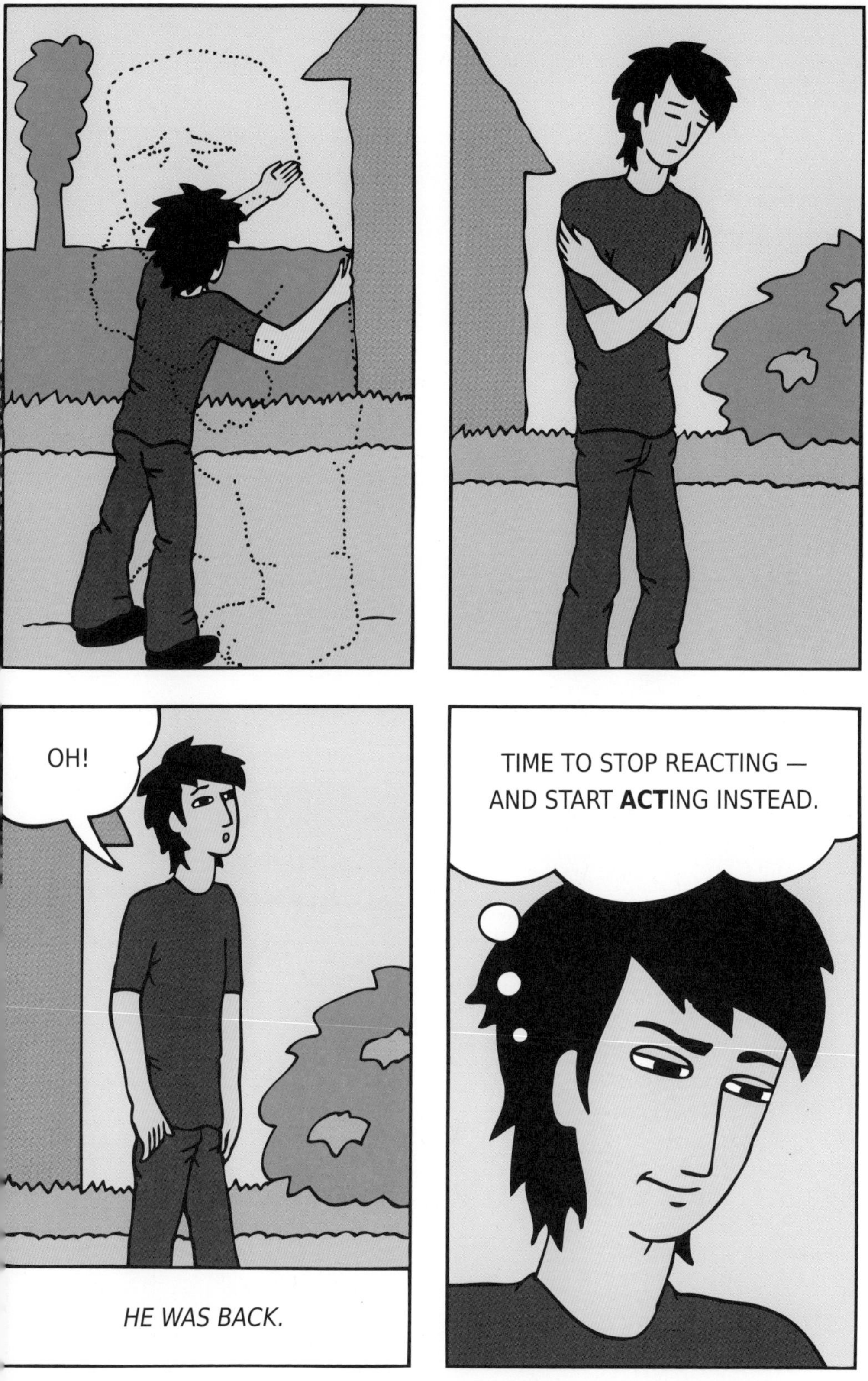
OH!
HE WAS BACK.
TIME TO STOP REACTING —
AND START **ACT**ING INSTEAD.

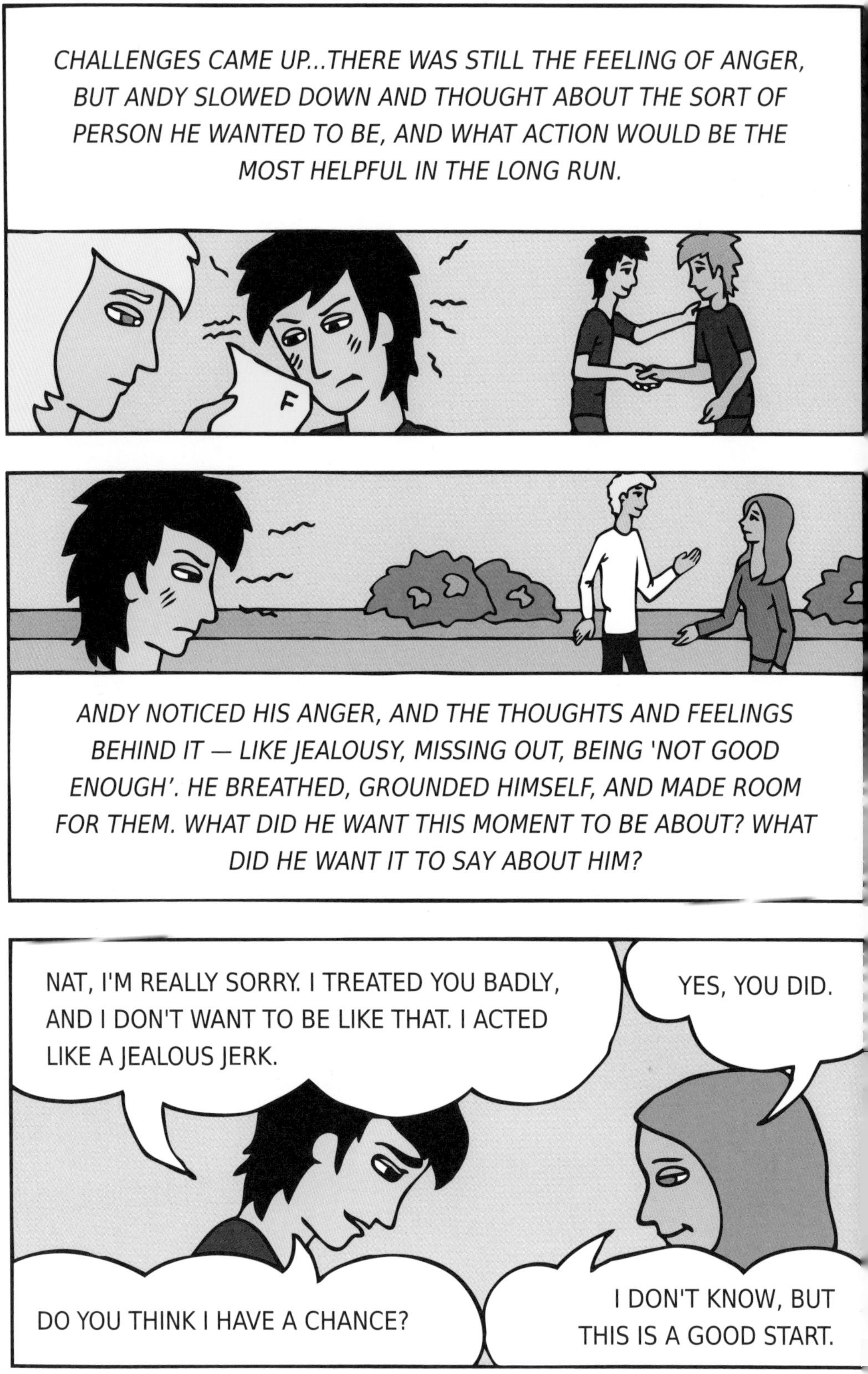
CHALLENGES CAME UP...THERE WAS STILL THE FEELING OF ANGER, BUT ANDY SLOWED DOWN AND THOUGHT ABOUT THE SORT OF PERSON HE WANTED TO BE, AND WHAT ACTION WOULD BE THE MOST HELPFUL IN THE LONG RUN.
F
ANDY NOTICED HIS ANGER, AND THE THOUGHTS AND FEELINGS BEHIND IT — LIKE JEALOUSY, MISSING OUT, BEING 'NOT GOOD ENOUGH'. HE BREATHED, GROUNDED HIMSELF, AND MADE ROOM FOR THEM. WHAT DID HE WANT THIS MOMENT TO BE ABOUT? WHAT DID HE WANT IT TO SAY ABOUT HIM?
NAT, I'M REALLY SORRY. I TREATED YOU BADLY, AND I DON'T WANT TO BE LIKE THAT. I ACTED LIKE A JEALOUS JERK.
YES, YOU DID.
DO YOU THINK I HAVE A CHANCE?
I DON'T KNOW, BUT THIS IS A GOOD START.

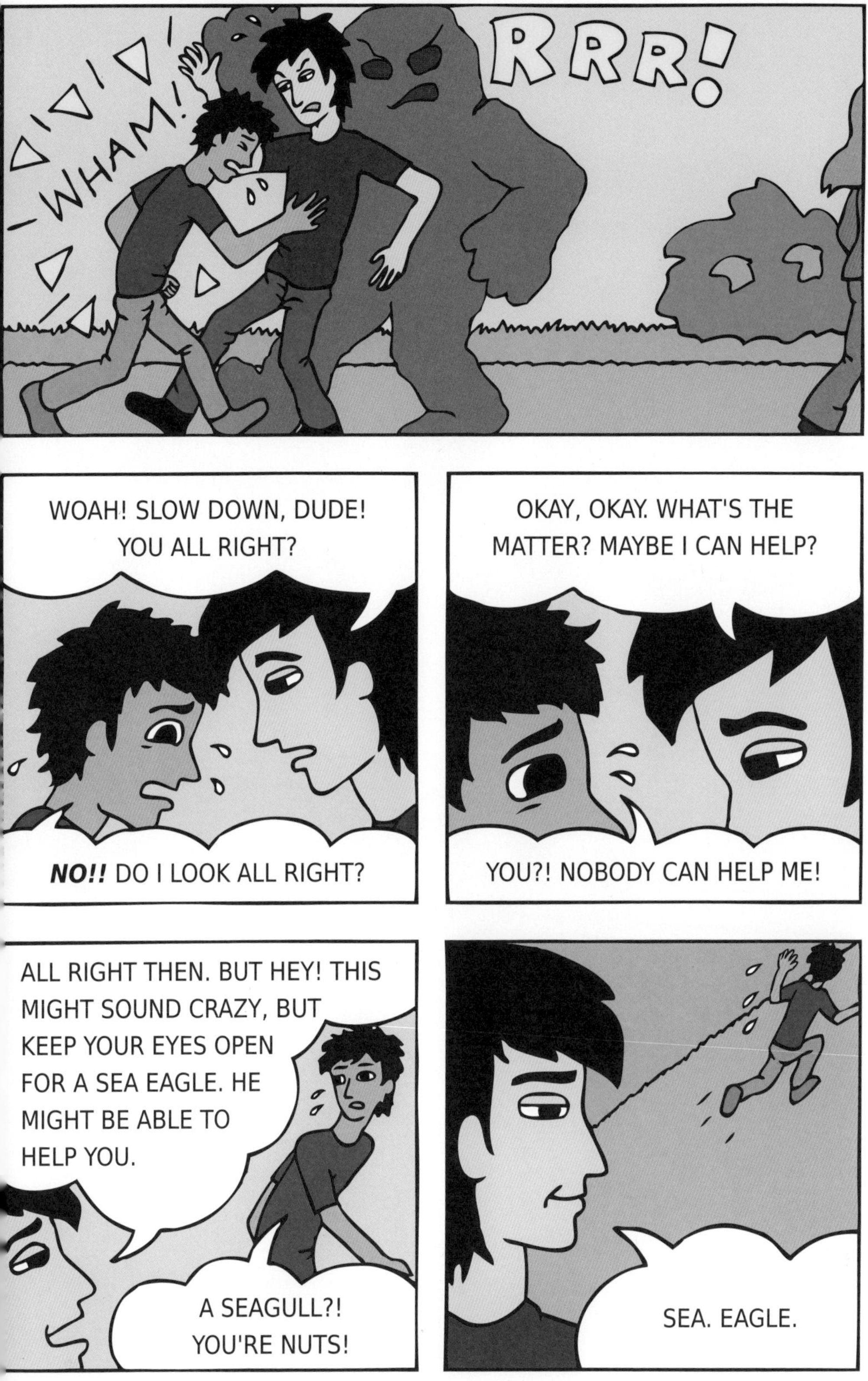
WHAM!
RRR!
WOAH! SLOW DOWN, DUDE! YOU ALL RIGHT?
NO!! DO I LOOK ALL RIGHT?
OKAY, OKAY. WHAT'S THE MATTER? MAYBE I CAN HELP?
YOU?! NOBODY CAN HELP ME!
ALL RIGHT THEN. BUT HEY! THIS MIGHT SOUND CRAZY, BUT KEEP YOUR EYES OPEN FOR A SEA EAGLE. HE MIGHT BE ABLE TO HELP YOU.
A SEAGULL?! YOU'RE NUTS!
SEA. EAGLE.

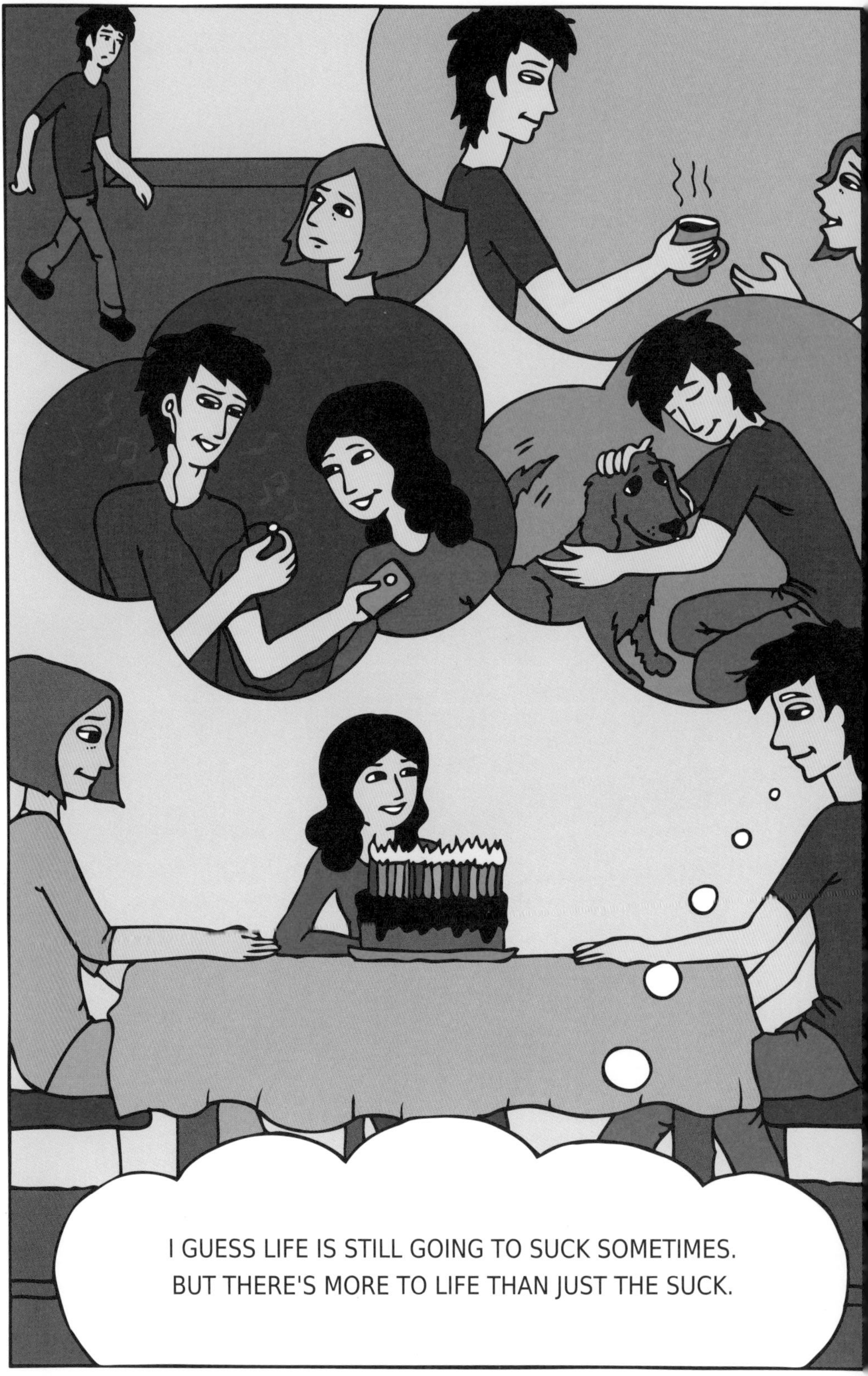
I GUESS LIFE IS STILL GOING TO SUCK SOMETIMES.
BUT THERE'S MORE TO LIFE THAN JUST THE SUCK.

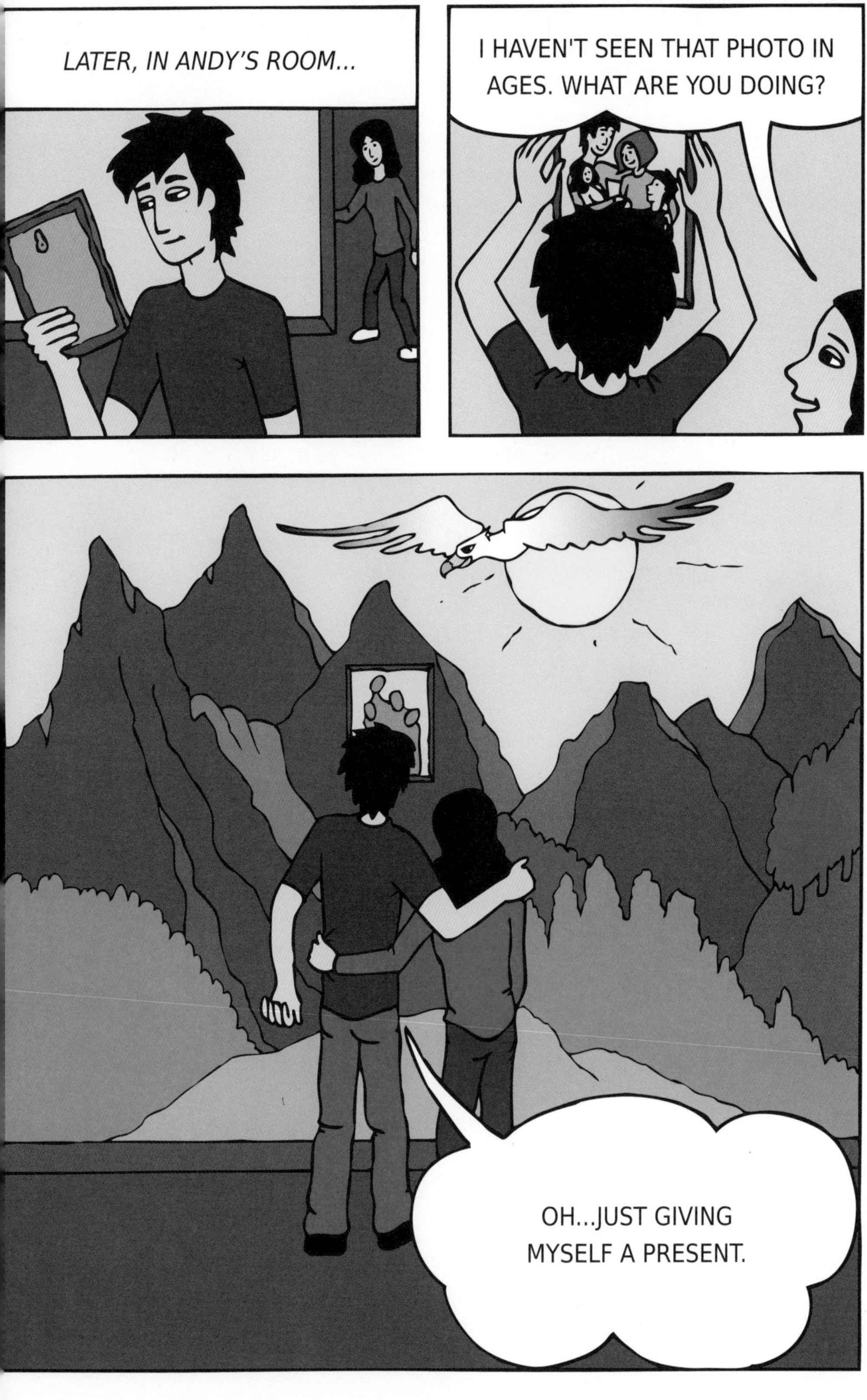
LATER, IN ANDY'S ROOM...
I HAVEN'T SEEN THAT PHOTO IN AGES. WHAT ARE YOU DOING?
OH...JUST GIVING MYSELF A PRESENT.

RESOURCES

To download free resources for use with *I Just Get So ... Angry!* and to find out about our other title, *I Just Want To Be ... Me!* (Exisle Publishing 2010), visit our website www.actonpurpose.com.au.

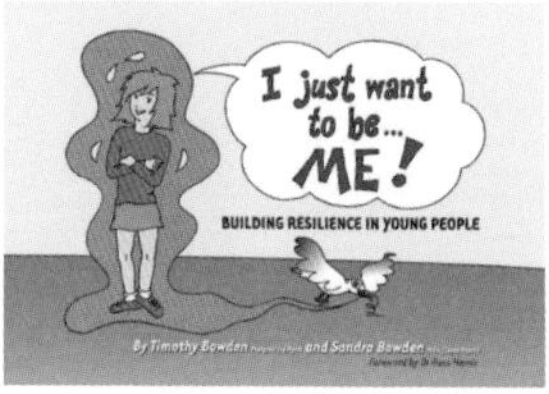
I just want to be... ME!
BUILDING RESILIENCE IN YOUNG PEOPLE

ANGER

UNDERSTANDING IT

Remember, anger itself is a natural and sometimes useful feeling you will be having for the rest of your life — it is what you do when you are angry that can be a problem.

- What has been the cost of angry behaviour to your relationships?
- What has been the cost of angry behaviour to your opportunities? How has it held you back?
- Context — when is it most likely to be an issue? Place? Time? Circumstances? (e.g. 'When I don't sleep well', 'When I miss breakfast.')
- Anger is a secondary emotion — it follows something else. What else are you feeling? What is anger covering over? What other feelings does anger get rid of?

WHEN YOU ARE IN IT

- What thoughts come up?
- What sensations are you aware of?
- What urges do you get? What things do you want to do with your hands, feet, mouth?

List some things you have been doing when you have been angry. Rate each for how workable it is in the short term and long term (that is, how much does it help to take you in the direction you want to go, help you to be the person you want to be, or help you to act in the way you want to act?). You may find that something seems to help in the short term but isn't very workable in the long term.

Action: ....

....

....

....

In the short term: ....

....

....

....

In the long term: ....

....

....

....

SOME EXPERIMENTS TO TRY

1. Slow down. Consciously slow down — don't move as fast, don't breathe as fast, don't answer as fast. Let there be a little space around things. Give yourself time to respond based on values, not urges.
2. Defuse from thoughts that are keeping you trapped. Notice your thoughts for what they are: just thoughts. Try adding the phrase 'I notice I am having the thought ...' to the front, or picture the words as fog drifting around you — let it sink down to the ground so you can see where you are.
3. Practise NAME (Notice, Acknowledge, Make room, Expand). Notice unpleasant feelings and acknowledge what you are feeling ('This is frustration.' 'This is fear.'). Make some space for unpleasant feelings — breathe into and around them, picture yourself opening up around them. Expand your awareness to what else you can notice outside yourself — use your five senses to bring yourself into the present moment.
4. Bring yourself back to your values. What do you want to be about in this moment, in this area of life? What is an action you can take that would serve that?
5. Act with kindness. Look for opportunities to do good for others. Why not look into doing some volunteer work? Remember to also practise being kind to yourself.
6. Consider forgiveness — it can be a powerful gift to yourself. It gives you permission to let go of something (not forget or excuse or condone, just let go) and get on with living your life.
7. Practise appreciation — take time to look at and be thankful for the things you have in your life, the people you care about, the things that mean something to you, the places you can go, things in the natural world.
8. Have compassion for yourself. Treat yourself with kindness (do you need to practise forgiveness for yourself?).
9. Look at your strengths and how you can use them.

ACKNOWLEDGEMENTS

We would like to acknowledge the fantastic work of Georg H. Eifert, Matthew McKay and John P. Forsyth on using Acceptance and Commitment Therapy as an approach to (as the title of their book says) *ACT on Life not on Anger* (New Harbinger 2006). Their work has guided our own approach to dealing with anger in adolescents.

A special thanks also goes to Fredrik Livheim for allowing us to adapt the Life Compass for use in our book.

We would also again like to thank Dr Russ Harris for all his support. We don't know where we would be without him.

Thanks also to the friendly folk at Exisle Publishing who have helped get this second book off the ground — Benny, Gareth and Anouska. And a special thanks to Al for his patience and expertise.